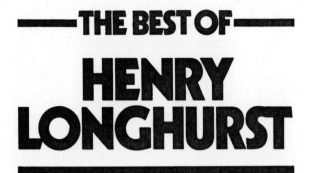

THE BEST OF
HENRY LONGHURST

THE BEST OF

HENRY LONGHURST

ON GOLF AND LIFE

With a Foreword by ALISTAIR COOKE

Compiled and Edited by Mark Wilson
and Ken Bowden

COLLINS
St. James's Place, London
1979

William Collins Sons & Co Ltd
London · Glasgow · Sydney · Auckland
Toronto · Johannesburg

First published in Great Britain 1979

ISBN 0 00 216163 X

Made and Printed in Great Britain by
William Collins Sons & Co Ltd Glasgow

NOONE LIKE HENRY

by Alistair Cooke

Everyone knows the special pleasure of discovering a new writer, even though the "new" man may have been mouldering in his grave for centuries. The joy of discovering a new columnist is rarer. A columnist is of our own time and is not likely to have a point of view so far removed from the standard attitudes as to provide us—like, say, Sir Thomas Browne or Max Beerbohm—with an unexpected brand of common sense, quaintness or indignation.

But from time to time it happens. Some years ago, in San Francisco, I had just finished riffling through the two more or less compulsory New York magazines (*The New Yorker* and *New York*) and turned to the San Francisco *Chronicle* and came on a column by an unknown—unknown to me. His name was Charles McCabe. His piece was called "The Good and the Chic." He, too, by some fluke of extrasensory perception, had in his hands the same two magazines. *The New Yorker* issue was 18 months out of date but there were things in it that were permanently good. The *New York* issue was only two weeks old, but McCabe was already gripped by the fear that he was dangerously behind in knowing what to eat, what to read, what to think. *The New Yorker*, he concluded, was a good magazine; *New York* was chic, the epitome, he wrote, of "boutique journalism." Since then, McCabe is the first item I turn to whenever I am out there.

It is so with Longhurst. When I took up golf, lamentably late in life, I plunged into the golfing literature for instruction and into golf journalism for entertainment. I was not entertained. Most of the reporting I would later recognize as the best required much more technical knowledge than I then possessed. Herbert Warren Wind impressed me with his subtle and accurate knowledge, which plainly I must try to acquire; but in the meantime, I was a kindergarten arithmetic student stumbling around in a text on astrophysics. Pat Ward-Thomas, too, offered tantalizing hints that in a year or two I might hope to appreciate why clover might require a hooded 5-iron or an innocent swale a lay-up. Of the others, Dan Jenkins was obviously having a lot of racy fun with locker-room know-how that was beyond me, and the American newspaper reporters seemed to be assembling and reassembling, week by week, a jig-saw puzzle of statistics.

But Longhurst wrote about the game as an entirely familiar exercise in human vanity. It is why, of all sportswriters, he had for so many years the highest proportion of non-sporting readers. Izaak Walton on fishing, Dickens on lawyers, Mark Twain on steam-boating, Cardus on cricket: they have appealed for generations to people who know nothing about baiting a hook, filing a suit, taking a sounding or flighting a googly. Longhurst is of their breed. He is recognizable in the first few sentences as a sly, wry, rheumy-eyed observer of human beings who happened to choose golf to illustrate their fusses and follies. He might just as well have chosen oil-drilling, toboggan racing, military service, being a member of parliament or the motives that propelled an old lady over Niagara in a barrel. That, in fact, he wrote about all these things only went to prove his particular virtue: a curiosity that centered not on a game but zoomed in on whatever was bold, charming, idiotic or eccentric about human behavior. After due meditation, he decided early on that as a weekly exercise of this curiosity, golf would do as well as anything.

In the beginning he served me, though he never knew it, as a canny uncle who was on my side against the commandments and prohibitions of my teachers. I was advised I must buy a "matched" set of clubs. Longhurst said you'd do better with whatever you picked up that felt right. A tiger of a young pro in Los Angeles told me it was "vital" to keep the right elbow practically knotted to the right waist. Longhurst said nothing was "vital" except delivering the clubhead to the ball at a right angle. I was solemnly told to memorize the entire book of rules. Longhurst said you mustn't blow your nose when your partner was addressing the ball, but otherwise the book of rules was mostly nonsense.

Very many of his readers, I should guess, never got so far with the actual dogma of this or any other game. They were wooed and won by Longhurst's reminiscences of caddies who ranged "from enchanting children to out-and-out brigands," by his affection for the praying mantis, by the boxing coach with "the traditional black cigar stub, unlit, who would have been ruled out of the average Hollywood film as a caricature," by the Dublin woman singing in the gutter and carrying a baby in her arms, "possibly her own." While his conscientious colleagues were calculating the yardage of the drives on the 18th at Augusta, Longhurst saw Weiskopf missing a tie by an inch and imagined him muttering, "We was robbed." It is the Hazlitt touch. Nobody remembers anything about the performance of the Italian jugglers who thrilled London in his day. But everybody remembers Hazlitt's remark that when anything at all is done so perfectly, you don't cheer, you cry.

From such an affable and sharp-eyed cynic, you must not expect starry-eyed tributes to the great ones of golf, or of any other game. Longhurst was as capable as any fan of a "Hear, hear!" or "Right on!" But there have been few sportswriters so unfooled by the motives and the sought rewards of professional sportsmen. He could write with relish about cunning, skill, ingenuity, physical prowess, but he did not mistake games for the Battle of Britain or The Pilgrim's Progress. You must look elsewhere for rhapsodies about the courage, heroism, endurance or bravery of even the best of their time. I suspect he always knew that these words are better reserved for Scott at the Pole, Solzhenitsyn in prison or the long marches of Martin Luther King Jr. As for the heroes of golf, he inclined to the scamps and the droll ones.

All these oddities, these agreeable and hilarious occasions, are written about in a prose style as effortless as falling out of bed: a more adroit achievement than some of his wordier rivals will ever appreciate. There are very few waste words in Longhurst.

Enough. No tribute—to an artist, writer, musician, golfer or character, come to that—can equal the simple remark that "there is noone like him." Of course, each of us is unique. But the ability to put that uniqueness—however engaging or obnoxious—onto paper or over the box is totally beyond the multitude of people who would like to have a go at television or muse that one day they must "write a book." Let them bow before the fact that—there was noone like Henry.

ACKNOWLEDGMENTS

Grateful acknowledgment is made to the copyright holders for permission to reproduce these extracts, which were originally published as follows:
Barrie & Jenkins; P. G.Wodehouse on Golf, in HOMAGE TO P. G. WODEHOUSE (1973);
Cassell: Available for work, Up the Tower, Golf Gives Me Up, in MY LIFE AND SOFT TIMES (1971);
Daily Sketch: 'Will I Give Ye the Daylight?' (1956);
J. M. Dent & Sons: Maiden Speech, Fiske Memorial, in I WOULDN'T HAVE MISSED IT (1945), Who's Going to be Second, The Lotus Eater, Death in the Forest, Sic Transit Gloria, in IT WAS WHILE IT LASTED (1940); A Person of Harmless Delight, Prisoners at Play, in YOU NEVER KNOW TILL YOU GET THERE (1949);
Esquire: That Rugged British Game (April 1955);
Evening Standard: The Average British Golfer (1938);
Golf Digest: A Long Love Affair With Ameircan Golf (1974), 'It'll Take Three Damn Good Shots to Get Up in Two Sir' (1975), Benevolent Dictators (1976), A Dramatic Finish (1975), The Yips – Once You've Had 'Em, You've Got 'Em (1973), A Plea for Smaller Greens and Tees (1975), Battleships, Blasting Powder and Golf Balls (1977), Practice Makes Perfect? What Rubbish! (1976), Yanks Challenged to Ringer Match (1975), Why Not Sudden Death? (1975), A Golfer's Best Friend is his Dog (1977), It's Getting too Costly to Remain an Amateur (1975);
Golf Illustrated: The Nineteenth (1958), ★★★★★★ !! (9.12.65), Admiral Benson Sails the Links (30.5.65), Seven Clubs Are Enough (1.9.60);
Bobby Jones Tribute: 'My But You're a Wonder Sir' (1979);
Wernie Laurie: Nightmare Over Niagara, in ROUND IN SIXTY-EIGHT (1953), A Hard Case from Texas, in GOLF MIXTURE (1952);
Stanley Paul & Co Ltd: Highlights of the Ryder Cup, in THE RYDER CUP 1965;
Punch: Castlerosse (1968), Golf Without Grass (1967);
The Sunday Times: First Principles (1958), Congenital Slice (1957), Peter Thomson Tells All (1959), So Much Flak (1956), The Greatest Tournament in the World (1960), A Case of Champagne (1964), Done it at Last (1959),

Bitter Pills (1965), Singing for Supper (1951), Comedy, Tragedy and Sharp Practice (1963), The Universal Amateur (1971), Beware the Martinis! (1961), Game Within a Game (1958), 'You Can't Let Them Do it, Barbara!' (1966), Chipers, Smudgers and Jiggers (1966), Goldfinger the Cheat (1969), Arnold Palmer – A Very Considerable Man (1967), Six of the Best (1966), Take a Pinch of Sand (1956), How Fred Ruined Golf and Won an Award (1968), Sluggers' Paradise (1964), 'What Club do I Throw?' (1955), As Rendered by Nicklaus (1968), Cannonball Accuracy (1960), Law of the Links (1961), Chicago Circus Master (1962), Them and Us (1966), 'I Can Always Dig Ditches' (1967), The Ltitle Man in the Tree (1968), Extraordinary Reluctance (1970), Agency Outside the Match (1964), Thinking of Sarazen (1958), Flat Out for Champions (1967), Sergeant Major Sheridan (1961), Three Penn'orth of Bard (1966), Tempting the Fates? (1953), A Bunch of Lousy Golfers (1962), Babe Zaharias (1956), The Genial Giant Killer (1967), Paralysis by Analysis (1967), Good Wishes from Henry Longhurst (1973). *World Sports:* His Golf Handicap – No Legs (1955).

EDITOR'S NOTE

The best time to be with and enjoy Henry Longhurst had always been in a bar at a golf event after the day's work was done, and it was on just such an occasion that this book was born. Henry was too unwell to work that week at Gleneagles, but was in attendance by invitation of the BBC and the organizers. Each evening after the dust had been washed away, the company would gather about his table in the Terrace Lounge for an hour, hopeful that he would feel like talking. Whatever his troubles, he never let them down.

Not being "up the tower," Henry was generally early for refreshment that week and, reminiscing one evening before the crowd arrived, he suddenly said: "You know, I really do wish I could do something for my American friends—I have so many of them and they have been so very kind to me."

"What about a book?" I said. "The best of all your writings."

And so, after much more talk and some reflection, it was done.

All Henry's closest American friends—those who know him well—will understand, and love, everything that is in this book. Those who know him less well or not at all, but who are opening the book mainly because it is about golf, will find equal pleasure in it, given two conditions. The first is that they enjoy not only what a writer says but how he says it—that they enjoy fine prose for its own sake. The second is that they do not believe the game of golf was invented by Arnold Palmer, or that the world would come to an end if the pro tour stopped tomorrow, or that the greatest joy the game can offer is six hours on a Florida resort course.

And if any golfer really does believe anything along those lines, then he should most *definitely* read this book—because he'll certainly know better afterwards!

—Ken Bowden

CONTENTS

NOONE LIKE HENRY by Alistair Cooke

EDITOR'S NOTE

INTRODUCTION

FIRST PRINCIPLES   19

HALCYON DAYS   19

AVAILABLE FOR WORK   21

A LONG LOVE AFFAIR WITH AMERICAN GOLF   24

UP THE TOWER   28

MAIDEN SPEECH   35

THE NINETEENTH   37

NIGHTMARE OVER NIAGARA   39

"IT'LL TAKE THREE DAMN GOOD SHOTS TO
    GET UP IN TWO, SIR"   41

BENEVOLENT DICTATORS   45

P. G. WODEHOUSE ON GOLF   46

THAT RUGGED BRITISH GAME   51

CONGENITAL SLICE   59

PETER THOMSON TELLS ALL   60

SO MUCH FLAK   66

WHO'S GOING TO BE SECOND?   67

THE GREATEST TOURNAMENT IN THE WORLD   72

A DRAMATIC FINISH   76

THE YIPS—ONCE YOU'VE HAD 'EM,
    YOU'VE GOT 'EM   78

A CASE OF CHAMPAGNE   82

DONE IT AT LAST!   84

HIGHLIGHTS OF THE RYDER CUP   85

THE LOTUS EATER   89

CASTLEROSSE   90

BITTER PILLS   94

SINGING FOR SUPPER   96

A PERSON OF HARMLESS DELIGHT   99

COMEDY, TRAGEDY AND SHARP PRACTISE   100

"WILL I GIVE YE THE DAYLIGHT?" 103
GOLF WITHOUT GRASS 105
THE UNIVERSAL AMATEUR 109
BEWARE THE MARTINIS! 112
A PLEA FOR SMALLER GREENS AND TEES 114
A HARD CASE FROM TEXAS 116
PRISONERS AT PLAY 119
GAME WITHIN A GAME 121
"YOU CAN'T LET THEM DO IT, BARBARA!" 122
CHIPERS, SMUDGERS AND JIGGERS 125
"MY BUT YOU'RE A WONDER, SIR" 127
BATTLESHIPS, BLASTING POWDER AND
   GOLF BALLS 129
CHEATING 131
ARNOLD PALMER—A VERY CONSIDERABLE
   MAN 133
SIX OF THE BEST 135
PRACTISE MAKES PERFECT? WHAT
   RUBBISH! 138
TAKE A PINCH OF SAND 139
HOW FRED RUINED GOLF AND WON
   AN AWARD 140
DEATH IN THE FOREST 144
SLUGGERS' PARADISE 145
"WHAT CLUB DO I THROW?" 147
AS RENDERED BY NICKLAUS 149
"SIC TRANSIT" GLORIA 150
YANKS CHALLENGED TO RINGER MATCH 153
WHY NOT SUDDEN DEATH? 155
CANNONBALL ACCURACY 158
******!! 159
LAW OF THE LINKS 161
CHICAGO CIRCUS MASTER 163
THEM AND US 165
"I CAN ALWAYS DIG DITCHES" 166
THE AVERAGE BRITISH GOLFER 167
HIS GOLF HANDICAP—NO LEGS 168

FISKE MEMORIAL   170
THE LITTLE MAN IN THE TREE   171
EXTRAORDINARY RELUCTANCE   174
AGENCY OUTSIDE THE MATCH   175
ADMIRAL BENSON SAILS THE LINKS   177
A GOLFER'S BEST FRIEND IS HIS DOG   179
THINKING OF SARAZEN   181
FLAT OUT FOR CHAMPIONS   181
SERGEANT MAJOR SHERIDAN   184
THREE PENN'ORTH OF BARD   185
TEMPTING THE FATES   188
A BUNCH OF LOUSY GOLFERS   189
BABE ZAHARIAS   191
IT'S GETTING TOO COSTLY TO REMAIN
    AN AMATEUR   193
SEVEN CLUBS ARE ENOUGH   195
THE GENIAL GIANT KILLER   195
PARALYSIS BY ANALYSIS   198
GOLF GIVES ME UP   200
GOOD WISHES FROM HENRY LONGHURST   203
AFTERWORD   205

INTRODUCTION

Jack and Jill make a majestic scene on their Sussex hill, standing together like proud guardians of the peace, splendour and heritage of the English countryside. It is an idyllic way of life, and one they deserve; for once, as beautiful, working windmills, they toiled to every wind. Now, in their years of rest, antiquity has given them a new stature: they tug at our hearts and remind us of a past age. So the laws of England have decreed that the two windmills must remain unmolested by progress; never to be vandalised by modernisation; always to be preserved among the nation's cherished historical riches.

Into such a gloriously reverent setting the figure of Henry Longhurst moulds well—indeed perfectly. Jack and Jill form part of the Sussex home in which Henry lived, and the three of them were marvellously suited. For nothing could have been more English than Henry, and he, too, is rightly acclaimed one of Britain's great treasures.

Like his beloved windmills, Henry in the last few years of his life was largely resting after an industrious, adventurous and congenial life based upon the compelling urge to "go everywhere and do everything" at least once. Those places he enjoyed at first acquaintance he visited again. It must therefore say much for the United States and its people that he commuted happily across the Atlantic for 40 years. The outcome of it all was an extraordinary life, filled—to overflowing on occasions—as a writer, speaker, golfer, soldier, traveller, member of parliament, pioneer, crusader, and much, much more.

Incomparable, many in Britain believe, as an essayist on the game of golf, Henry spurred the discerning Lord Brabazon to declare passionately: "I cannot leave my bed on a Sunday morning without first having read Longhurst in the newspaper." And the golden rule for ensuring a successful, standing-room-only club dinner in Britain had always been: "Persuade Henry to come and speak."

Golf was always his highway through life, from the moment he paused while struggling with his Greek verbs, gazed out of the school window and envied the freedom of the boy caddies he saw on a nearby links. Occasionally, being a man of most inquisitive nature and adventurous spirit, he explored a detour, and so it was, while soldiering during the war, that he became a member of parliament. It was a brief but lively distraction. His political opponent thought it fair to use as ammunition the fact that Henry had won the 1936 German Amateur Championship. "Do you want to vote for a man who has actually played golf in Germany?" he kept asking. The constituents answered that they did, and Henry swiftly found himself as one of Winston Churchill's supporters in the House of Commons.

It is as a TV commentator, of course, that Henry is best known to the world of golf, especially in the United States. He was a naturally modest person but he could not hide the pleasure afforded by such moments as the one at an airport in South Africa where, in his unmistakable voice, he asked that his shooting stick be given good care in the luggage hold. Overhearing the exchange, an American passenger tapped him on the shoulder and said: "Hey! Aren't you the guy that does the 16th at the Masters?"

To say that Henry has given pleasure to millions can be no exaggeration; and by doing so he has earned moving tributes from his professional peers, among them Jim McKay of ABC sports. I trust he will not object to my revealing the inscription I found in a book he gave to Henry, because I think it tells so much: "To Henry Longhurst—whose writing delights me, whose spoken commentary I quote more often than my own, and whose friendship I cherish." What more could one man say of another?

Frank Chirkinian, the celebrated CBS golf director, was moved to declare after a Masters at which Henry excelled himself from the 16th tower: "I just don't know what it is about the guy. He looks like W. C. Fields in drag. But he happens to be the best in the business." Then our own Peter Alliss paid this eloquent tribute: "The one man who gives me my supreme pleasure is without doubt Henry Longhurst. His sense of humour, his little asides, are to me a joy. I am aware that he may well have belonged to a different era, the days of 'send a gunboat up the river, give 'em a good flogging, Rhodesia for the whites,' but I for one am glad he wasn't born 50 years earlier or else I should not have been able to enjoy his sense of the ridiculous, nor his beautiful command of the English language."

The Walter Hagen Award and a royal summons to Buckingham Palace to be made a Commander of the British Empire by the Queen Mother have also recognised his vast contribution to golf. But he has given so much I suspect we will forever remain in his debt.

If his intriguing way of life created any regret at all, it must be that no biographer can hope to do it full justice. We can only try to convey an impression of it all, and I hope that this random selection of Henry's writings on a multitude of subjects and people will help others appreciate why we in Britain hold him in such esteem for having been more than just a brilliant commentator on television.

He was an extremely brave man who, in recent years, continued to inspire others through his work while bearing the most severe attacks upon his own health. Not for a moment, however, did he allow his wit to fade. I remember the Masters when Henry was first taken seriously ill, and detained in an Augusta hospital which, to any visiting Englishmen, must give the impression of a Hilton Hotel with its reception desks, cashiers' windows, and gift shops in the foyer. Henry was in a bad way when I reached his bedside but, as always, he opened the verbal batting. "What do you think of this place?" he whispered with difficulty. "I couldn't afford it. They've just charged me 25 cents to park the car and come in," I said, hoping to amuse. Henry fought to raise a hand and stretched out in search of his wallet on the cabinet next to the bed. "I'll give you 50 cents in case you come again. Now do you feel better?" he quipped.

Then in 1973 he left the Open championship, won by Tom Weiskopf at Troon, and returned to Jack and Jill to prepare himself for a cancer operation. The comeback he achieved five months later with the "Best Wishes from Henry Longhurst" revelation was a fantastic personal victory which all Britain gratefully applauded.

Through it all, as might be expected, his sense of the ridiculous proved unscathed, remaining as sharp as the day at yet another Masters when I drove him and four more British golf writers to our Augusta home for the week. As anyone might well do in such circumstances, I misjudged the width of our king-sized limousine and collided with the gates at the entrance to the driveway. It did no good to the gates, the front wheels of the car, or to the nerves of my jet-lagged passengers. The four hurriedly got out, leaving me in no doubt as to what they thought of my driving prowess. Henry, however, sat still for a full minute, composing himself. Then, gathering his papers together, he slowly climbed from his seat, saying: "Wilson, my dear fellow, I have been in a great many motor accidents in my time. But this is the first ever to be caused by a teetotaller. I find this disgraceful."

There are some things Henry could not forgive, though in my case I'm not sure whether it was being a poor driver or a non-drinker which upset him more. But for me and many others, he could do no wrong. I think you will be better able to understand why through these writings: the work of an incredible man, the memories of an extraordinary life.

—*Mark Wilson*

Mark Wilson is an outstanding journalist who is currently the golf correspondent for the London Daily Express. He was privileged to have known Longhurst for many, many years.

1958
FIRST PRINCIPLES

I often think that one's attitude to the game of golf is subconsciously conditioned for a lifetime by the circumstances in which one is first introduced to it. Those of us who see it first in its elementary, primitive form, knocking a ball along with one club, or perhaps even two or three, cheerfully encountering all manner of unorthodox hazards on the way until eventually we get it into the hole, seem to me to have captured a basic outlook on the game which can never later be revealed to those who travelled first class from the start.

My own beginnings were primitive in the extreme. I was introduced to the game before breakfast one morning on the common at Yelverton, Devon, by two other small boys whose parents were taking their holiday in the same hotel. They had devised a triangular course of three holes—no tees, flags, fairways or any other such nonsense, of course—and with luck we could get in two rounds before breakfast.

None of us, therefore, was baptised in the faith that, if we drove onto the fairway, we were entitled to a "fairway lie," and that, if we did not get it, we had been robbed. Ours was a simple creed. You played the ball where you found it. The only true disaster in golf was when you could not find it.

1941
HALCYON DAYS

In the Autumn of 1927 I went up to Clare College, Cambridge, which Elizabeth, Lady of Clare, founded as Clare Hall in 1347 and which is to my mind one of the most beautiful colleges in either university. Here I fell at once into a different and heavenly world, for of all the transitions that one undergoes in this life, that of schoolboy to undergraduate is assuredly the best. Now, at last, one was no longer a schoolboy; one was out on one's own, a man. At Cambridge you live out of college at first and move in later, and so it was that I found myself lodging in Park Street, which is a little street off Jesus Lane, under the roof of Miss Hardstaff. Though these were comparatively modest rooms, her other lodger was none other than Prince Alex Mdivani, a member of a family known on account of their matrimonial adventures as the Marrying Mdivanis. When Miss Hardstaff admired the portraits of two exceptionally beautiful women in his bedroom, Alex said, "Ah, yes. They are my sisters-in-law." They were the two great film stars of the day, Pola Negri and Mae Murray.

It would be doing myself an injustice to say that my only thought at Cambridge was to get a place in the university golf team—I did indeed get a modest Honours Degree in Economics—but I confess that golf was never long out of my mind. Every Saturday and most Sundays the university had a 12-a-side match against some of the best-known clubs in the whole of the country, mostly around London, and it was these matches that helped to make golf beyond doubt the best game, I will not say to play, but to have played, for the university. Very soon I managed to get a place in the team and eventually settled at No. 7. It seems hard to credit it now but we travelled at first to our matches by train, the 7:47 from Cambridge, players in the not too distant colleges actually humping their clubs to the station in the half-light on foot. Then it was all across London from Liverpool Street, generally to Waterloo, and home again by the last train, known then and, I trust still, as The Fornicator.

Later one acquired a second-hand car costing perhaps £50 and when we arrived at the course our hosts and opponents would often say, "You don't mean you've driven all the way from Cambridge 90 miles this morning?" Equally distinctly I remember thinking, "I suppose the day will come when one gets so old and decrepit as to think it remarkable to drive 90 miles from Cambridge for a golf match, but I can hardly believe it." At the end of the spring term we played the great match against Oxford, and the first of the four in which I played was at Princes, Sandwich, myself little knowing that this was to be the scene only four years later of the first Open Championship that I should ever see and write about. I can see, as though it were yesterday, the olive-skinned features of Gene Sarazen coming down the last fairway to win.

So for three and a half blissful years this life went on. Our next university match was at Rye, where my partner in the foursomes and dear friend and travelling companion was Eric Martin-Smith. When he went down from the university he proceeded through round after round of the Amateur Championship at Westward Ho! and at last miraculously reached the final. A Cambridge contemporary sent him a telegram saying, "Ridiculous but stick to it." This appeared in the press as having come from me and, though I have always given credit where credit was due, this particular credit has always stuck to me. Eric went on to win and on the plinth of the vast trophy you will see, "1930 R. T. Jones, 1931 E. Martin-Smith."

Next year it was the Royal Liverpool Club at Hoylake where in fact Bobby Jones was to win the Open as part of his Grand Slam in 1930, and this match will always be remembered by the fact that the rain poured down and filled up the bunkers and despite the efforts of the Hoylake Fire Brigade nothing could be done about it. The two captains, Eric Prain for Cambridge and Oxford's Bob Baugh, a diminutive American from Alabama, decided upon a complicated set of local rules which got them into terrible trouble with the authorities, with hostile comment on the lines of, "Who do they think they are to tamper with the sacred Rules of Golf?"

And so at last for my final effort, when by this time I was captain, we played at Royal St. Georges, Sandwich, the scene of two of Walter Hagen's wins in the past, in one of which he was followed by the then Prince of Wales, and at the conclusion gave the first prize of £50 directly to his caddie.

—1971—
AVAILABLE FOR WORK

In 1931, Henry Longhurst captained Cambridge in the University match against Oxford at Sandwich. He won his singles easily but, as he recalled in his autobiography, "My Life and Soft Times," instead of pleasure at his own success, a huge wave of depression came over him:

This then was the end; the end of the halcyon days; the end, it seemed, of the only life I had ever known. The future seemed to stretch out bleak and unpaid. I had no job. Indeed, I had hardly given it a thought. I knew neither trade nor profession, and such was the anticlimax that I lay on my bed in the Bell Hotel in Sandwich and wept, before getting up to dress for the dinner.

From here I embarked on a number of false but in the end not unvaluable starts, beginning with the family business. Eventually there occurred to me a fantastic piece of good fortune, and I am ashamed to admit that I cannot for the life of me remember how it came about or to whom to lift my hat in retrospect. Somebody introduced me to an amiable, easy-going character called George Philpot, who later had the irrelevant distinction of being in the only carriage in the London Underground to be involved in a serious accident in 40 or 50 years. George edited a little monthly golf magazine called *Tee Topics*, of blessed memory, and, as a result of our meeting, the light of good fortune shone upon us both. George, who was by that time old enough to look upon work rather as I do now, was enabled to stay for most of the afternoon playing billiards with his cronies in the London Press Club, while I, a square peg in an absolutely cut-to-measure square hole at last, settled down to what every instinct told me was the kind of life I was going to love. Not yet, perhaps, the kind of living, for the arrangement was that I should be on probation for three months, after which, having practised at editing the paper while George was playing billiards or lunching with a potential advertiser, it would be ascertained what salary I should command, if any.

In the meantime I had a family allowance of £4 (then worth some $20) a week and this, unbelievably, enabled me to move to the Connaught Club near Marble Arch and to dine as often as desired at the Praed Street premises of "William No. 1 Harris, the Sausage King, also at Brighton"—sausages, chips and an extra shovel of onions, for less than 30 cents. I was back in the world of golf where there was still so much to be seen and learnt, and so many people to be met, and where at least I knew basically what I was talking about and people still knew my name. As for this new world of writing and printing and editing and seeing the glossy result at the end of the month, I felt rather as a woman must feel when she picks up a dress and says, "This is me." Furthermore, it turned out that it *was* me, whereas the woman so often takes the dress back with, "I knew the moment I bought it that it wasn't me." The fact that elementary insight into the finances of *Tee Topics* showed that, however much the amiable George might wish to pay me, there was nothing with which to do it, did not seem to matter. This at last was my world and somewhere there would be a niche for me in it.

Writing now in the later stages of the more than agreeable life into which I had at that time just been initiated, I marvel at the good fortune which continued to dog my unworthy footsteps. The Depression was still very much with us and there had not, of course, been the golfing "explosion" which is such a feature of the sporting scene today. The Sunday Times, then sister paper to the Daily Telegraph in the Telegraph's present Fleet Street building, carried, broadly speaking, no golf other than agency reports. Someone suggested that a modest outlay on a man of their own might be justified and Sir Herbert Morgan, who has something to do with the Sunday Times, mentioned the matter to James Braid one day at Walton Heath. Braid said he did not know of anyone suitable, but a young fellow who used to be captain of Cambridge had, he understood, taken to writing about golf in some magazine and from these simple circumstances was born the turning point of my life.

It was the last week of my three probationary months with *Tee Topics* and there was arising between George Philpot and myself a certain unease, not impairing what had become a delightful and informal camaraderie between us but stemming from the awareness that the day of reckoning was approaching and he knew I knew there was nothing in the kitty and I knew he knew I knew, and indeed that he must have known all along. Neither of us was anxious to broach the subject, though I was in the stronger position of the two since I knew, and he didn't, that I should be only too happy to go on in this new life, Micawber-like, until something turned up. The problem was solved by the arrival of a courteous little note from what proved to be an exceptionally courteous little man who signed himself, on the headed paper of the Sunday Times, W. W. Hadley. I was not to know, though I like to think I immediately appreciated, that here was one of the great, almost legendary, editors of Fleet Street. He sat dwarfed behind a large and rather untidy desk and revealed that the Sunday Times was considering including on the sporting pages a short regular piece about golf and that my name had been mentioned. Was I, he wondered with that curious humility characteristic of men of his stature—and I shall always remember his words—available for further work? I revealed pretty rapidly that I was, and a few days later there began at six guineas a week [$31.50] a relationship which is now, as I write, in its 40th year.

I have always had a sneaking sympathy for the chap in the Bible who got the most frightful stick for thanking God that he was not as other men are, but at the risk of incurring the divine displeasure, I must reveal that from this time onwards I never went to a regular place of work and even now I am either entirely at home or entirely away, probably in some far distant, sunnier clime, in pleasant places among mostly pleasant people who are anyway at their pleasantest in the circumstances in which I meet them, and all this almost certainly at someone else's expense. Furthermore, I have never in my life, never, worked during the afternoon. So it may be forgiven if sometimes, when I go down to see friends in the City and observe these hideous glass-box buildings and reflect that it falls to thousands of people to spend their whole working life therein, and in the same few square feet at that, I tend to feel, "There but for the grace of God . . ." and a sort of guilty shiver comes over me in case Providence gives me the same sort of stick as the Pharisee. Still, nothing can take it away now and all one can do is to be truly thankful.

────────1974────────
A LONG LOVE AFFAIR
WITH AMERICAN GOLF

It gave me immense delight to be given the Walter Hagen Award, not only because I had the honour and pleasure of knowing the great man and enjoying many a glass, or "hoot" as he always called it, in his company, but also because I really can call myself an old and faithful customer of the United States now, believe it or not, of some 44 years' standing. The Good Book tells us that it is more blessed to give than to receive, in which case my American friends, with their unbounded hospitality which I have enjoyed for so long, must be a great deal more blessed than I.

In 1930, when I was captain of the Cambridge University golf team, someone had the brilliant idea that we might band ourselves together and tour around that fabulous land of prohibition and plenty, the United States. Thus in August of that year, 10 of us set sail in the good ship Caronia. Those who could not touch their fathers for £150, equivalent in those days to $750 (which, again believe it or not, covered the fare and five weeks in America), were aided by the father of one of our number, Billy Fiske, who is commemorated by a plaque in St. Paul's Cathedral in London as the first American to lose his life in the service of the Royal Air Force in the Battle of Britain. Already he held the world record for the Cresta bobsled run and had captained the winning American bobsled team in the Olympic Games. He was also the owner of a car which enthusiasts will recognise as one of the great motors of all time, the 4½-litre supercharged Bentley.

Our first port of call was the Huntingdon Valley Club, near Philadelphia, where we at once experienced the "sea legs" which in those days had the same effect on new arrivals as the "time change" does on those who fly the Atlantic in jets today instead of travelling like gentlemen in luxurious ocean liners. The ground seemed still to be moving and no matter how slowly one swung the club it never seemed to come down in the same arc twice (and when I come to think of it, I doubt whether it has ever done so since). We could make little of the big, undulating greens and were duly beaten 4-1. But the big moment really came in the locker room afterwards when one of my opponents said, "I guess you boys would like a little drink."

Awful warnings had been sounded before we left. It would be all right for them; they were used to it. Others talked of "delayed action" and people dropping as though poleaxed. Many, it was said, went instantly blind from wood alcohol. I opted for gin and tonic and raised it with a lively surmise. It tasted exactly like gin and tonic, which in fact was what it was.

Not always, however, were we to come out unscathed. At the Mt. Kisco (N.Y.) Club, our charming host, Donald Carr, for whom I formed a profound admiration and respect, had laid on a special bottle of port for two of us who were his house guests. What was in it we shall never know, but in the morning neither of us was able to raise his head from the pillow or, indeed, to move, let alone get up.

Perhaps because we were mostly staying among the sort of people who had reliable bootleggers, this was the only occurrence of its kind. Nevertheless, it is salutary to have seen Prohibition in action, to have seen leading citizens in the finest clubs in the land reduced to drinking furtively in the locker room, and to have actually proceeded to an address with the classic instruction, "Knock three times and ask for Charlie."

In Camden, N.J., which we passed through on our day of arrival, a character had been warned by certain other characters that a "pineapple" was liable to be cast through his window. Wondering where he should have his dinner, he decided the safest place to be a crowded restaurant. One may imagine, however, his feeling as his dinner drew to its close. As he came out, a black sedan motorcar passed slowly by and the sidewalk echoed to the fire of machine guns. After innumerable pictures, "X" marking the spot, and column after column on the victim's lurid past, the local newspaper account ended with the memorable words, "A by-stander was also killed." He never even got his name in the paper.

Our humble team was also flattered to be noticed by the press and I still possess references to us as the "invading British collegiate linksmen," and even, let me tell you, "famed stars from the dear old country." We were taken, too, to an enormous banquet given by the City of Philadelphia for Commander Byrd, lately returned from remarkable exploits in the Antarctic. But my principal memory, I am afraid, is of the master of ceremonies announcing that only two pieces of music had ever been written for 12 women harpists, and that the 12 women harpists he was about to introduce would play them both.

The ladies came on draped in long classical robes and started to pluck at their strings but, alas, the clatter of knives and plates and the incessant chatter was such that eventually they rose in a body and swept out. I have thought ever since in terms of a sweep of women harpists.

Our second match was at Pine Valley in New Jersey. Since that time I've played some 400 courses in more than 30 countries, yet I still look upon Pine Valley as unchallengeably the greatest inland course in the world. There I had the good fortune to play, and be duly defeated by, the club's president, the legendary John Arthur Brown, whom I was to see again riding briskly around a Miami course in a car at an age much nearer 90 than 80.

From Philadelphia we moved up to Boston, where we were at once knocked off, 8½-3½, by Harvard. Since we had been in a sleeping car all night, and furthermore lost five matches by a single hole, perhaps it wasn't too bad. I cannot see any British university team beating Harvard today, but I still believe we might have done it then. They had a mighty slugger, James B. Baldwin, with whom I still stay from time to time at Hilton Head Island, S.C., and with whom I share the fast play record for the No. 2 Course at Pinehurst, a record which clearly will stand forever—2 hours and 25 minutes.

We sallied forth to play a number of clubs around Boston, of which I remember particularly the Myopia Hunt Club on account of the remarkable variety of liqueurs which they openly offered us after lunch. At The Country Club, Brookline, I found myself matched against none other than Francis Ouimet, who on that same course had beaten Vardon and Ray in the playoff for the 1913 U.S. Open. He beat me by one hole and, if only I could have saved a stroke or two here and there, I am convinced that he still would have beaten me by one hole. In 1951 Francis was accorded the highest golfing honour perhaps that we in Britain can offer when he became the first American captain of the Royal and Ancient Golf Club of St. Andrews. I shall never forget the moment at the dinner when Francis paused in his speech and, his eyes glinting genially through his glasses, said slowly, "It may interest you to know, gentlemen, that it is 38 years ago, this day, that I beat Vardon and Ray." Francis, I like to think, became a lifelong friend and in 1963 I was privileged to join with Joe Looney, of the Boston Herald, in presenting him with the Walter Hagen Award. Ouimet was just about the nicest, gentlest man I ever knew.

My second visit to America was to accompany the 1936 Walker Cup team to Pine Valley and such was the impression it had made on me before that I was able to leave behind from memory a complete description of every hole. We travelled on the old Transylvania (sunk, alas, in World War II) which wallowed its way across the Atlantic in 11 days, every man except two being prostrated by seasickness.

On arrival at Pine Valley I was walking across the little bridge to the 18th green when I felt an appalling stab in my right thumb and, on looking down, saw my trousers crawling with wasps, whose nest had been hanging from the bridge. At the same time the club pro, Ted Turner, suddenly started executing a series of wild leaps, yelling like a frenzied dervish. He had, he said, yellow jackets in his pants. For myself, I bolted and it was perhaps symbolic of what was to come that I should have lost my trousers within 30 seconds of entering the clubhouse. We were beaten without winning a single point.

From Pine Valley we went on for the U.S. Amateur at Garden City, N.Y., a delightful club which I still associate with the most marvellous lobsters. After getting through the first round I played our own best player, the late Jack McLean, in the second and furthermore was 2 up on him at the turn. He came on and beat me, which was a good thing, for I assuredly should never have got to the final as he did—only to be beaten for the title on the 37th hole by Johnny Fischer, now a pillar of the USGA.

No fewer than 31 years later, I was sitting up in an ABC-TV tower at the U.S. Open at Baltusrol and beside me was a handsome young fellow assisting with the scoring. "Didn't you play in the 1936 Amateur at Garden City, sir?" he said. (It makes you feel your age when they start calling you sir!) "Yes," I said. "Do you remember who you beat in the first round?" "I'm afraid I don't really." "My father," he said. That really did make me feel old.

Writing and television assignments have brought me the incredible good fortune of getting to know many of the finest American clubs. I can look back on events not only around New York, but at Boston, Philadelphia, Baltimore, Atlanta, Buffalo, Detroit, Dayton, Chicago, Portland, Pinehurst, Houston, Palm Springs, San Francisco, Tulsa and Oklahoma City—the last unforgettable! I was there for the U.S. Amateur in 1953 when Oklahoma was still a dry state. The amount of hard liquor they consumed was a revelation, even to one who, like myself, had seen the "6 o'clock swill" in Sydney, Australia, before they, too, civilised their licensing laws. I was hard put to keep up with them, though I enjoyed doing my best.

Having been brought up in the more "simple" clubhouses of Britain—one or two of them still so disgracefully simple that I should hesitate to let any American friend inside them—I have always had an instinctive preference for those in the United States that are golf clubs pure and simple, such as The Country Club, Pine Valley, Cypress Point, and, above all, still the favourite of all who attended the 1953 Walker Cup there, Kittansett, of Marion, Mass. On the other hand, the one that made the biggest impact on me was the scene of the Ryder Cup Match of two years later. This was Thunderbird, in what was thought to be the California desert, till they found, with a jest that is now corny but was new at the time, that all you had to do was "sow the seed, apply the water, and jump back."

Though there are 20 or more such courses now, Thunderbird was then only the second desert course and it was multi-coloured, gay and new. The club bar, with the bartender "sunk" behind the bar to the level of the seated customers, remains the best designed I have seen anywhere in the world. What impressed me most, however, was not the bar or the sunshine or the grapefruit trees lining the fairways, or even the 200 electric cars in the "buggy stable ," but a single local rule. "Players on foot," it said, "have no standing on the course."

Now, I thought, I have seen everything.

I haven't, of course, but I have seen a lot, and am duly thankful.

1971
UP THE TOWER

Life is a mixed bag—chances offered and taken, more often chances missed or not even noticed. Successes are sometimes to be scored by honest toil and solid worth, more often by happening to be standing somewhere, thinking of nothing, at exactly the right time. In the latter category may be placed my entry into broadcasting, which for about 35 years has been one of the most pleasurable activities of my life.

Television is, by comparison with radio, a pushover. In television—I am talking, of course, of golf—in times of local difficulty, which means quite often, you can always intersperse what Sydney Smith, referring to the loquacious Macaulay's conversation at dinner, called "brilliant flashes of silence," and, indeed, as I hope to show in due course, this may gain you much merit. In other words, you can always sit back and let them look at the picture. In radio, if your mind goes blank for three seconds, they think the set has gone wrong. It is essential, therefore, in an emergency to possess the ability to "waffle on," and with this from the first I never had any great difficulty—on the radio or anywhere else, come to that!

I believe I can claim to have done the first "live" outside radio broadcast on golf when the BBC (British Broadcasting Corporation) set up a glass box on stilts at some vantage point far out on the Little Aston course outside Birmingham, overlooking two greens and three tees. In a way we were not unsuccessful. We saw plenty of play, chopping and changing from one hole to another, and had an added piece of good fortune when a past British Open champion, Arthur Havers, completely fluffed a short approach shot in front of our window. Perhaps he was unnerved by the thought of being on "live" for the first time in history.

Then the BBC brought in a portable apparatus with which it was to be possible actually to follow the golf, and here the initiator, at the English Amateur Championship at Birkdale the year before the war, was the doyen of our profession, Bernard Darwin. He set off onto the course accompanied by two engineers, one carrying a portmanteau-shaped apparatus strapped to his back with a long aerial sticking up vertically behind his head, and the other lugging around the batteries. I naturally listened with professional interest, having been invited to carry out a similar venture at the Amateur Championship at the Royal Liverpool Golf Club at Hoylake later on.

It was soon pretty clear that the venerable Darwin was finding it heavy going and it was no surprise when he declared, on returning to the clubhouse, that golf, so far as he was concerned, did not lend itself to this type of broadcasting.

At Hoylake on the morning of the Amateur Championship quarterfinals, we tried to follow the play but soon came up against the elementary stumbling-block that in order to describe the play you had to see it, and in order to see it you had to be within range of the players, and they could therefore hear what you were saying, which was not only extremely embarrassing but led to persistent cries of "Sshhhh" from the silent spectators. For the afternoon semifinals, we set ourselves up on a knoll beside the fifth fairway, well out of the way but with a reasonable view of the distant play. It seems incredible today but the signal for us to start was to be the lowering of a white handkerchief by an engineer perched on the roof of the Royal Liverpool clubhouse.

The exact hour of the broadcast in those days had to be printed in advance, so there was no flexibility in time. The first semifinal came to us and passed, then came the second. At this point the engineer raised the white handkerchief and we were under starter's orders. He lowered it briskly, and we were "off"— whereupon the second match vanished from sight, leaving our little trio silent upon a knoll in Hoylake, unable to move since our range was only a mile. I state with confidence that I gave an absolutely splendid and dramatic eyewitness account of the play, understandably interspersed with a good deal of the "Wish you were here . . . lovely view across the bay" sort of stuff, and I could not help feeling that not everyone could have waffled continuously or to such effect for 10 whole minutes about non-existent play. I thus returned to the clubhouse feeling that a congratulatory hand or two might well be extended. Instead, we met the engineer. He was most apologetic. "We had to fade you out after a minute or two," he said, "on account of a technical hitch."

Much as I respect the club, Hoylake has never been my happy

hunting ground for either radio or television. In 1936, when golf on the radio was comparatively new, the engineer and I were stuck in a tiny, glass-fronted box situated among the guy-ropes at the back of the refreshment tent, with barely room for ourselves and a suspended microphone. Firstly, one day's play in the Open was cancelled on account of a snowstorm—in July—and I had to do three 10-minute pieces on a program going out across the British Empire, filling in for a whole day's play that had never taken place. Then a couple of friends espied me from afar and with schoolboy delight advanced upon our humble box.

I was in full spate when they came and made rude two-fingered gestures outside the box, pressing their noses against the glass and generally carrying on as though provoking a monkey in a cage. Finally, when once again we were in full flow, a waitress came out behind the refreshment tent carrying an enormous pile of plates. The strange spectacle in our little box so distracted her attention that she tripped over a guy-rope and sank with a crash that reverberated throughout the Empire. I explained what it was and gather that it gave innocent pleasure as far away as New Zealand.

The first serious attempts in Britain to televise live golf were directed by Antony Craxton, who used to do the Queen's Christmas broadcasts. Many were from Wentworth, which, in summer, with the trees in full glory and a shirt-sleeved crowd moving from hole to hole enjoying themselves in the sunshine, can present a magnificent picture. I remember Craxton saying how golf even then attracted quite a large "rating" by comparison with what had been expected, and how many housewives on housing estates said that they knew nothing about it but liked to watch because "it seemed such a lovely place." Nowadays, of course, this holds good to a much greater extent and some of the scenes in colour—on British television so much superior to the American colour, for once, due to different "line" standards—can be really heavenly.

For myself I always thought the "beauty shots" and the little irrelevancies—though we seem to have time for few of them these days—added to the appeal of golfing programmes: the 360-degree panorama of, say, Turnberry, with the Clyde and the Isle of Arran and the long encircling arm of the Mull of Kintyre and Ailsa Craig; or Muirfield, with the distant tracery of the two great Forth Bridges and the Kingdom of Fife on the other side of the Firth; or St. Andrews and the bay and the snow-capped Cairngorms; or, again, the small boy at the eighth at Wentworth who, immediately after the last match had passed by, emerged from the undergrowth and started fishing in the pond; or the lark's nest focused upon by an alert cameraman at Muirfield during the Open. The producer had to sacrifice this camera for quite a while before the mother lark returned to the nest to feed the young, and there were many who afterwards said that this was the best bit in the programme, never mind Jack Nicklaus. The same cameraman's roving eye and tele-photo lens discerned a couple on the sandhills just outside the course and it was nip and tuck whether their subsequent union would appear, live and in colour, for the first time on this or any other screen. If only the producer had been under notice from the BBC at the time, he might have risked his arm and given the world a most entertaining exposure—and I sometimes wonder what I should have made of the commentary.

What we put up with in the early days of TV golf never ceases to surprise me. For a Walker Cup match at St. Andrews I was stuck up on a tall tower out by the "Loop," where the holes crisscross over each other at the far end of the course, making it almost impossible on a small monitor to detect who is playing which hole and who is crossing over playing a different hole. Once again the wind howled in, direct from the North Sea and twice as strongly at 40 feet up as on the ground, and soon it was so cold that one became numbed. Nor were the senses quickened by the fact that the British team lost every match on both days. For the second sitting I borrowed a fine, fur-collared flying-coat from the barman at the Scores Hotel, but once again I gradually froze, to such an extent that I eventually found myself huddled over the blurred picture, thinking how poor it was and that there wasn't even a commentary. It was quite a time before the penny dropped. I suppose I can claim the doubtful distinction of being the only BBC commentator who has actually forgotten to do the commentary.

Another time, at St. Andrews, it was the picture that failed and I heard frantic voices from London saying, "Tell him to do a sound commentary till we get the picture back." This was really like old times and the "lovely view across the bay" stuff came back as naturally as though it were yesterday. In fact, at St. Andrews, there *is* a lovely view across the bay. I kept this up for about 25 minutes till eventually we got going again, and at the end of it all strolled back from my perch at the 17th to the Royal and Ancient for refreshment, which I felt had been well earned. As I got inside the door, the porter handed me a telegram. It was from the Nore Golfing Society. FIRST RULE OF ELECTRONICS, it read; IF IT DOESN'T WORK, KICK IT.

What can be the mentality of the man who actually rings up the BBC during the course of a transmission, as did a doctor during the playoff for the British Open between Peter Thomson and Dave Thomas at Lytham? We were in full voice when the producer came in with: "There's a doctor who has just rung the BBC in London with a message saying, 'Tell Longhurst there is no "p" in

Thomson.' " This is a moment for instant decision. The answer comes immediately to mind, but do you give it? Do you say, "I understand a doctor has just rung the BBC to say there is no "p" in Thomson, and if it is of any interest to him this is by no means the only thing in which the p is silent"—or don't you? I didn't, but I still have a sneaking wish that I had.

Gradually it came to be appreciated that, if you wanted to "show the winner winning," the thing to do was to concentrate, as the Americans were already doing, on the last five holes, together with any "bonus" holes that the same cameras might be able to cover elsewhere—as, for instance, at St. Andrews, where the first five and the last five all share a common strip of ground.

It was also realised, as was really known all along, that the commentator need not be able to see what he was talking about, since his first task is to watch the monitor, the cardinal sin being to talk about something the viewer cannot see, thus driving the latter into absolute frenzies of frustration. Thus at last we began to be pitched nearer the clubhouse rather than miles out on the course, and up only one ladder, and the hand of civilisation was extended towards us in the shape of little glass boxes to sit in.

It was to producer Ray Lakeland, and to the fact of happening once again to be in the right place at the right moment with my mouth open—literally, and with the right elbow lifted, at that— that I owe another experience in television which has given me more delight than I can say and has turned out to be a compliment not only, if I may say so, to me but also to "us." Lakeland was for some reason at the 1965 Carling tournament at Pleasant Valley outside Boston. I was also there but, having no work to do until the Friday, was idly sitting around having a drink, when he informed me that CBS, who were televising the event, wondered if it would interest me to go up one of their towers, it being their rehearsal day, and "see how they did it." I was naturally intrigued, and did so, joining John Derr, one of their announcers, as they call the commentators in the U.S.

So far as I remember I only said a few words into their microphone, but to my astonishment I got a note from the producer, Frank Chirkinian, inviting me to do the 16th hole next day. This turned out to be a long short hole of some 210-odd yards, where the players drove from an elevated tee down between two bunkers and onto a huge green, behind which we sat under a big parasol on a tower no more than 20 feet high.

"After all I've been through," as my mother is fond of saying, I soon discovered the luxury that is the lot of the American television announcer by comparison with home. Firstly, we ascended our little tower by a broad set of steps instead of a death-trap ladder. The next luxury was the thought of having only one hole to pay attention to, and a short one at that, so one did not even have to watch drives as well as second shots.

At any rate, at Pleasant Valley I did all I was called upon to do, which heaven knows did not seem very much, naming the players and their scores correctly as they came up to the tee, which one could hardly fail to do in view of the fact that a very efficient young fellow had already put a piece of paper in front of one's nose containing the information, and occasionally adding some commonplace comment before being told to "throw it to 15."

It transpired, however, that completely unwittingly, I had managed to cause two minor sensations in our limited little world. One was when, towards the end, a young golfer called Homero Blancas came to the 16th hole with the prospect looming before him of picking up, if everything went right, the equivalent of some £12,000 ($33,000). It proved to be a little much for him and, taking a 2-iron, he hit the shot that a good many of us would have done in the circumstances; in other words, he hit it right off the sole, half topped, and it must have stung like the devil. "Oh, that's a terrible one," I said instinctively. "Right off the bottom of the club." In fact, it scuttled down the hill and finished on the green, but that wasn't the point. I had said it was a bad shot—which of course, it was—but no one, it transpired, had ever said such a thing before, at least in such downright terms.

This, though it took some time for the penny to drop, and I can sometimes scarcely believe it still, was the first "sensation."

The second took even longer to dawn on me. Golf being, like billiards, a "silent" game—that is to say that silence is expected while a man is making his stroke—it had never occurred to me from the very beginning that one should do other than remain silent while the golfer was actually playing his shot, so that "talking on the stroke" had always seemed to be one of the cardinal sins of golf commentating, even though, heaven knows, I have found myself often enough guilty of committing it. This had not been, up to that time, the accepted principle in America it has since become, and the "brilliant flashes of silence" turned out to be the second "sensation."

Also, of course, the most commonplace little expressions in one man's country may seem strange and catch the attention in another's. Towards the end of this (for me) momentous day, for instance, I announced that the eventual winner, Tony Lema, later so tragically killed in a private plane accident, had a very "missable" putt. This, I was told, was greeted with much applause by the crowd watching in the locker room: "You hear what the old guy said? He said, 'He's got a missable putt.' " For some extraordinary reason this commonplace and self-explanatory expression seemed never to have become part of golfing language in America.

Anyway, it was all good for trade, and not only was I invited again by CBS, this time to the Masters at Augusta, which must have a separate mention of its own, but also by ABC who handle such "prestigious" events as the U.S. Open and the PGA Championships. This has meant not only a minimum of four visits to various parts of the States each year but also a whole host of new friendships among the general camaraderie of television, which, though I hope it does not sound pompous, is the team game to end all team games, since there are so many links in the chain between the original product and the viewer's screen that a single incompetent or bloody-minded link can ruin the whole enterprise.

In a modest way, too, my name has gone into the language of television, for by the time we all met in America I had already grown portly enough to wonder what I was doing, climbing these ladders at my weight and age, and made so bold as to wonder whether it would not be possible to somewhat civilise this mode of ascent. From that time onwards a form of staircase, complete with handrail, has been the order of the day, for which I and all my successors may be truly thankful. What I am really proud about, though, is the fact that, in the directions to the scaffolders who erect the towers, these staircases are ordered by ABC under the name of "Longhurst Ladders."

Such is immortality!

As a result of the pleasant episode at Pleasant Valley, CBS, as I have said, invited me the following April to cover a hole at the Masters at Augusta, Ga., and for years I have had the honour, to say nothing of the aesthetic pleasure, of sitting on a little tower at the back of the 16th there, too. It is once again a short hole and clearly, I should have thought, among the first half-dozen in American golf.

Who christened this tournament "the Masters" no one seems quite to know, nor is it certain that the pious founders would ever have started it at all if they had known what eventually they would be letting themselves in for. However that may be, the tournament they created remains unique. No advertisements are allowed to disfigure the scene either inside or outside the grounds —except when some supporter of Arnold Palmer (not, we may be sure, the great man himself) hired an aeroplane to fly noisily over the scene all day trailing a banner with the words GO ARNIE GO. Nor is any mention of filthy lucre permitted, and this really is something when you consider that the "leading money winner" seems to be the chief focus of interest in American golf. All the television directors and commentators have to submit to a solemn lecture forbidding mention of any tournaments other than the U.S. and British Open and Amateur championships and the American PGA (other tournaments on the professional tour simply do not exist) and especially forbidding them to mention money in any form. No prize money is announced beforehand and none presented at the time, it being held sufficient for the winner to have won the Masters and to have been invested with the traditional green blazer, which, thenceforward, even though he be a millionaire, he wears with justifiable pride. Only later is it revealed that the first prize came to $40,000, or whatever it may be.

Perhaps I may add one final comment on my own modest operations in television, namely that, whatever you may say, it is nice to be recognised, even if only by one's voice. This is not vanity. It adds much to the pleasure of a taxi ride (as well as to the tip!), for instance, if the driver says, "I'd know your voice anywhere," and starts talking about golf. Only the other day, hailing a cab opposite the American Embassy in Grosvenor Square, I said, "I wonder if you could take me to Cricklewood Broadway?" to which the man at once replied, "I'd take *you* anywhere."

Like so many London taxi drivers he was an avid golfer—they have a golfing society of their own—and actually had a golf magazine beside him in the cab, open at a picture of Arnold Palmer, who once, he said, the biggest day of his golfing life, he had driven in this very cab. All this is not, however, the irrelevance to the subject of the Masters that it may seem, for my peak was reached, and you can hardly blame me for relating it, when, on handing in my baggage at Cape Town airport in South Africa, I had had time to say only, "I wonder if you could check in this shooting stick as well as the suitcase?" when a transAtlantic voice behind me said, "Hey! Aren't you the guy that does the 16th at the Masters?"

—1945—
MAIDEN SPEECH

I defy any member of parliament in living history to declare that he was completely confident and at ease as he sat in the House waiting to make his maiden speech. All the same it is a tremendous thrill. You know that, for what it is worth, it is a milestone in your own little history. In a few minutes you will have joined that select band of citizens who on their death-beds can say: "Well, at least I once addressed the House of Commons!"

I remember being told: "The Speaker hopes he will be able to call you at about two o'clock." Obviously, that meant no lunch. One can't risk the brain being dulled by the processes of digestion.

A large, pink gin seemed indicated instead. This was duly sent down, followed by another, engendering a well-known, if wholly illusory, feeling of confidence.

I think I knew my humble words pretty well by heart—most "maiden" speakers would admit to that—but I took the precaution of getting them typed out and cut up into small sheets, to fall back upon in the event of that nightmare of orators and broadcasters, the total "blackout." Clutching them in moistened palm, I took my seat on the third bench below the gangway—and from that moment all trace of them vanished from the memory.

Not only could I not remember what I wanted to say, I could not even remember what it was about. Something to do with America—or something. Hastily re-reading the first paragraph, I essayed a desperate silent rehearsal, but concentration is impossible when someone else is addressing the House. Three-quarters of your attention is lured away towards what he is saying. I confess that unworthy thoughts of another pink gin flashed across my mind to be succeeded by the delicious idea of slipping out of the Chamber and postponing the whole ghastly business to a more favourable occasion.

The previous speaker sat down and, rather as the bather plunges into the pool after testing it with his toe, and finding it even colder that he had dared to contemplate, I recall rising to my feet. Rarely in the history of parliament would an Honourable Member have been happier not to catch the Speaker's eye. Memories came surging back of the old days on a more humble back bench, when one had not prepared the overnight translation and the baleful eye of the headmaster searched the class for the next victim.

"Captain Longhurst," said the same kind of voice. This was it.

Perhaps the shock cleared the brain. At any rate, I will say no more of my own maiden speech than that I remembered what I wanted to say, and then, for what it was worth, said it. I don't think it altered the course of history, nor did our foreign affairs take a sudden upward turn as a result of it. If it had not the distinction of Lord Birkenhead's maiden oration, well, at least it was not as big a flop as Disraeli's. Perhaps the best thing about it was that it was over!

My knowledge of golf club bars is somewhat limited, as I am naturally out on the course most of the time. However, I do confess to wishing that I had been in the bar of the North Middlesex Club when the driverless, runaway car came in! Nothing such has occurred in my experience and it is almost too much to hope that it ever will. The nearest I can claim to it is, so to speak, in reverse. I was delivering an impressive harangue at the opening of a certain club's new clubhouse, when the mayor of the town, overcome either by my oratory or the heat, fainted and was passed out of one of the big windows, chair and all, to recover. I then resumed my speech, but it was never quite the same again.

For the golf correspondent numerous human hazards lie in wait in the bar. There is always our old friend who says, "Ha! I see you do your watching from the bar. Ha, ha!" Very witty, sir, and so original! Also, every kind of bore lurks in the bar, anxious to engage you in a one-sided conversation and tell you the story of his life or his round. Of these the worst—to me, though some people find it genuinely interesting—are those who come up and pose problems relating to the Rules of Golf. I feel rather ungracious in saying this, because very often they are flattering enough to begin by saying, "Here—you'll know the answer to this one," and I therefore have to maintain some sort of show of interest, difficult though it may be.

I do not know the Rules of Golf, I never have known them, and I am too old to begin learning them now. I think it is ridiculous that we cannot hit our little balls round with our little sticks without 93 pages of rules and an ever-increasing volume of case law in the form of Decisions, many of them, so I am assured, contradictory to each other. I am afraid I am something of a spoilsport in this connection. I put a damper on the discussion by saying, "Why not look in the book of rules and see?" They have never thought of this—and anyway, as I say, it spoils the fun.

Nevertheless, I confess to enjoying the period before lunch at the golf club bar on a Sunday morning as one of the most enjoyable times of the week and I believe that this goes for a great number of people to whom golf is their recreation after a hard week's work. I am always sympathetic with the clock-slaves who have to creep away just when the talk is getting interesting, for no better reason than that their wife's clock says five to one, or whatever. The answer to this one is surely to alter the wife's clock.

I like to think of myself as something of a connoisseur of bars. What to drink presents me with no problem, for I have long ago settled for pink gin and soda before lunch—or champagne if I can afford it—and whisky and water after 6 o'clock(5:30 in winter), but I think that the surroundings in which you drink make a great deal of difference and that many golf clubs have been very unimaginative in the siting and decor of what after all is the "happiest" room in the club.

Though it is not every club that is lucky enough to have the opportunity, there is nothing in my opinion to touch a bar with a view. The finest bar I have seen in any club in the world—and I have said this many times—is at the Thunderbird Club in the desert in California, where the Ryder Cup match was played some years ago. The course is flat as a pancake, but there is a fine view of the mountains a few miles away, and as the sun sets behind them a magical peace comes over the scene, as in a tropical twilight, and even our American friends, if they will forgive my saying so, tend to fall silent.

The bar at Thunderbird runs the length of a big room, parallel with the window looking out towards the mountains, but here is what makes it different. You sit down to the bar not on high stools but on low leather chairs and settees. Behind these the floor is raised so that those who sit at tables or stand up can see over the heads of those who are sitting down. Furthermore, the floor behind the bar itself is sunk a foot or 18 inches, so that the barmen, as they stand up, are about on the level, face to face, with those who are sitting down and do not obstruct the view.

I have always wished that, while they were spending money on new bars at Turnberry and Gleneagles, where the views in their different ways are both "out of this world," they had adopted this principle. Nor can I see why, if we have got to have these frightful skyscrapers which have now transformed our beloved London scene and in my opinion ruined it, we should not at least have the consolation of being able to sit in a bar at the top of them, just as one does in the "Top of the Mark" in the Mark Hopkins Hotel in San Francisco. We have not yet come to skyscraper clubhouses. All the same, many clubhouses possess splendid views and it seems a pity that so few should make real use of them.

NIGHTMARE OVER NIAGARA

Many years ago the women held their Curtis Cup golf match against the Americans at Buffalo and in the course of it, like any good tourist, I went to see the Niagara Falls, to become at once intrigued not so much by the Falls themselves, which, as Oscar Wilde said, would be much more impressive if they flowed upward, as by the extraordinary antics of folly, nerve and self-destruction performed by mankind under, in and over them. Of those who went over the Falls in barrels, rubber balls, and the rest of it, and even the boy who recently went over by mistake with nothing and still lived, I will mention in passing only two, because I wish to come to the Awful Moment.

The first was one of the most unlikely figures, perhaps, of all time, a tight-waisted, corseted, thoroughly Victorian, middle-aged schoolmistress, Mrs. Annie Taylor. Having inserted a kitten in her barrel, she sent it over the Falls in a trial run. When she opened the barrel, the kitten was dead. Next morning, October 4, 1901, sharply reminding would-be dissuaders to mind their own business, she eased herself into her barrel and, in front of a crowd of several thousands, was cast off. Meanwhile, her manager retired to a bar and averted his eyes. Three hours later, bruised, battered but by no means bewildered, and with the bun on her head still neatly in place, she was hauled alive from the barrel. Having sacked the manager for dereliction of duty in retiring to the bar, she set herself up as the Queen of the Mist and, posing beside her barrel, made a living signing autographs.

We come now to the tightrope walkers and the Awful Moment, and my excuse for including them is the fact that I have dined out successfully on this particular episode for years.

The greatest of all tightrope walkers was a thin, cadaverous man with matted hair and beard, Jean François Gravelet, who was the son of one of the heroes of Napoleon's army, and who was otherwise known as Blondin. He first walked Niagara in 1859. A year later he was back, his name a household word all over the world, with the Prince of Wales (later Edward VII) and former President Millard Fillmore among the spectators. He put on such a show as made women tear handkerchiefs to shreds and strong men bite their nails to the quick. He ran to and fro, slipping deliberately in a swirl of legs and arms and recovering himself. He walked across backwards; with baskets on his feet; and on stilts. He lowered a mug, and, hauling it up, drank the waters he defied.

He held out his hat at arm's length and the local sharpshooter from the boat, Maid of the Mist, put a bullet through it. Finally, he took out a portable stove, squatted on the rope, and cooked and ate an omelet. At last there was nothing more for him to do. At this moment there steps into the picture a man who to me is one of the unsung heroes of all time—Blondin's manager, Harry Colcord, of Chicago.

It was the manager's idea. Somehow they had to go on attracting the crowds. What about taking a man across on his back? Splendid, said Blondin—and we may imagine the scenes that followed. "What about you, sir? Nice chance to achieve fame and fortune . . . All over in a few minutes . . . No? Well, *you*, sir? Come along, sir . . . No? . . . ."

At what point the dreadful inspiration entered Colcord's head we do not know. We may surmise, without doing him posthumous injustice, that he had been drinking at the time.

"I suppose," he said, "I shall have to do it myself."

Now Colcord had never in his life stepped onto a tightrope. So, while we may never envisage ourselves in Blondin's position, we can without the least stretch of imagination see ourselves in the manager's.

When the great day came, 100,000 people assembled on the banks. Betting was fast and furious. The odds were even money.

The manager, as big a man as Blondin, took off his coat and mounted the maestro's back, and a moment later the pair embarked on the frightful expedition. On the downward journey all went well, but, as they mounted the slope on the other side, their pace was seen gradually to slacken. Amid a muttered rumbling of speculation among the watchers on the cliffs they came to a full stop.

Let us leave the watchers and focus our attention upon the nightmare predicament of the two figures balancing over the abyss. This is the Awful Moment.

"It is no good," Blondin is saying, "I am exhausted. You will have to get down!"

The reader may be left to imagine for himself what surged through the manager's head; the appeals to the Almighty to spare him but this once, and never again . . .; the urging-on of his exhausted steed; the dread realisation; the frantic groping of his shiny shoes for the rope invisible behind and below.

Somehow he dismounted, and for minutes they stood upon their awful perch, the maestro panting to recover his strength, Colcord clutching his hips from behind, and speculators on the bank advancing the odds to even money Blondin, 6-1 the manager.

The latter, of course, had no chance of walking up the steeply inclined rope. How was he to remount? A sort of creeping, furtive, one-knee-at-a-time action suggests itself, though whether you can climb on a man's back with the remaining foot balanced only on a swaying steel hawser is open to doubt. Yet the full-blooded leap—"Allez, oop!"—with its attendant probability of the whole ensemble disappearing in a flurry of arms, legs and 20-foot pole, gyrating slowly as they fell and vanishing with a scarcely visible splash in the swirling torrent below . . . no, I cannot think they would have decided on that.

The lonely, desperate conference has never, alas, been recorded, nor the method by which the manager at last climbed back, but get back he did and the picture shows the pair of them with 10 yards left to go. Colcord's eyes have vanished into their sockets; his mouth is agape; his cheekbones stand out like a skeleton's. And the caption calls him the "Timorous Manager!"

"I break out into a cold sweat," he recorded later in life, "whenever I think of it."

So, for that matter, do I.

—1975—
"IT'LL TAKE THREE DAMN GOOD SHOTS TO GET UP IN TWO, SIR"

As I look back on a life of golf which started when I was about 10 and has taken me to many parts of the world which I otherwise would never have seen, I often think that one of its more rewarding aspects has been the association with the long and miscellaneous crew, ranging from enchanting children to out-and-out brigands, who have carried my clubs.

A wonderful fellow-feeling can arise between a man and his caddie, and at its best the relationship can hardly, I think, be matched elsewhere in sport. In common with royalty, editors and boxing managers, the good caddie instinctively talks of "we" and "us"—e.g., "We was robbed at the 14th"—instead of using the third person. It is indeed a question of the two of us against "them."

Nowadays it is nothing for a caddie to be working his way through college towards a degree which his employer could never have obtained, but in my younger days such a thing would not have been held "respectable," especially in England. My first feeling towards caddies, however, was of sheer envy. Attending a school below the first hole on the Royal Eastbourne Course in Sussex, I used to seek relief from Greek irregular verbs by peering furtively at the golfers on the skyline and especially at the young caddies so lucky as to be trailing along behind them.

These boys, incidentally, were subject to stern discipline and a savage system of fines for misdemeanors, which I only wish I had space to quote in full. Suffice it to say that they had to attend six days a week for the equivalent sum of about 20 cents a day, plus 20 cents per round of 18 holes. On the other hand, the penalty for "Fighting: Throwing stones: Rough or coarse play: Ill-treating any caddie: Shouting or annoying any member: Smoking in the club-room or workshop, or Using obscene language" was 20 cents, while "Laziness: Inattention: Rudeness or smoking while carrying the clubs, or Asking for gratuities(!)" was 20 cents for the first offence and 45 cents for the second, which must have made a nasty hole in one's weekly wage.

My first experience with a caddie came in a junior competition, I being 13 and he about 15. He admired a pair of white shoes I was wearing and in a burst of fellow-feeling I said that if we won—I am sure I said "we," not "I"—I would give them to him. We did, and I did, and a national golf writer rather charmingly reported that "the traditions of kings and cobblers who were companions on the links never had happier expression."

Later, when playing matches each Saturday for Cambridge University against the better-known London clubs, one graduated to the real Artful Dodgers of the caddie world, men of ready wit and nimble fingers, not above carrying, when the stakes were high, a second ball with the same markings, ready in emergency to be dropped down the trouser leg through a hole in the pocket. A friend of mine, playing at Walton Heath, found himself in an appalling divot mark in mid-fairway. "That'd be a nice one to get in the Medal," he said—to which his caddie replied darkly, "You'd never 'ave 'ad it in the Medal."

The London caddie is liable to come out with comments which he may or may not appreciate for their real worth. One, leaning up against the wind at a long par-4 hole, observed in my presence, "Take three damn good shots to get up in two today, sir." We all knew what he meant and you could hardly put it better. Tom Webster, a well-known sports cartoonist in his day, remarked to his caddie on the size of the cemetery marking the out-of-bounds on a long hole. Having announced that it was the biggest in North London, the caddie added, "And furthermore, we have some very well-to-do people buried here."

Visitors to Britain are often astonished at the age of some of the caddies, especially at St. Andrews. In a tournament there, when I fortunately had a small bag and an abbreviated set of clubs, they were carried for me by an obviously senior member of a local family. When I ventured to ask his age, he revealed that he was 81. He did 18 holes in splendid style but the family would not like it, he said, if he came out again in the afternoon.

The most celebrated caddie in British golf was old Skip Daniels, nearer 70 years old than 60, with whom Walter Hagen and later, in 1932, Gene Sarazen won the Open at Sandwich, and about whom Sarazen wrote so movingly with Herbert Warren Wind in *Thirty Years of Championship Golf*—the best book of its kind I ever read. Later there came an almost tearful goodbye. "I waved to him as he pedaled happily down the drive," Sarazen wrote, "the coat I had given him flapping in the breeze, and there was a good-sized lump in my throat as I thought how the old fellow had never flagged for a moment during the arduous grind of the tournament and how he had made good his vow to win a championship for me before he died." They were destined never to see each other again.

One of the finest caddies in Britain, always in demand, was "Aunt Polly," or Mrs. M. Mitchell, aunt of the Ryder Cup player of the early '30s, Abe Mitchell. She compiled her reminiscences of caddying at the Royal Ashdown Forest Club in a school exercise book, in flawless hand, spelling, punctuation and grammar, a collector's piece if ever there was one. I quote only the singular episode involving the Rev. Mr. Williams and the big red cow with the long horns. The reverend gentleman, having driven into the ditch at the seventh, picked out and dropped in a bad spot:

"He almost missed the shot and hit the cow, who was standing directly in front and swishing her tail to keep off the flies, and the ball lodged under her tail.

"The poor cow, getting more angry every minute, ran off in the direction of the green. The Rev. Williams said, 'What do I do now?' I told him to drop another ball. I said, 'I don't suppose the cow will go far away, so I can get your other ball.' But the man on the mowing machine, waiting to mow the fairway, was doubled up with laughter at my predicament and, of course, he was back at the golf club before I, so my fellow caddies had the laugh on me."

There ought to be many more female caddies, of course. On the continent of Europe they are commonplace, some of them elderly grandmothers of whom there seem to be only a skinny pair of legs visible when they have cheerfully shouldered some indifferent player's enormous bag; others maidens of such good looks as to make it difficult to concentrate on the business at hand. One such was Gertrude, a blonde beauty who caddied for me in the German Amateur Championship before the war. I mention her not only in gratitude, but as an excuse to inform you that I—I beg Gertrude's pardon, "we"—won the championship.

Girls, of course, excel as caddies in Japan. After the then Canada Cup at Kasumigaseki, outside Tokyo, it is understood that Sam Snead had to be deterred from leaving his clubs behind and bringing his caddie home in the bag in their place.

On the whole, though, it is boys who are the most entertaining companions on the links. At Hong Kong soon after the war no fewer than nine children, most of them in big conical straw hats, insisted on accompanying me round as caddies, at a few cents apiece, and it was more like taking the kindergarten for a walk than playing golf. The lies in which I found my ball, however, were outstanding and the only reason I did not find it actually on a peg tee in the rough was that the boys possessed no peg tees.

In Lagos, Nigeria, the caddies are black boys, some of them so black that I found myself staring at them fascinated and wondering whether it was humanly possible. On their heads they wear ridiculous little "school" caps, bright red, each with his own number on. As caddies they are splendidly, magnificently idle. They do not care. And, thinking it over, one cannot see any possible reason why they should. As a disturbing force, however, they are to be reckoned with. I defy any man to give of his best if, just out of the corner of his eye as he addresses the ball, he sees an enormous big toe, jet black, wiggling up and down. As for finding a lost ball, not a hope. "I look 'um. I no see 'um. No dere!" Followed by a vast, engaging ear-to-ear grin.

The United States caddie, on the other hand, is often highly conscious of his responsibilities and the player may have a choice of marking him Good, Fair or Poor. Further, in the example I have before me from a game at Rochester, N.Y., many years ago, he may mark a cross against any or all of the following: "Does not replace divots/Does not mark ball/Does not take flag/Lags behind/Does not rake traps/Moves on green/Inattentive/Talks to players."

The boy who accompanied me at Rochester had just, he informed me, got a basketball scholarship, I forget where, and was full of a thirst for knowledge. He put me through a continuous interrogation in our leisurely 4½ hours on the course together. Topics ranged from the effects of the industrial revolution in England, the bombing of London, to the House of Lords, London fogs, and had I met Montgomery and did I know Winston Churchill?

By the time we reached the 17th green—and we were now in the fifth hour—I had decided with reluctance that a cross against "Talks to players" was indicated. At this point, however, curiously enough for the third time, I exploded a ball from the bunker to within a yard of the flag. "Gee," said the boy, "I ain't never seen no one get out of traps the way you do!"

I marked him "Excellent and Attentive."

BENEVOLENT DICTATORS

There are all sorts of ways of running a golf club and I cannot help feeling that, having played at some 400-odd clubs in more than 30 countries, I must have seen most of them. At the end of it all I come to the conclusion that the most effective of the lot is the "benevolent dictator." Of course, there is no such thing really as a one-man club, but the reader will know what I mean.

At one club your request is greeted with, "You will have to bring that up at the annual general meeting." At another it is a question of "You had better ask Mr. So-and-So and, if he says it is all right, go ahead." For myself I infinitely prefer the latter. Even if Mr. So-and-So is liable at times to give you a stony stare and a firm negative, at least you know where you are.

Three examples of benevolent dictators come at once to my mind, two in the United States and one in Britain. The first is the now almost legendary John Arthur Brown, whom I had the privilege of meeting, and being soundly beaten by, at Pine Valley. A few years back I met him driving his own golf car over the slopes of George Fazio's magnificent new creation, the Jupiter Hills Course near Palm Beach, Fla. John Arthur Brown, at past 80, was still, they assured me, most definitely in charge at Pine Valley.

Then, of course, there was the redoubtable Mr. Clifford Roberts, Chairman of the Augusta National Golf Club since before the course was even built.

"How wonderful to have done it all alone," someone remarked of Lindbergh's flight over the Atlantic. "More wonderful,' was the reply, "if he had done it with the aid of a committee."

My own British benevolent dictator, and he really did dictate, was the late J.F. Abercromby, universally known as "Aber" and certainly one of the outstanding architects in all golf, as the many visitors who have played the two London courses he designed at Addington will agree. About 40 years my senior, he used to wear a green velour porkpie hat and habitually carried under his arm an ancient wooden putter.

We younger members were in considerable awe of him. I was standing beside him at the bar at Addington one Sunday morning when a member came in and pre-emptively demanded of the steward, "Where's the suggestion book?" Aber turned slowly around and prodded the luckless fellow with a bony finger. Then, pointing to himself, he said, "I'm the suggestion book!"

That's the way to run a golf club.

P. G. WODEHOUSE ON GOLF

"It is one of the chief merits of golf," says the Master—writing as an 18-handicap man who has "got to look extremely slippy if he doesn't want to find himself in the 20's again"—"that non-success at the game induces a certain amount of decent humility, which keeps a man from pluming himself on any petty triumphs he may achieve in other walks of life . . . Sudden success at golf is like the sudden acquisition of wealth. It is apt to unsettle and deteriorate the character."

"Golf," says the Oldest Member, ruminating on the terrace, "acts as a corrective against sinful pride. I attribute the insane arrogance of the later Roman emperors almost entirely to the fact that, never having played golf, they never knew that strange chastening humility which is engendered by a topped chip shot. If Cleopatra had been ousted in the first round of the Ladies' Singles, we should have heard a lot less of her proud imperiousness."

It is no surprise, then, that so many of the characters in P.G. Wodehouse's golfing stories are, in the golfing sense, humble performers. One thinks, for instance, of the Saturday foursome which the Oldest Member observes "struggling raggedly up the hill to the ninth green. Like all Saturday foursomes it is in difficulties. One of the patients is zigzagging about the fairway like a liner pursued by submarines. Two others seem to be digging for buried treasure, unless—it is too far off to be certain—they are killing snakes. The remaining cripple, who has just foozled a mashie shot, is blaming his caddie."

Supreme among the foozlers, however, must be the Wrecking Crew, who feature in what is almost my favourite story, "Chester Forgets Himself." Chester Meredith, needing a 4 to beat the record, comes upon them moving up the 18th fairway with their caddies in mass formation, "looking to his exasperated eye like one of those great race migrations of the Middle Ages." The star performer of the Wrecking Crew—"if there can be said to be grades in such a sub-species"—was the First Grave-Digger. "The lunches of 57 years had caused his chest to slip down to the mezzanine floor but he was still a powerful man, and had in his youth been a hammer-thrower of some repute. He differed from his colleagues—The Man with the Hoe, Old Father Time, and Consul, the Almost Human—in that, while they were content to peck cautiously at the ball, he never spared himself in his efforts to do it a violent injury."

How often have I made use of that last phrase—generally, I may say, with acknowledgment—both in writing and on the television! That and Mitchell Holmes, who "missed short putts because of the uproar of the butterflies in the adjoining meadows." Every writer delights in occasionally getting precisely the right word in the right place, and there are, of course, innumerable instances in the Wodehouse canon. None, surely, is better than "uproar."

What a wonderful character is the Oldest Member, introducer and narrator of the series! There he sits, with his venerable white hair, under the chestnut tree overlooking the ninth green, from which he can also look down on the duffers putting ball after ball into the lake at the second and enjoy to the full "that perfect peace, that peace beyond all understanding, which comes at its maximum only to the man who has given up golf."

To him comes a succession of young men, crossed in love or so unsuccessful on the links as to cause them to threaten to give away their clubs, or even, in extreme cases, to blaspheme against the sacred game itself. He always has a parable to tell and pins them relentlessly down while he tells it.

"Did you ever hear of the Ancient Mariner?" says one of them.

"Many years ago," says the Oldest Member. "Why do you ask?"

"Oh, I don't know," says the young man. "It just occurred to me."

"Can you name a single case," cries one distraught youth, "where devotion to this pestilential game has done a man any practical good?"

The Sage smiled gently. "I could name a thousand."

"One will do."

"I will select," said the Sage, "from the innumerable memories that rush to my mind, the story of Cuthbert Banks."

"Never heard of him."

"Be of good cheer," said the Oldest Member. "You are going to hear of him now"—and thus is introduced what must by common consent be the greatest of the stories, *The Clicking of Cuthbert.*

This with its companion episodes was published in 1922, and *The Heart of a Goof* in 1926, and this means that, though the author can give me the best part of 30 years, he is writing of the world of golf that I knew when I "came in."

The characters call clubs by their proper names: the driver, the brassie, and the baffy; the mashie, the mashie-niblick and the niblick. They wear plus-fours and still play stymies. They all have caddies, either venerable gentlemen, as on so many English courses in those days, or small boys who sneeze or hiccup at the critical moment. They still use sand tees, and the ball nearly sliced in two by a member of the Wrecking Crew is a blue-dot Silver King—the ball of my early golfing days.

"You, ordinary?" cries Cuthbert to Adeline . . . "You can't have been looking in a glass lately. You stand alone. Simply alone. You make the rest look like battered repaints." Only my generation is left to remember the repainting of an old ball by rolling it in a film of white paint in the palms (its distinctive smell comes back to me as I write) and laying it out to dry on a board of upturned nails like a fakir's bed.

How refreshing to read through all the stories and find not a single mention of how much money a professional has won. The duffers look with awe upon "the pro"—the club pro, that is—as an almost godlike creature, and their respect for such distant heroes as the Great Triumvirate of Vardon, Braid and Taylor may be likened to that of a minor curate for the Archbishop of Canterbury. Jane Packard and William Bates ("The Purification of Rodney Spelvin") call their little son Braid-Vardon Bates, while Adeline, a heretic now converted to golf, is only prevented by Cuthbert's earnest pleading from christening their firstborn Abe Mitchell Ribbed-Faced Mashie Banks.

It is with the pro at Nijni-Novgorod that Vladimir Brusiloff, the Russian literary sage, is partnered in his epic match against Lenin and Trotsky, when Trotsky has a two-inch putt for the hole *(The Clicking of Cuthbert)*: ". . . but just as he addresses the ball, someone in the crowd tries to assassinate Lenin with a rewolwer—you know that is our great national sport, trying to assassinate Lenin with rewolwers—and the bang puts Trotsky off his stroke and he goes five yards past the hole and then Lenin, who is rather shaken, you understand, he misses again himself and we win the hole and the match and I clean up 396,000 rubles or 15 shillings in your money."

Our Author, we are told, went to America in 1904 and again in 1909, when he sold two short stories for $100 apiece and decided to remain there, so all the golfing stories will have been written in America. It is amazing, therefore, not only that they retain their almost wholly English background and character—or should I say British, since at that time in America "all pros are Scotchmen"—but also that the American public (the stories were all first published in the *Saturday Evening Post*) should have appreciated and lapped them up as they did. Sometimes I wonder, rather basely, whether there were two versions, adjusted for each side of the Atlantic.

How otherwise could the vast *Saturday Evening Post* audience have appreciated the Oldest Member's homily on the beginning of great friendships: "Who can trace to its beginnings the love of Damon for Pythias, of David for Jonathan, of Swan for Edgar? Who can explain what it was about Crosse that first attracted Blackwell?" They will have understood when told that no open champion had yet been known to have gone to prison, but what would they have made of the theory that the sort of men who tee up their ball in the rough are "in and out of Wormwood Scrubs all the time. They find it hardly worthwhile to get their hair cut in their brief intervals of liberty?" Would the Cornish Riviera on its way to Penzance have struck a chord?

And what would they have made of Mortimer Sturgis, who wanted for his nuptials "a somewhat florid ceremony at St. George's, Hanover Square, with the Vicar of Tooting (a scratch player, excellent at short approach shots) officiating and 'The Voice that Breathed O'er St. Andrews' booming from the organ?"

The younger reader of today may be forgiven for suspecting the Vicar of Tooting to have been a rather feeble jest on the Master's part, but not so. The Tooting Bec Club, long since built over, was in the heart of suburban London, only a mile or so from Peter Sellers's immortal Bal-ham, Gateway to the South, and was thought worthy of inclusion in Horace Hutchinson's *British Golf Links*. It was founded on Tooting Common in 1888 with the Rt. Hon. A.J. Balfour, a future Prime Minister, as president, and in 1891 became the first home of the Parliamentary Golf Handicap, a tournament which is still played today. "Only players who use their iron deftly," Hutchinson wrote, "can expect to get round under three figures."

Whether Wodehouse would have credited, when he was writing in the early 1920's, that the day would come when we should have "proettes" in the United States, touring on a regular "circuit" of tournaments and winning tens of thousands of dollars, I very much doubt. Most of the stories have female characters in the shape either of formidable wives or ex-wives or, more likely, doe-eyed heroines, who mostly do not play golf but walk round, like Barbara Medway, whom in a most satisfying conclusion Ferdinand Dibble "folded in his arms, using the interlocking grip." Nor, of course, must we forget Mrs. Podmarsh, who said of her son, "Rollo is exceedingly good at golf. He scores more than 120 every time, while Mr. Burns, who is supposed to be one of the best players in the club, seldom manages to reach 80."

Another female inspired perhaps the best of Wodehouse's dedications to his books, in this case to *The Heart of a Goof*:

To
My Daughter
LEONORA
without whose never failing
sympathy and encouragement
this book
would have been finished in
half the time.

The dedication in the *Clicking of Cuthbert* bears witness to the author's respect for the history and traditions of golf:

To the immortal memory of
JOHN HENRIE AND PAT LOGIE
who at Edinburgh in the year
AD 1593 were imprisoned for
'Playing of the gowff on the links of
Leith every Sabbath the time of
the sermonses',
also of
ROBERT ROBERTSON
who got it in the neck in
AD 1604 for the same reason.

A cat, they say, may look at a king, and in that spirit I may perhaps add the respectful opinion that a great majority, even of the most devoted Wodehouse fans, tend, in chuckling at his characters and the ludicrous situations into which they contrive to get themselves, to overlook just what a master of the English language he is. This occurs more forcibly, of course, to those of us who struggle to extract a living from it ourselves, so I will content myself with quoting something which I wrote in an autobiography:

"Another great writer of English, as I see it, is P. G. Wodehouse, and from him I learnt two things, one of them particularly comforting, namely, that to write well you did not have to write on a serious subject, so there was no reason why I should not try hard just because I only did little pieces about golf. The other was that good writing *flows*, in other words, you may well have the right words but not have them in the right order. Although it is poetry, not prose, the classic example is, of course, 'The ploughman homeward plods his weary way.' There are, I believe, dozens of orders in which the words can be put—but only one right one. However trivial or hilarious the subject, Wodehouse's writing always *flows*."

"A trivial subject?" I seem to hear the Oldest Member saying. "That varied, never-ending pageant that men call golf—a trivial subject? My boy, you are not yourself!"

THAT RUGGED BRITISH GAME

Many thousands of Americans, we hope, will be paying us a visit in Britain this year. We hope so, not merely because the war sentenced us to spend much of our lives searching for dollars and this is one of the most congenial ways of extracting them, but also because, contrary to our reputation for standoffishness, in the bottom of our hearts we are delighted to have people come to see us. I hereby add my own personal hope that as many as may be permitted by their wives will bring their golf clubs with them for, whatever may be our failings in other directions, in this small island we do possess indisputably the golfing treasure house of the world.

Golf in Britain has two supreme merits, both accidents of geography. The first is that, while one American country club course presents the player with much the same golfing problems as another, over here you'll play four or five different species of golf all presenting different problems and demanding different degrees of golfing intelligence. You may play, for instance, on some of the great championship links beside the sea—on the "linksland" left as a sort of no man's land when the sea receded 15 million years ago. It left those folding valleys between the sand hills and that unique, crisp, seaside turf designed by Providence for rabbits and golfers, and useless, fortunately, for anything else. We tend to think that golf by the sea is the real golf and that everything else is a somewhat indifferent man-made substitute. Nevertheless, we can offer a formidable range of these substitutes: heath and heather; woods and forest; moorland; ancestral parks; and the Highlands of Scotland.

Our second geographical advantage lies in distance, or rather lack of it. Golf in Britain is "get-at-able." The United States is so vast that no one, however enthusiastic or well endowed, can cover the whole field in the way that is possible over here. Indeed, I dare say that I, myself, have seen as many of America's best courses as most Americans. They include clubs as far apart as Winged Foot, the National, Pine Valley, Pinehurst, Augusta, Oklahoma City, Tam O'Shanter, Pebble Beach and, for good measure, Honolulu. In Britain, in effect, all our courses are compressed into an area equivalent to the state of New York. Four hundred miles, or one night in a railway sleeper, would cover the lot.

Also important to the visitor, though not so important to the natives, is the fact that golf in Britain happens to divide itself conveniently into half a dozen neat compartments, each containing a selection of the most notable courses, all reachable from the same base. These are London, Sandwich, Liverpool, the West of Scotland, Edinburgh, and the triangle of Gleneagles-Carnoustie-St. Andrews.

The first London course that comes to the visitor's mind is usually Sunningdale and here at once we are confronted with another intriguing aspect of golf which, again for reasons of geography, cannot be paralleled in America. Pressed by justifiable claims from clubs all over the States, the U.S. Golf Association has to spread its championship jam somewhat thinly. It cannot return constantly to a small rota of championship courses. In Britain the Open Championship has been played on only 13 different courses in more than one hundred years. Thus there grows up around all the great links a historical background based not on musty textbooks but on vivid personal memories of the great figures of golf in their moments of triumph and disaster.

Furthermore, golf being the only game in which one can perform on the very battleground on which the mighty have made history, the humble can stand exactly where the great man stood, facing the same problem, and their solution may well be superior to the one which, in the event, lost him several thousand pounds. No one, broadly speaking, can play tennis at Wimbledon or Forest Hills. Anyone can play at St. Andrews tomorrow. Thus, if you know your way around, the thrill of playing the great courses is much intensified by the procession of shadowy figures who seem to step out from the past and tag along beside you. This applies particularly to American visitors, since it is your compatriots who, for the past 40 years, have written the more exciting pages of golfing history in Britain.

Golf clubs in England and Scotland are not, of course, as lavish as the average country club in the States. As a rule they are golf clubs pure and simple, like your Pine Valley or Cypress Point. They do not cater to the whole family and, largely on account of the climate, you will find no swimming pool at these clubs. Indeed, some do not even boast showers. What is more, however explicit your instructions to the barman, you will never get a decent martini—but please do not blame us for that. The reason, little appreciated by Americans, is that, whereas you make the best martini in the world with our exported gin, we can't get the same gin for love or money. Ours is only 70 proof. What we send to you is 83 or more; it's all a matter of taxation, too painful to go into.

On the other hand, golf in Britain, particularly in Scotland, retains much of that original, indefinable "feel" or atmosphere which is necessarily sacrificed amid the trappings of a luxurious country club. Without a doubt it makes a greater demand on the player in the way of inventiveness, ingenuity and the variety of strokes at his command. On a fast-running seaside course with a stiff breeze, short-cropped turf and greens like lightning, the wedge, which by sheer repetition has dimmed the wits of American golfers and removed so much of the artistry from the short game, may spell absolute disaster. To master the Old Course at St. Andrews you require no fewer than five distinct strokes from 40-yards' range, only one of which, and probably the least frequent, is the high-flying wedge.

Around London, which is generally the first port of call, there must be a hundred presentable courses, but the best are about 25 miles out, in the heather-and-pine belt in Surrey. The one that comes first to mind is, I have said, Sunningdale. A mile or two before reaching the club, look out for the inconspicuous white gates leading to Fort Belvedere, from which the Duke of Windsor made his abdication broadcast. It was at Sunningdale that the greatest American of them all played what is still regarded as the greatest round of all (not the lowest, that is, but the most nearly flawless). It was a qualifying round for the Open of 1926. The player was Bobby Jones and the score was 66: 33 putts, 33 other shots; no 5's, no 2's. He holed a long putt for a birdie at the fifth and bunkered his tee shot at the short 13th, though pitching out for a 3. These were the only two "unorthodox" strokes in that qualifying round. The rest were par personified.

An easy pilgrimage out of London by car is the 70-mile journey to Sandwich, taking in Canterbury Cathedral on the way. Golfers and cathedrals are not perhaps a usual combination, but Canterbury is something apart. Anyway, I seem to remember a story about Gene Sarazen being shown over a cathedral and, on being informed that some part of it was built in 1170, remarking, "Gee, it's older than Hagen!" Both of these two in their day have made Sandwich a happy hunting ground. There are three courses: Royal St. George's and Prince's, beside each other at Sandwich, and Royal Cinque Ports a little way along at Deal, a mile or two from where Julius Caesar landed in 55 B.C. Deal, low-lying, is protected from the sea by a pebble ridge and the ships seem to be higher than the golfers—as indeed they are. On the sixth green, hard beside the foreshore, you may care to recall the man who, on missing a short putt there, brandished his club aloft and cried, "How the devil can a man be expected to putt with all this traffic going up and down the Channel!"

Deal saw the first appearance of Hagen in England. It was the Open of 1920 and, though he survived to the final day, he spent it in a private and unpublicised contest with his partner as to which of the two would finish last. It was at St. George's two years later that he won the first of his four British Opens and, as you walk out across the clubhouse lawn, you may imagine him there in his camel's-hair coat, receiving the trophy from the then youthful Prince of Wales and giving the prize money straight to his elderly caddie Daniels, thus launching the first of the "Hagen stories" which connoisseurs collect and cherish.

Across the way is Prince's. Can it really be well over 40 years ago that we watched Sarazen striding up the last hole followed by his vast gallery, serene in the knowledge that no one could beat him now? By his side was the same old Daniels; Daniels is dead now and so for a long time was the Prince's that Sarazen knew. It was battered to pieces as a target range in the war and pigeons nested in the remains of the clubhouse. Then, when everything had been rebuilt, the sea came in and flooded the course four feet deep. Now at last it seems home and dry.

The northwest corner of England is another locality where several golfing birds can be killed with one stone: the Royal Liverpool Club at Hoylake, Formby, the various Southport courses, and, higher up the coast, Royal Lytham and St. Annes— all enriched for the visitor who cares to recapture beforehand something of their past. Jones's Grand Slam of 1930, for instance, included the British Open at Hoylake.

As you play that last hole there, you may like to imagine a really colossal crowd lining it from tee to green with Frank Stranahan on the tee. He had a 2 to tie with Fred Daly for the Open, and his second shot really did finish inches from the pin. It produced the biggest roar I ever heard on a golf course in Britain.

Best of all, though, I like to imagine an incident at Hoylake that happened before I was born. It was, I believe, the first professional tournament ever to be played there and the hero was an old Scottish pro called Jamie Anderson. As does everyone who plays Hoylake more than once, he drove out-of-bounds at the first hole. Reaching in his pocket, he drew out another ball—and sliced *it* out-of-bounds. In silence he reached for another. Out-of-bounds. "Ma God!" he said. "It's like playing up a spout!"

At Lytham you will see more concrete evidence of the past, literally concrete, in the shape of a kind of "tombstone" marking the spot, and of all the great scenes of the past this is perhaps the easiest for the visitor to recapture. It is the Open of 1926, the one for which Jones had qualified at Sunningdale, and here he is, partnered with Al Watrous, coming up the 17th in the final round. The championship lies between the two of them and they are level. The hole bends to the left and Watrous, correctly, drives to the right edge of the fairway. Jones hooks into the sand. Watrous plays a good one to the short edge of the green, whereupon Jones, as the "tombstone" bears evidence, hits his ball from the sand to the green, a direct carry of 170 yards. He went on to win by two shots; the mashie iron (hickory-shafted, of course) with which he played his historic stroke hangs in the clubhouse today. And as you play the 18th hole, spare a thought for Hagen. They talk of it still at Lytham—how, needing a 2 to tie with Jones, he sent his caddie all the way up to the pin and then, with every window and balcony crammed, hit his ball into the geraniums under the clubhouse windows.

Perhaps, instead of starting from London, you will fly into Britain via Prestwick, thus alighting a mile or two from the first tee of the course on which the first 11 British Opens were played, beginning in 1860. The one-time calm of this little Scottish holiday town is now shattered by a procession of airliners from all over the world, but it is no small convenience for transAtlantic golfers to be deposited, so to speak, on the doorstep. Arriving from Sussex for the 1952 Amateur Championship, won by Harvie Ward, I was disconcerted to find that Jimmy McHale had taken rather less time to get there over the broad Atlantic from Philadelphia.

Prestwick, a little archaic perhaps by modern standards, but on no account to be missed, has seen two of the greatest crowds in golfing history. One reason for this is the desperate partisanship of the local Scots, who will turn out in thousands in the hope of seeing one of their men beat an Englishman, an American or a man from the East of Scotland—in that order of preference. The other is that they can get in for nothing via the "Aberdeen Gate," i.e., the sand hills beside the beach. The first of Prestwick's great crowds was the one that trampled their compatriot, Macdonald Smith, into taking 82 for the last round of the 1925 Open when he needed only 78 to win. The other, a more happy occasion, was the first of Lawson Little's victories, in the 1934 Amateur, when his opponent was a local artisan (or public-links golfer, as you would call him), James Wallace. Little flashed round in 66, started 3-3-4-3-3 in the afternoon, and won by a record 14 and 13. The match was advanced to enable him to catch the boat to America and people were pouring in by the hundreds an hour after he had gone.

Down the road from Prestwick is Troon, another typical seaside links whose difficulty depends on how hard the wind is blowing. When Sarazen came over in 1923 (he was then U.S. Open champion), it blew so hard in the morning that the fishing boats could not leave the harbor. Having blown Sarazen into an 85, it completely subsided; the rest of the field came in with low 70's, and Sarazen failed to qualify. He said he would come back even if he had to swim across—which is one reason for his persistent popularity in Britain.

My own favourite is Turnberry, which, though owned by the nationalised railways, is one of the finest hotels in the country and should be your base in the West of Scotland. It overlooks a view of surpassing beauty: the two courses stretched out below, the white lighthouse out on the Point, and in the purple distance the Isle of Arran and the long protecting arm of the Mull of Kintyre. Believe it or not, both these lovely Turnberry courses were flattened for an airfield during the war. Modern implements, government money and Mackenzie Ross, the architect, have done such a good job that one can hardly tell now where the airfield runways were.

Incidentally, when driving from Turnberry, stop on the slope marked Electric Brae. "Brae" means a hill in Scotland and this one slopes down towards a wood into which the road disappears. As you release the brake, the car begins to move with gathering speed *upward*. A golf ball laid on the road does the same. The thing is quite uncanny. Some say it is an optical illusion due to the configuration of the hedges.

The chain of courses lying along the southern shore of the Forth, a few miles outside Edinburgh, is in every way the equal of those in the West. They include Muirfield, North Berwick (call it "Berrick"), Longniddry, two courses at Luffness and three at Gullane (which you call "Gillan"). I remember them with special affection because, on taking a job with a North Berwick family during a vacation from Cambridge University years ago, ostensibly to teach the boy Latin and arithmetic, I found myself playing with the golf-mad father on all these eight courses in the first week. It was at Muirfield, more properly known as the Honourable Company of Edinburgh Golfers and perhaps a little more "aristocratic" than the rest, that Big Bill Campbell, U.S. Walker Cup captain in 1955, was surprisingly beaten by Douglas Bachli of Australia in the Amateur Championship final—an event of which my own outstanding impression is that of the lanky Campbell bicycling bandy-legged up to the club each morning on a hired machine that was two sizes too small for him.

The Gullane and Luffness courses are perhaps the most "natural" you will find in Britain. Seeing the heather and gorse and soft green turf from afar, instinct tells you that, if this is not a golf course, it ought to be. The No. 1 Course at Gullane, where the late Babe Zaharias won the Women's Championship before turning pro, takes you to the top of a hill from which you can gaze down on long stretches of golden sands, the Archerfield Wood immortalised by Robert Louis Stevenson, and in the distance the dim tracery of the Great Forth Bridge. With the wind in your hair and the wild flowers under your feet—and plovers nesting in the bunkers— you seem to revert at Gullane to the original, simple golf, and a wonderful feeling it is.

And now at last we move on for the final pilgrimage—to the Royal and Ancient Golf Club of St. Andrews and the Old Course.

Your base for this pilgrimage is the Gleneagles Hotel in the heart of the Scottish Highlands, one of the few establishments in Britain in which we can lay our hands on our hearts and promise you will be satisfied with the plumbing.

Gleneagles is heaven. As you play golf you can see 70 miles to the Grampian Mountains on one side, 50 to the coast of Fife on the other. The turf is like a green edition of the thick pile carpet in the hotel, and the two courses, Kings and Queens, are "sympathetic" towards the visitor. They seem to want you to do well—unlike, say, Hoylake or Carnoustie, which defy you for 13 holes and hammer you over the last five.

Carnoustie is a "must" for the golfing expert or connoisseur. Duffers, wives and camp followers should be left behind at Gleneagles with instructions to proceed to nearby Auchterarder and buy tweed. Carnoustie is the opposite of sympathetic. The inhabitants are small, dour and oppressed by liquor-licensing laws superior only to those in Oklahoma and Australia. If you are thinking only of golf, and there isn't much else to think about, Carnoustie is terrific. Since the game began to boom in the United States just before the turn of the century, no fewer than 400 of Carnoustie's sons have left to spread the golfing gospel and seek their fortune as professionals in America. They include Stewart Maiden and Macdonald Smith. As to the course, try playing it off the championship tees, as Hogan did, and see what you think of a man who, playing for the first time in Britain with the small ball, could score 73-71-70-68.

Now, at last, St. Andrews. The University, which was founded in 1411, has many links with America, not the least of which is James Wilson, part founder of the American Constitution, but it is as the golfing capital of the world that we come to St. Andrews now. There are four courses—the Old, the New, the Jubilee and the Eden—all of them are public links and open to anyone. Clustered round the last hole are a number of clubs: the St. Andrews Club, the New Club, for women the St. Rule's Club and, finally, behind the first tee, the Royal and Ancient.

It is the Old Course which every visitor wants to play, though few are worthy of pitting their wits and skill against it. Even the experts would not claim to appreciate the full quality of a masterpiece of painting or music at the first time of seeing or hearing, and so it is with the Old Course, which is assuredly the masterpiece of golf. Bobby Jones, who hated it at first sight, lived to declare: "If I was set down to play on one course for the rest of my life, I should choose the Old Course at St. Andrews." Sarazen, although he had suffered the greatest disappointment of his life on it, said virtually the same.

What is the secret? Partly, I think, that before playing any shot you have to stop and say to yourself, not, "What club is it?" but "What is it exactly that I am trying to do?" There are no fairways in the accepted sense of the word; just a narrow strip of golfing ground which you use both on the way out and the way in, together with huge double greens, each with two flags. So from the tee you can play almost anywhere, but, if you have not thought it out correctly according to the wind and the position of the flag, you may find yourself teed up in the middle just behind a bunker, and downwind. At this point fools say the course is crazy. Others appreciate that the truth lies nearer home.

Perhaps its greatest quality is what the golf architects call "indestructibility." Whatever the changes in clubs and balls, whatever the changes in the wind, the Old Course seems to stand up to them. What was a good par 5 with a guttie ball is still a good par 4 with the rubber-cored. The good par 5 against the wind yesterday is still a fine par 4 with it today. And what a difference the wind can make! I have seen strong men take a brassie to the short 11th, 152 yards, and with a gale behind play it as a low run-up. As you play the long fifth, take a look at the bunker you have not quite reached with your second. In 1953 Craig Wood drove into it, just under a quarter of a mile from the tee, and lost the Open in a playoff.

After playing on 400 courses in 30 countries, I have come to look on the Old Course as being a different class from all others. To master it requires not mechanical precision but a combination of skill, nerve and intelligence not demanded on any other course. On the other hand, don't be too disappointed. Few people begin to see it this way till they have played it 20 or 30 times—and some never see it at all. But if at first sight you do not capture some suspicion of its magic, I shall be very surprised.

One last point. How exclusive are golf clubs in Britain? The answer is: much less exclusive than before the war and to American visitors hardly exclusive at all. Most clubs are wide open to fee-paying visitors. In the case of some of the older ones, including even the Royal and Ancient, a letter or phone call to the secretary (not the "manager") will nearly always do the trick. You have come thousands of miles to pay us a visit and we are truly delighted to see you. Golf is the Esperanto of sport, the language we all understand.

CONGENITAL SLICE

We have served out our self-imposed 14-day sentence and, subject to good report by the Governor and the Chaplain, will be issued with our civilian suit and released in the morning. It has been, as always, an interesting and beneficial experience. Like any other delicate piece of machinery, the human body has from time to time to go in for repairs and what the soldiers always called "maintenance," and this for the past fortnight is what we have been doing at the so-called "health farm."

The rations have been meagre in the extreme—an orange for breakfast, tomato juice for lunch, tea for tea, and a cup of soup for dinner, which is "on," roughly speaking, at 6:59 and off at 7:00. No alcohol, of course, but to a near-teetotaller like myself this is of little account—though I confess to a suspicion that, having so often walked past it with pious and averted eye during the morning exercise, I shall not readily pass by the nearby White Hart Inn during opening hours again.

One of the objects of this curious business, though by no means the only one, is the melting of our too, too solid flesh and those who go through life admitting cheerfully that they are "a stone (14 pounds) or two on the heavy side," may come to reflect that a stone represents, within an ounce or two, a full set of 14 golf clubs and a medium-sized bag. Touching on this at Rye the other day with a stout and rubicund friend, I shook him, I like to think, by observing that he was caddying permanently for half the British Walker Cup team.

At any rate, mounting the scales is an essential item of the daily routine and great are the sacrifices, not least in dignity, that we make to ensure a favourable reading. We even sit, in corpulent rows, in little "sitz baths" of hot water with our feet in a bowl of cold, each watching his own little clock for the dread moment when it "pings" to tell him to go and sit in the cold one with his feet in a bowl of hot. Still, it has its rewards, and I shall not lightly forget the jubilation of the noble naked lord who, on the sixth day, declaimed that he had "lost all the irons and two of the woods."

Smoking is frowned upon, and addicts are herded together to puff furtively in a communal cell. I mention it only in order to pass on a simple, perhaps rather childish but remarkably effective way of cutting one's smoking by half at a cost of twopence. When the cigarette is half way through—which is all you want at a time anyway—you lay the lighted end on a penny. You then lay another penny gently on top. Within seconds the cigarette goes out—don't ask me why—and may be re-lit later, tasting exactly as good as before. With this I have been able to keep easily within the daily quota of 10, except for one day when James Mason's thriller, "The Man Between," combined with a Hollywood film so moronic as to defy description, cost me the whole of the unexpired portion of the day's ration, and I had to open another packet.

Though golf was to be forgotten, the past fortnight may have had for me a profound golfing significance. On alternate days we go to have our necks ricked and such like—"never broken one yet"—by the osteopath. The other day, lying on the slab, I presented so interesting a phenomenon that he called his colleague from the adjacent cubicle to come and look. They peered learnedly together at I knew not what. No doubt about it, apparently. Yes, yes, of course. You could see it without even measuring. Right leg shorter than the left.

No wonder I have had a slice all my life! Now I know, dammit, I was born with it!

1959
PETER THOMSON TELLS ALL

I say without hesitation that this is just about the best, and certainly the most succinct, piece of golfing instruction that I have ever read. There is no lack of modesty in this assertion, since, as you will see, Thomson's contribution is everything and the writer's virtually nothing. My own part in the proceedings was to spend a couple of half-hours with him in the lounge of Rusack's Hotel at St. Andrews and then set down what he said almost precisely as he said it. As seen, described, and played by Thomson, golf is indeed a simple game. It is the rest of us who make it so difficult!

All this began in a practise round before the Bowmaker tournament at Sunningdale. Though I had watched him many dozens of times, this was the first time that I had had the pleasure actually of playing with Peter Thomson. I had always found it difficult to describe his style to other people because it seemed so straightforward. There was nothing peculiar about it. It turned out not only that his ideas about the golf swing were as "simple" as his method but also, as I hope to prove, that he was equally good at communicating them.

I asked him, naturally, to cast an eye over my own manifestly unsatisfactory efforts and he said at once, "Well, for a start you are set up all wrong."

This expression, "getting set up right," constitutes the absolute basis of Thomson's golf. "If you get set up right and look like a competent golfer, you won't go nearly so far wrong." Your setup consists of how you stand, where you are aiming, your "triangle" (i.e., the two arms and shoulders), and where you put the ball in relation to your feet.

The nearer you are, before you start, to the position in which you will be when you hit the ball, the fewer adjustments you will have to make in the course of the shot. "Think how your body has to be when you strike the ball," he says, "and work back from there." Lest this sounds too obvious, take a look on the first tee on a Sunday morning and see how many people's starting positions bear any relation to any position in which they should conceivably be at impact!

There is no reason why any of us, tall or short, fat or thin, should not get set up right. The stance, about which volumes have been written, is a piece of typical Thomsonian simplicity. Lay a club down on the ground, pointing to the hole and put your toes against it. That is the end of that.

Now put the ball opposite your left foot with your left arm and the club in a straight line, as they will be, or should be, as you actually hit the ball. Your arm and the club will now be at right angles to the imaginary club on the ground against which you have lined up your toes. If they are not, you have got the ball—as almost everyone has—too far back. (We are talking at the moment of wooden club shots.)

We now come to the critical point, the make-or-mar of the entire setup. Your right arm is not long enough. It won't reach. How are you going to get it on to the club?

You do it instinctively as nature tells you, the easiest way. You reach over with the right hand, bringing the right shoulder forward in the process, and at the same time, probably without realising it, you bring the left hand back a bit to meet it. This is perfectly comfortable, but, to make it more so, you probably move forward a couple of inches at the last moment, thus, in effect, bringing the ball two inches back.

The whole setup is now wrecked.

Let us retrace our steps. The right arm once again is not long enough. This time, keeping your right shoulder back and tilting your left shoulder up, you reach under with the right hand and attach it to the club. (This was accompanied in the Sunday Times by a picture of myself, taken on my lawn and bearing the caption, "I don't care what you say—I at least look like a golfer."

I tried this experiment on many willing subjects and in every case, regardless of handicap, in this position they at once looked like a golfer. If it feels awkward at first, it only shows how wrong you were before. You can apply a simple test. When you have got "set up," keep your body still, lay the club flat across your chest and see where it is pointing. In the "easy" position you will find that it points yards to the left of the hole. If you are set up right, it will be pointing straight at the flag.

How Far Away From The Ball Should You Be?

Thomson often uses the expression "measuring off," and he himself measures off quite deliberately before each shot. Stand relaxed, leaning slightly forward, with your knees slightly bent and the whole body in balance. Extend the left arm and the club in a straight line, not stiff as a ramrod, and you are now measured off. "Picture in mind your position as you strike the ball and make final adjustments from that." This applies to every club.

How Do You Grip The Club?

Again, delightfully simple. Get set up right and you won't notice! Take it as you find it.

How Hard Do You Hold Onto The Club

"Often," says Thomson, "you can actually see the tension in a man's hands. You should start with a light touch, barely enough to lift it off the ground, so that it feels heavy. It is just like using an axe. You lift it with a light grip, just enough to raise it, and it feels heavy. As you bring it down, your grip tightens without your thinking about it and reaches its tightest at the moment of impact.

"There is another likeness with golf. Using an axe, you do not hit with it; you accelerate it. That is exactly what you should do with a golf club."

How Do You Start The Club Back?

"Well, you just draw it straight back. Never mind about what the books din into you about turns and pivots. Just draw it straight back as far as is comfortable and let nature take its course. Don't turn away; just draw it back—but keep your weight squarely on both feet and make sure you don't sway back with it yourself."

Finally, what Thomson describes as the key axiom in the golf swing, namely, to be behind the ball when you strike it—not all of you, maybe, but certainly your head. "A plumb line from your nose as you strike the ball should hit the ground several inches behind it"—a sobering thought for us lurchers and swayers, to whom, as we heave forward, the ball so often appears to be moving rapidly backwards.

As a postscript I might add that, with the first shot in which Thomson was satisfied that he had got me satisfactorily "set up," I ricked my back—probably using muscles which had not come into play for 30 years—to such an extent that we almost had to terminate the game there and then. This in no way shook my faith in his principles and I wish you the best of luck. You have been warned!

A few days after publication of the above, in July, I had a letter from a reader in Yorkshire. He had tried it on the lawn on a wet day, he said, and, having only slippers on, had fallen flat on his face. He had retired to the house, changed into spiked shoes and tried again. "I then had to be helped back into the house. The doctor was summoned and he says that, given reasonable care, I should be able to play again in October."

I have described the emphasis placed by Peter Thomson on how important it is to get set up right before making a golf shot. The example taken was a wooden club shot, but the same principle applies to all.

We are to imagine the position in which we shall be, or ought to be, when we hit the ball, and set ourselves up as nearly in that position as possible. It will involve, as always, the left arm and the club in a straight line, rather as though one were about to play a one-armed shot with the left arm.

The position of the ball with the driver was simple. It was opposite the left foot. Where is it to be with the other clubs? Again there are no complications. His answer is, "roughly an inch farther back for each club."

This finds the ball midway between the feet with a 5-iron and about off the right heel with a 9-iron. With the driver you hit the teed-up ball an ascending blow, the clubhead having already passed its lowest point. With the short irons you hit it a descending blow, taking a good-sized divot after the ball.

How far away do you stand? Again the same principles apply throughout. You "measure off," as before, with the left arm extended, and yourself poised and in balance, though naturally stooping a little more with the shorter clubs than you did with the driver.

Thomson also likes to have his feet progressively closer together as the shots become shorter. It all seems to fit into a very simple and intelligible pattern. As the shots become short enough to require judgment rather than power for their execution, he likes to open the stance slightly, drawing his left foot back a little.

For the short game his maxim, typically, is that one should always look for the simplest way. He describes the high wedge shot, which we so much admire when played by professionals, as, for most people, "a form of lunacy." The more you can picture a short approach as a kind of extended putt, he says, the better.

The ruin of most handicap players' short games comes from their efforts to hit the ball up. It is the golfer's job to hit it forward, the lofted club's job to hit it upward. It is an old professional trick, in trying to teach this to beginners, to put a lofted club into their hands and invite them to try to hit the ball along the ground into a bunker between them and the flag. They concentrate on hitting the ball forward, whereupon it sails over the bunker.

Thomson is a supremely good bunker player. Perhaps his finest exhibition of this art was when he won the Open at Lytham, where they have innumerable bunkers, of which he encountered at least his share. I have always remembered his remark afterwards that he had "never seen such a beautiful sand." He sincerely regards "splashing" the ball out of the sand as the simplest shot in the whole game, if only because there is so much greater margin for error than with a similar shot off grass.

"The chief factor is the club itself. There are some atrocious old sand irons about that even Snead could not play with. You want one with a wide sole, with the back edge considerably lower than the front." He thinks little or nothing of most of the so-called "dual-purpose" clubs.

He reckons to stand well behind the ball and to measure off carefully to the exact point that he wishes to hit the sand. Instead of hitting the ball first and the turf afterwards, you hit the sand first and the ball afterwards. You can hit the sand anything from two to six inches behind and it may well be sometimes that the clubface never actually touches the ball at all. So far as you are concerned, at any rate, you are playing a shot at the sand rather than at the ball. His only golden rule is "swing very slowly."

Thomson is also—again in an unostentatious and "simple" way—a supremely good putter. I spent a long time drawing him out on the subject and from this I think three main points emerge. He does not think that the grip matters unduly—indeed, he used the words "almost any grip will do"—but he has no doubt about his own method.

To initiate it, take a normal grip, then rotate your left hand to the left so that the back of it is at about 45 degrees to the ground; do likewise with your right hand to the right, and then stick your right thumb firmly on the shaft. He also reckons to stand with his eyes vertically over the ball. All this is common ground but there are many who might vastly improve by giving it a trial.

His second point interested me because I have so often referred to it as one of the main secrets of Bobby Locke's phenomenally successful putting and because it is something that we can all so easily do and, even when we mean to, so often don't. It is to carry out a sort of drill: in other words, to find a set of motions that suits our own particular eye and temperament and carry them out, without exception, every time we putt.

Locke's will be familiar to all who have seen him either in person or on the television: two practise strokes, a step up to the ball, one look at the hole and away it goes. Even with "this to tie for the Open," his drill never varies.

For his third point I quote Thomson's own words. "It must incorporate some sort of determined tap. What kills putting is the old so-called 'stroking' method. You don't stroke a putt like you stroke a cat. If you do, it is usually timid and damned lucky if it goes into the hole. The most natural way is to give it a tap, like a child instinctively does.

"None of the people who follow through like poor old . . . (and here he named four distinguished players who shall remain anonymous, two British and two American) have ever really been any good on the greens." He named as the world's best putters Rosburg, Casper, Ford, Palmer and Venturi—all Americans who hit the ball with a firm tap rather than a smooth stroking movement. This, I need hardly add, is not to be confused with a quick jerk or jab!

Like Locke, Thomson thinks it essential to hold the club loosely with a very light, sensitive grip and he likes to have the feeling that he is playing the same stroke every time, increasing the length more by lengthening the backswing than by hitting harder.

I believe all good putters, and the rest of us during our "on" days, have this feeling, though whether we are any longer capable of a very light sensitive grip remains to be proved. I did not have the heart to ask him the $64,000 question: How, if at all, can you cure the "jitters?" After all, he was due next day to play in the Open Championship.

SO MUCH FLAK

The more I see of other games and sports, the more I am struck by the similarity of their underlying principles and psychology with those of golf. The thought comes to mind because one or two kind friends have in the past invited me to help in slaughtering their pheasants—though that is perhaps an optimistic term regarding my own part in the proceedings. I like to think I generally succeed in making them swerve, or at least fly faster, but can never quite get out of my mind cartoonist Osbert Lancaster's wartime drawing with the caption: "I suppose you realise, Sir Henry, that to the pheasant you and I are just so much flak."

I regard myself as about a 12 handicap at shooting, or, as our American friends call it, "hunting." Usually I am a little "off my game," though like the golfer on a celebrated occasion I could with justice add: "Come to that, I suppose I am never on my game." Still, it is an exhilarating and provocative pastime, alternately luring you, like golf, into a ludicrous idea that you have "Got it at last," then casting you back into the depths of humiliation and despair.

Yet my last memory, as we left the field of battle near Mildenhall the other day, is of firing 10 shots at five pheasants—all flying, as we used to say in sterner anti-aircraft days, at a "constant height, course and speed"—and not a single feather floating down from any one of them.

At golf you do have one indisputable advantage. You may slice it out-of-bounds over the railway line and be very angry indeed, but at least you can see where the damn thing went. If you know you are slicing, at least you can lay on such anti-slice precautions as you may be aware of next time, but when you fire carefully aimed shots and absolutely nothing happens whatever, it is as though you hit your drive up the middle and the ball vanished in mid-air. It makes you feel like throwing the offending weapon to the ground and walking in, as Lord Castlerosse once did at Walton Heath, with the splendid words: "Pick that up, have the clubs destroyed, and leave the course."

In both pursuits the heart cry is the same—"What do I do to get length?" Ted Ray's immortal answer "Hit 'em a . . . sight harder, mate" will not do in respect of shooting. I suppose the only answer is, "Point it a . . . sight straighter, mate."

WHO'S GOING TO BE SECOND?

If I were cast upon a desert island, which the Lord defer, and were permitted to choose one man as my companion in exile, I sometimes think I should call for that great philosopher and good companion, Walter Hagen.

The prospect of being cast upon a desert island with a golfer is one to fill the mind with a horrid anticipation. But to Hagen, third greatest golf player of all time, golf was only a means to an end. He used it as Gene Tunney used prize-fighting, and as Henry Cotton, as I think you will find, will turn out to have used golf.

Hagen was bigger than the game by which he rose to fame. In any walk of life into which he might have drifted he'd have been a success. He probably stuck to golf because it brought him with the least trouble the things he most desired from life: wealth, luxury, travel, the limelight, and the company of famous men—and women—on level terms.

That he made a million dollars from golf is certain. It was equally certain that he would not die a rich man. "Easy come, easy go," was Hagen's motto with money, and maybe he was right.

My own affection for Hagen bordered almost on hero-worship. What a character! Staggering self-assurance; wit and good humour; a bronzed, impudent countenance with a wide-open smile; inexhaustible zest for life; and a unique ability to combine wine, women and song with the serious business of winning golf championships—that was Hagen. A fellow whose like you meet once in a lifetime.

His golf exactly matched his personality. Often brilliant; never, never dull. He won the Open Championship of my country four times and of his own United States twice, and he made more bad shots in doing so than the man who finished second would make in a month. He finished at the top because his powers of recovery were almost superhuman. When he won his first championship at Sandwich, he went through six rounds without taking a 6, yet four times he was still in a bunker beside the green in 3.

It was only natural that such a man should capture the imagination of the crowd. At first they resented his swagger and his multi-hued attire. On one regrettable occasion in the early days they even clapped when he missed a shot. But that soon passed when they came to understand the real Hagen, and long after he was past his prime they flocked round with him like sheep.

He took them through all the emotions. He would play a

succession of holes as though divinely inspired, while they marvelled at his skill. Then from a clear sky would come a stroke of unbelievable inaccuracy—a wild slice, or a top, or a quick, semi-circular hook—and the heart of the duffer warmed to the god that could descend to the level of man. And then, when all was apparently lost, he would extricate himself with a recovery which to the faithful seemed nothing less than a miracle.

Where other men strove vainly for consistent perfection, it was part of Hagen's philosophy, typically enough, to expect his quota of downright bad shots in every round he played. He expected them, so they did not upset him, as they did the others, when they came.

He was, of course, the showman par excellence, the master golfer-entertainer. No matinee idol ever had a stronger hold on his audience. I recall a tournament at Porthcawl, when his days of winning championships were already over. Hagen, still in London, was informed that he was to be partnered next day with a certain British Ryder Cup player and that they were to start at 10:30 a.m.

"I'll start at three," said Walter.

He is the only man in the game who would not have been disqualified. Instead, they meekly replied: "Very well, you shall start at three."

Word went round the little town, and no one bothered to watch the morning play. They stored their energy for the afternoon. The master arrived in a huge Daimler saloon—I can see him now—seated in the small space left by a number of cabin trunks. He had his feet up, and genially waved a large cigar. In the front seat sat his 16-year-old son Junior.

Hagen knew he had not the remotest chance of winning the tournament. So did everyone else. But did that make any difference? Not a bit. Every spectator on the course was there at three to see him drive off. They followed him eagerly to the end. He took 81.

Next day they were there again. Hagen by this time had no chance of even qualifying for the final day's play, but who cared? He played deplorably and again took 81. Everyone was happy. They had seen Hagen play golf.

Hagen was the dandy of the links. "Sir Walter," they called him. His clothes were immaculate, if sometimes a trifle bizarre, according to Savile Row conceptions, and frequently he'd change his whole outfit at lunchtime. I think he'd as soon have scratched as appear in clothes that offended his sartorial eye.

Was it vanity? Twenty-five percent of it, maybe. The rest was a part of his astute sense of publicity. He knew that making money from golf did not depend only on winning the titles. It depended on being noticed, talked about, quoted, criticised—anything, in fact, but ignored.

It wasn't only natural indolence that made him late where-ever he went. He liked to set the world asking: "Where's Hagen?" Had he arrived? Would he be disqualified? By the time he appeared, the stage was set for his entrance, his name on every-one's lips. "Ah, there he is! Good old Walter!" In all the times I watched him play, I never knew him to reach the first tee before his opponent.

Hagen had an overwhelming confidence in his own powers. "Waal, who's gonna be second?" he would drawl as he strolled out to the first tee. Then he would win—and win against the best competition the world could offer. His imitators cried: "Who's going to be second?"—and then finished 20th.

Innumerable tales, some of them true, are told of his irrepres-sible self-assurance. Perhaps the most characteristic concerns the finish of his Hoylake Championship. He frittered the shots away in his last round and was out in 40 or 41. At any rate, he had to come home in 36, and knew it, to beat Ernest Whitcombe's total of 302—and there is no tougher finish in the world than the last five holes at Hoylake.

He got by the 10th with a 4 and drove into a bunker at the Alps (the short 11th). He blasted it out and holed the putt. Bunkered again at the 12th, he holed a whopper for his 4. Then his tee shot to the short 13th floated away into the sand, and that, surely, was the end. There were no strokes to be picked up on the last five holes, even by Hagen, and a 4 at the 13th must cost him the champion-ship. He flipped the ball neatly out to within a few feet and got a 3.

And so he came to the 17th needing two 4's to win the Open. At the 17th he played what must stand as one of the greatest iron shots of all time, a long, low shot that ran nimbly through the narrow opening and lay eight feet from the hole. A 3 there would clinch it, but he rolled the ball casually along and missed it. Four to win! Every man in Hoylake, and half Liverpool, as it seemed, crowded round the last green. Watchers craned their necks from every window.

Hagen hit his second shot right over the back into the long grass. His approach, not bad in the circumstances, ran within eight or nine feet of the hole. One putt to win!

Where most men would have spent an age in preparation, Hagen strolled up to his putt and with scarcely a preliminary glance ran it into the hole.

As he walked from the green, having duly been embraced by his wife, a colleague of mine said to him: "You seemed to treat that putt very casually, Hagen. Did you know you had it to win?"

"Sure, I knew I had it to win," drawled Walter, "but no man ever beat me in a playoff!"

Then again they'll tell you the tale of how Hagen was left with a long putt to tie with Leo Diegel for a tournament in America and insisted that Diegel should be summoned from the clubhouse to see him hole it—to be suitably impressed before the playoff on the following day. Of course, he holed it. The only trouble about this tale, which I have been told by several people who actually saw it happen, is that they saw it happen at several different clubs and the other man was not always Diegel.

All the same, I fancy that Hagen must have holed more crucial putts deliberately than any man who ever won a championship. Indeed, I recall no instance on which, in his prime, he missed one that he knew would win or lose him a title. Yet he was never a man to waste effort. The rich streak of idleness in his makeup saw to that. Thus when, at Muirfield in 1929, he was left with a putt of four feet to win the Open Championship, he missed it by inches. So great was his lead that he could have taken seven putts and still have won. But not a man doubted that he would have holed that putt if the title had hung on it.

They do say that Hagen that day played the greatest golf ever seen in the Open. On the previous day in calm weather he had gone round in 67, the lowest score hitherto recorded in a championship. (This prompted a friend of mine to send a wire to the green committee of the Honourable Company of Edinburgh Golfers, i.e., The Muirfield Club, saying: "Suggest play off back tees for remainder of championship.")

On the final day there blew a mighty gale. Scores shot into the 80's and all day the best round was 74. But the gale only showed Hagen as the supreme artist, a man who could juggle with a golf ball as though it were tied to a string. He produced from somewhere a mallet-headed, deep-faced driver, and they say that for 36 holes he steered his ball along within 20 feet of the ground. Cannily, craftily, he was round twice in 75. Starting two strokes behind Diegel, he finished six shots ahead of the field.

As for the rules of training and physical fitness, Hagen defied the lot of them. He was the only man who could stay up till three in the morning playing bridge, smoking cigars, and stoking up with whisky, and go out and win a championship in the morning. Others tried, and great was their downfall. His power of concentration, too, was exceptional. Even in the closing stages of a tournament, when a false step might cost £1,000 or more, he could converse with his friends as he walked along between shots, breaking off suddenly when he came to within a few yards of his ball and switching his mind completely over to the business in hand. The only thing I ever knew to put him off was when, at Sandwich, they told him the Prince of Wales had arrived to watch him. He topped his next shot 40 yards. Then he pitched up and holed his putt for a 4.

It was at Sandwich that he made perhaps the most famous of all Hagen gestures. Having won the Open Championship of Great Britain, he handed the first prize, then a meagre £50, straight to his caddie. He knew he could cash in on the title for thousands of dollars in America. As for the caddie, he died some years later, and his friends have told me that, following the celebrations with Hagen's cheque, he was never the same man again.

Walter's first love, they tell me, was baseball, and he might have made a great pitcher. Later he became crazy on shooting and fishing, both of which sports he pursued with the eager enthusiasm of a boy with a catapult, and big game hunting, in which he indulged as a sideline during his golfing tours round the world. I remember sitting in the lounge of a Carnoustie hotel at half-past one in the morning during the 1937 Championship, when in walked Hagen with a basket under his arm. In it were half a dozen trout. He was lying well up in the championship, but that had not stopped him driving 70 miles for an evening's fishing. He took the fish down to the kitchen, gutted them, and solemnly cooked them for his supper.

Two of his matches over here will never be forgotten. One will never be forgiven. It was in 1928 that he stepped off the boat and went straight to play Archie Compston over 72 holes for, it was said, £500. He was out of practice after the voyage, and was beaten by the staggering margin of 18 up and 17 to play, an all-time record. A lesser man would have struggled to keep the margin of defeat down to reasonable proportions. Hagen, I suspect, when he saw he could not win, saw to it that the margin was so colossal that the world would discount the result of the match. Be that as it may, the following week he went down to Sandwich and won the Open Championship. Compston was third.

The other match, against Abe Mitchell in 1926, brought all manner of abuse on his head and added a phrase to the English golfers' vocabulary—"Doing a Hagen"—in other words, keeping a man waiting for the purpose of putting him off. In the first 36 holes at Wentworth, Mitchell finished 4 up. The second was played at St. George's Hill, and Hagen was half an hour late, a circumstance to which Mitchell's friends, though not so far as I know Mitchell himself, ascribed his ultimate defeat by 2 and 1. Hagen said his driver lost his way in the fog, and, indeed, St. George's Hill is difficult enough to find on a clear day. Hagen's record for being habitually late makes it likely that, as usual, he had simply not bothered to get there in time. I doubt if he had any ulterior motive. In any case I always think the suggestion that Hagen won this match almost by cheating reflects at least as badly on Mitchell. It portrays him as a man of such meagre calibre as to lose six clear holes in a day for no better reason than that the match started half an hour after the advertised time. I don't believe it. Be that as it may, it took Hagen years to live the incident down.

Life has been very much the richer for having known Hagen. He was the most colourful, spectacular personality cast up by the game of golf, and will take his place in sporting history with the giants. Their statistical records may have been surpassed, but they stay on their pedestals, men who became legends in their lifetime.

—1960—
THE GREATEST TOURNAMENT IN THE WORLD

"I shall never forget my first visit to the property . . . The long lane of magnolias through which we approached was beautiful. The old manor house with its cupola and walls of masonry two feet thick was charming. The rare trees and shrubs of the old nursery were enchanting. But when I walked out on the grass terrace under the big trees behind the house and looked down over the property, the experience was unforgettable. It seemed that this land had been lying here for years just waiting for someone to lay a golf course upon it.

"Indeed, it even looked as though it were already a golf course, and I am sure that one standing today where I stood on this first visit, on the terrace overlooking the practise putting green, sees the property almost exactly as I saw it then. The grass of the fairways and greens is greener, of course, and some of the pines are a bit larger, but the broad expanse of the main body of the property lay at my feet then just as it does now. I still like to sit on this terrace, and can do so for hours at a time . . . ."

Thus wrote the immortal Bobby Jones, on what is now Augusta National in Georgia, which he and Clifford Roberts, for so long the presiding genius, founded in 1930, the year in which Jones at the age of 28 retired from competitive golf, having no further worlds to conquer.

As a club they wanted to create "a retreat of such nature, and of such excellence, that men of some means and devoted to the game of golf might find the club worthwhile as an extra luxury where they might visit and play with kindred spirits from other parts of the nation."

As to the course, they sought "the greatest good for the greatest number." As co-architect they incorporated Dr. Alister Mackenzie. "The doctor and I," wrote Jones, "agreed that two things were essential. First, there must be a way around for those unwilling to attempt the carry; and second, there must be a definite reward awaiting the man who makes it. Without the alternative route the situation is unfair. Without the reward it is meaningless."

They made big, undulating greens and were, I believe, the first in America deliberately to make four different "pin positions"—a practise now common on nearly all new American courses of any consequence. This means that a shot good enough to stay near the flag leaves a comparatively simple putt for a birdie, while one that only finds the edge of the green leaves the player hard put to get down in two more. Furthermore, they try to keep the pace of the greens sufficiently fast so that a well-struck shot will hold, whereas one slightly skimmed, or "thinned," as they put it, will shoot over the back.

Four years after they started, Jones and Roberts decided to hold an invitational tournament, little knowing, I fancy, into what it was going to develop. They invited all the accepted masters of the game and almost from the beginning it became known as the Masters Tournament.

For a while they themselves decided who should be invited, but such was the immediate prestige of the tournament that a complicated system of qualification had to be devised, encompassing home and overseas players, professionals and amateurs. The sponsors nevertheless retain a power of discretion, and I suspect that anyone who started throwing clubs or tantrums in one year would not be invited the next, even if he were an Open champion.

"As far as I am concerned," Arnold Palmer has said, "there will never be another tournament like it." The winner is invested with a green blazer, almost the most distinguished emblem in American golf, and becomes a member of the Masters Club, which dines once a year, at the expense of the previous winner.

Most people, furthermore, seem to look upon the Masters as the best-run tournament in golf. "Any club that wants to see how a tournament should be conducted should dispatch a few emissaries to study the Masters," Gene Sarazen once commented. "The galleries are intelligently marshalled. The spectators as well as the golfers are treated as gentlemen. Jones will not tolerate the faintest suspicions of burlesque-show atmosphere . . . The flavour at the Masters reflects the personality of Robert Tyre Jones Jr., and Bob has always epitomized the best in golf."

It was during the second Masters Tournament in 1935 that Sarazen played what might almost be described as the most historic single shot in golf. As he walked towards his second shot at the 15th—then 485 yards long and rated par 5—a tremendous roar from the clubhouse signified that Craig Wood had finished with a birdie 3.

Consulting with his caddie Stovepipe—so called after the battered tall silk hat he always wore when caddying—Sarazen found that he needed four 3's, against a par of 5-3-4-4 to win.

He decided to take a 4-wood to get the ball up and over the intervening pond and "rode into the shot" with all his might. A moment later the spectators behind the green were jumping wildly in the air. He had holed out from 220 yards for 2! Poor Craig Wood. Sarazen tied and beat him in the playoff.

The Masters, regarded by so many as the greatest golf tournament in the world, has everything. A course which, as set for the players, is a tremendous test of nerve and skill; an organisation second to none; provision for the comfort and information of spectators that has grown steadily better every year; and an atmosphere all of its own, which has grown up perhaps through a combination of the qualities mentioned above. It is an event which is greater than any individual who participates in it.

The course is laid out among a combination of vast pine trees, shorter firs, and flowering trees and shrubs, including particularly azaleas. These are in full bloom for the tournament and the sight of the second part of the long 13th hole will live in my memory as long as I live. The hole is a dogleg to the left and a creek crosses the fairway and then proceeds up the left-hand side, turns with the dogleg and runs all alongside the second shot, finally turning again to cross directly in front of the green and wind away round the right-hand side of it. Meanwhile, along the left of the second shot the ground rises steeply and this bank is covered with the most magnificent orange, red and purple azaleas, all around the foot of pine trees which must be every inch of a hundred feet high. I spent much time there on my first visit, just gazing at it and committing it to memory.

We were fortunate too in the weather, the best they had ever had, I was told: four successive days of blazing sunshine that brought everything out, including the spectators, in gorgeous Technicolor. The grass, as green as could be, is an expensive combination of basic Bermuda, which provides an almost invisible brown and dormant undermatting to the vivid green rye, which at this time of year grows so fast that they have to mow it twice a day. Soon the winter rye will die and the course will be closed until October, when it is resown.

There is no rough on the Augusta National course, though of course there are plenty of trees and sand traps, especially round the greens. What makes it such a tremendous test is that from the Masters tees you have to be very long—the day of the "good little 'un" has long since gone in American golf—and you are then faced with the flag in any one of four pin positions on sharply sloping greens. On the final day the pins are put in really hideously difficult positions, sometimes only four yards from a slope rolling down into a trap, so that only a desperate man dares "have a go." It is this aspect more than any other, or so I felt, that means that no one can fluke a win in the Masters. To play at these tiny targets knowing that you are playing for many hundreds of thousands of dollars is a strain which anyone can understand.

On the left of the clubhouse, as you look out towards the putting green and the first and 10th tees, there is a series of white so-called "cabins," all in the same charming Colonial architectural style as the clubhouse itself. The second on the left was Bobby Jones's, and here I was able to pay my respects again to the great man. In a prominent place on his walls were the cartoons that Tom Webster did day by day as Jones was winning his Open Championship at Hoylake.

The first cabin, which is, in fact, a most exquisite and substantial country house, was presented, anonymously, by about 50 members to General Eisenhower on his election to the Presidency in 1952. I was shown all over it by Clifford Roberts, and it did not take long to realise why, as President, Eisenhower so often managed to take both his work and his relaxation there. When his term of office came to an end, they gave him a dinner attended by those who had subscribed to the house and who thus for the first time revealed their identity.

It so happened that I was billeted during the Masters in the same hospitable house as the young South African player, Retief Waltman. I was impressed with both his golf and his attitude to life. He started the tournament with a par 72, which was highly satisfactory, but then fell back with a 77. With the course laid out as it is for the Masters, this is not a particularly bad score, but his total of 149 put him out of the running and he failed to qualify for the final 36 holes.

He thereupon handed his clubs to David Thomas and quietly, deliberately and inexorably gave up golf. It was the only grown-up life he had known. At the age of 25 he had already won the South African Open twice and had with great pride represented his country in the Canada Cup. It was clear that, apart from Gary Player, who did much to help him on his way, he would soon become accepted as South Africa's leading golfer. The game would give him an excellent and, one would have thought, a congenial living for the rest of his life. The whole world lay before him.

Perhaps if he had not been so good and so dedicated—his "god" was Ben Hogan and he even wore a flat white cap in imitation of the great man—he would have settled down happily as a club professional in his native land. Ambition, however, took him further afield and drew him into the rat-race of tournament golf. Gradually the sheer materialism of this form of life and the unceasing emphasis on money began to sicken him, as it must have done so many before him. The difference was that he did not threaten to give it up. He just gave it up.

He came home on the second evening—I shall always remember it—and said quietly, "Well, I have given my clubs away and this is the last tournament golf I shall ever play." I seem to remember that for good measure he had even given his golf shoes away, too.

Our host and I naturally pressed him for his reasons, though neither of us thought of trying to reconvert him to golf. He was obviously very sincere. He replied that, while golf had given him much, he had never really learnt anything, and that quite simply what he wanted to do was to "go to school" and start again where he should never have left off. He already had thoughts of going into the Church. Like a surprising number of golfers, and I say it in no flippant sense, he sincerely believed that in winning, in his own case the South African Open, he was in receipt of divine help and guidance. I am sure that everyone joined in admiration of this strength of character and wished him well.

——1975——
A DRAMATIC FINISH

I suppose that any golfing impressario, including Mr. Clifford Roberts himself, if he had had a chance of "staging" the finish of the 1975 Masters, would have said, "I think we will have Nicklaus safely in the clubhouse in the lead, with only two players left to come in. These will be Weiskopf and Miller. They will each be one stroke behind. Both will hit spectacular second shots to the 18th and the world will then hold its breath as each in turn putts down the slippery slope with this to tie." So it came about, and it is a matter of history that both missed by a hairbreadth to conclude the most dramatic scenario of the year in golf.

The build-up to all this took place, however, round the 15th and 16th greens, at which I was privileged, sitting up in the TV tower behind the 16th, to enjoy a ringside seat, and it remains one of the outstanding memories in a lifetime of watching golf. For those not familiar with Augusta National, let me say that the two holes in question form a sort of capital letter T. The par-5 no. 15, generally reachable by the big hitters in two, forms the upward shaft of the T, and the par-3 no. 16 the crossbar, from left to right at the top.

The 16th green is about 50 yards deep from back to front, sloping sharply up toward the back. On the last day the pin is placed right at the back, only 12 feet from the fringe. From the tower behind the green it is possible to look across through the Georgia pines to the 15th green.

Tournaments these days have to be by stroke play, for the benefit of the television. All the same, no one can deny that when, as sometimes happens, an old-fashioned, head-to-head match-play situation develops, the pulses quicken. Mine certainly did, for here was a real heavyweight contest between Nicklaus, the world's No. 1 of the day, and big Tom Weiskopf, whose turn after so many near-misses in the Masters must surely now be due. Miller, though in the end he nearly tied, seemed to play a background part.

The curtain goes up with Weiskopf on the 15th green faced with a 20-footer across the slope, and Nicklaus on the 16th tee. At this moment they are level with each other, but Weiskopf has his birdie putt yet to come.

Nicklaus plays his tee shot to the 16th first and, with due respect to the great man, a very disappointing effort it was, woefully short on the left and well within the three-putt area.

As Nicklaus reached the green, he stopped and looked back across the water, no more than 90 yards or so, to see, or rather to hear, what happened to Weiskopf's putt. He was left in no doubt. Masters spectators are a notably well-behaved company. They stampede not, neither do they run. What they do do, however, in order to vent their enthusiasm, is to yell. A colossal yell, reverberating among the pines and audible in the clubhouse away up at the top of the hill, told Nicklaus that Weiskopf's putt had crept across the slope and into the hole, giving him the lead.

Weiskopf moved to the 16th tee and waited for Nicklaus up ahead. He was one ahead now and in a minute might well be two. Nicklaus's huge putt had to go up the hill—first across a right-hand slope, then a left, and then, in the pin area, who could quite tell? The putt lined up in exactly our direction, and our little party on the tower agreed on "fully 45 feet." To get it within four feet would have been quite a notable putt. If you had tapped Nicklaus on the shoulder at that moment and said, "Will you accept a par 3?" he most assuredly would have picked up the ball and moved smartly to the 17th tee.

At last he struck it, straight up towards us, curving first over one slope then another, and then—No, no! But, yes! Straight into the very center of the hole. The caddie jumped in the air, the pin

jumped in the air, and even Nicklaus jumped in the air. If the yell
that had greeted Weiskopf a few minutes earlier could be heard in
the clubhouse, this one must have been heard in downtown
Augusta.

Away in the distance stood the tall, silent figure of Weiskopf.
Having got his opponent, as he might well have thought, against
the ropes, he suddenly found himself reeling from a near knockout blow. Far from needing a 3 to be possibly two ahead, certainly
one, he now had to have 3 to stay level. The narrow top end of the
green, never a great target, must now have seemed like the eye of a
needle.

I remember watching his shot soar up against the blue sky and
down through the dark green background. Dead straight but, oh
dear, oh dear, it did not even reach the green, let alone the pin.
Once again we agreed on the figure 45—but this time yards, not
feet. His pitch was nearly there but not quite, and his putt was
nearly there, too, but it all added up to 4, and now, suddenly, he
was one behind.

All credit to Weiskopf for hanging on and so nearly tying on
the 18th, but, if every stroke over those vital 15th and 16th holes is
so firmly entrenched in my own memory, how much more indelibly must they be impressed on Weiskopf's! Nicklaus's putt on 16
really was the most monstrous, diabolical and perfectly timed putt
I ever saw. If ever a man was entitled to say, "We was robbed," it
must be Weiskopf.

---------------------1973---------------------
THE YIPS—ONCE YOU'VE HAD 'EM, YOU'VE GOT 'EM

There can be a no more ludicrous sight than that of a grown
man, a captain of industry perhaps and a pillar of his local community, convulsively jerking a piece of ironmongery to and fro in his
efforts to hole a three-foot putt. Sometimes it is even a great golfer
in the twilight of his career, in which case the sight is worthy not of
ridicule but of compassion. He will battle on for a year or two, but
twilight it is, for "Once you've had 'em, you've got 'em." I refer, of
course, to what Tommy Armour was the first to christen the
"Yips."

When he wrote a book called *The ABC's of Golf,* he had no
difficulty with the letter Y. The yips drove Armour out of tourna-

ment golf. On a somewhat humbler level they drove me out of golf, too, and a long and agonising process it was, ending on D-Day 1968, the anniversary of the invasion of Europe. On that occasion I put my 25-year-old clubs up into the loft with the water tanks, because I am too mean to give them away.

Armour wrote graphically of "that ghastly time when, with the first movement of the putter, the golfer blacks out, loses sight of the ball and hasn't the remotest idea of what to do with the putter or, occasionally, that he is holding a putter at all." This confirms the description of that most distinguished of all sufferers, Bob Jones, who recorded that just before the moment of impact the ball "seemed to disappear from sight." Jones also recorded how he once was partnered with that sterling character of the late 1920's and early '30s, Wild Bill Mehlhorn. Poor Mehlhorn! He was only three feet from the hole, said Jones, but gave such a convulsive twitch at the ball that it shot across the green into a bunker. He then had the humiliation of exchanging his putter for his niblick, and, we may assume, without being unkind, that was the last seriously competitive round he ever played.

Contemporary with Jones and Mehlhorn was Leo Diegel, whose extraordinary spread-elbowed putting style put a new phrase into the golfing vocabulary, "To diegel." I watched him on the 18th green at St. Andrews in 1933 when, from some yards above the hole, he had two to tie for the British Open title. While his partner holed out, Diegel paced up and down, much as an animal in its cage, repeatedly taking off his felt hat and mopping his brow. When his turn came, he charged the ball down the slope, several feet too far, chased after it, and, almost before it had come to rest, yipped it a foot wide of the hole. Everyone knew, as I am sure he did, too, that Diegel would never win an Open now.

Armour wrote, "Yips don't seize the victim during a practise round. It is a tournament disease." Here the great man was certainly wrong. My mind goes back to a conversation at Augusta with Craig Wood, who was robbed of the 1935 Masters by Gene Sarazen's historic double eagle. Craig told me that he even got the yips on the practise green, all by himself and with nothing at stake. Again, Armour says, "I have a hunch that the yips are a result of years of competitive strain, a sort of punch-nuttiness with the putter." Wrong again, surely, for you will see any number of compulsive yippers, though many may not admit it, in Sunday foursomes whose members never play serious competitive golf.

In winning the 1931 British Open, Armour, having perpetrated a most frightful yip to miss from two feet on the 71st hole, found himself faced with a three-footer to win: "I took a new grip, holding the club as tightly as I could and with stiff wrists, and took a different stance . . . From the instant the club left the ball on the backswing I was blind and unconscious." Next day that greatest of golf writers, Bernard Darwin, recorded in the London Times that he had never before seen a man so nonchalantly hole a three-foot putt to gain a championship!

Who, would you guess, wrote the following, and in what book? "As I stood addressing the ball I would watch for my right hand to jump. At the end of two seconds I would not be looking at the ball at all. My gaze would have become riveted on my right hand. I simply could not resist the desire to see what it was going to do. Directly, as I felt that it was about to jump, I would snatch at the ball in a desperate effort to play the shot before the involuntary movement could take effect. Up would go my head and body with a start and off would go the ball, anywhere but on the proper line."

That was written by Harry Vardon, winner of six British Opens and one U.S. Open, indisputably the greatest golfer that the world had yet seen, in the book entitled *How to Play Golf*.

Americans sometimes refer to the yips, rather unkindly, as "whisky fingers," and sometimes no doubt they are. Perhaps the last word on "whisky fingers"—and almost my favourite golfing quotation—was uttered by Vardon to a lady who was trying to persuade him to sign the pledge. "Moderation is essential in all things, madam," said Vardon gravely, "but never in my life have I been beaten by a teetotaller!"

Sam Snead, whose fluent style has lasted longer than any other man's in the history of the game, was reduced to putting between his legs, croquet-fashion—and he was a total abstainer for years. The croquet putter gave many a golfer, myself included, an extended lease on life, and the banning of it was an act of cruelty to many hundreds of miserable wretches for whom the very sight of a normal putter set their fingers twitching. The ease with which you could line up one of these croquet putters to the hole was quite remarkable. By holding the club at the top of the shaft, and loosely lower down with the right arm stiffly extended, the most inveterate yipper could make some sort of a four-foot putt which would not expose him to public ridicule. We did not ask to hole it; all we wanted was to be able to make a stroke at it, and this we could do. The United States Golf Association not only decided to ban a method which had brought peace to so many tortured souls, but the group let its decision become public before the Royal and Ancient Golf Club of St. Andrews had time to consider it, thus putting the latter in the impossible position of either banning the club or falling out with the USGA. So they banned the club.

Further proof that the dread disease is not traceable to a dissolute way of life was furnished by the "Iron Man" of golf himself, Ben Hogan, who, of all the men who have played golf since the game began, would have seemed most likely to be immune. The rot set in, so eyewitnesses have assured me, on the 71st green at Rochester in 1956, when he was well-placed to win a record fifth U.S. Open. Not only did he miss the three-footer, which anyone could do, but he yipped it, and that was the beginning of the end. At any rate, my last memory of Hogan in competitive golf is at the Masters some years ago. Every green, as usual, is surrounded with spectators and, as the familiar white-capped figure steps through the ropes, everyone spontaneously rises to give him a standing ovation. And a moment later he is struck motionless over the ball, as though hypnotised, unable to move the ironmongery to and fro.

Is there any cure for this grotesque ailment? Few people can have made a more penetrating research than myself. The first led me to a psychiatrist-cum-hypnotist, who solemnly tried through my inner self to talk the ball into the hole. This, of course, was ridiculous, since all I was seeking was that, on surveying a four-foot putt, a massive calm should automatically come over me instead of the impression that I was about to try to hit the ball with a live eel.

Better hope came from an Austrian doctor, who wrote to say that he knew the solution and would be willing to reveal it to me. Within a matter of hours I was visiting him in his rooms in London. "It all comms," he said, "from ze angle of ze right ell-bow."

Something in that, I thought, recalling how, with the right arm stiffly extended, one could at least make some sort of stroke with the croquet putter. The theory seemed to be supported by the fact that, if you have difficulty in raising a glass to the lips, it is when the arm bends to approximately the putting angle that your drink is most likely to make its bid for freedom.

What he said next, however, blissfully unaware of the full horror of his words, was "Violinists very often get it." We may imagine a silent audience of 6,000 people in, say, London's Albert Hall, and the maestro in the spotlight, his right arm fully extended, drawing the bow delicately across, when suddenly, the elbow having arrived at the putting angle . . . A-a-a-ah! He nearly saws the instrument in half and his career is ended. I once told this ghastly little story to Ben Hogan during a World Cup match and thought his eyes began to turn glassy. Only later did I suspect why.

Innumerable "cures" for the yips have been tried and passed on from one sufferer to another. Looking at the hole instead of the ball; putting left-handed; putting cross-handed with the left hand below the right, and putting with the hands wide apart (probably the best bet of the lot). A friend of mine has his hands about a foot apart, with the left below the right, and then pulls down as hard as he can with the left and up as hard as he can with the right—and he a one-time runner-up in the British Amateur!

As an ancient and finally defeated warrior—three putts from a yard on the 18th at St. Andrews, and only as few as three because the third hit the back of the hole, jumped up and fell in—I listen politely to all their tales. But the bitter, inescapable truth remains.

Once you've had 'em, you've got 'em.

1964

A CASE OF CHAMPAGNE

Anthony David Lema, the new Open champion, is really rather a splendid fellow, absolutely in the Hagen tradition of not wanting to be a millionaire but possessed of a strong determination to live like one. Gay, debonair, handsome and, at the age of 30, something of a reformed character, he now has the world before him.

In the past few weeks he has won four tournaments and $20,000. The advertised prize for winning the Open is a mere £1,500 but in effect it ranges between £3,300 and £19,500, since the winner is entitled to a place in the four-man television World Series, for which the first prize is £18,000 and the last £1,800. In addition, with the aid of an old friend of mine, Fred Corcoran, who is one of the most experienced managers and organisers in the game, he should "cash in" on his victory to the tune of many thousands of pounds.

Lema's father, a labourer of Portuguese descent, died when the boy was 3, leaving his mother, widowed and penniless, to bring up four children "on the wrong side of the tracks" in an industrial area of Oakland. Lema's boyhood was marked by playing truant from school, getting into fights and picking up the odd dollar when and where he could.

Soon, like so many American pros, he started caddying at the local municipal course and golf became the abiding passion of his life. On the spur of the moment, when he was "just batting around," he enlisted in the Marines and with them spent two years in Korea, gaining 20 pounds in weight and becoming a fine athletic figure of a man.

After this he became an assistant at a club in San Francisco, then a teaching pro and finally secured a businessman backer—to whom, on account of his liking for first-class travel and the good things of life, he was soon owing some $11,000. In the whole of

1959 he won only $6,000 and in 1960 it sank to $3,000.

At this period there was no doubt about his being a fine swinger of the club, with the beautiful and natural rhythm that characterises his style today, but he was temperamentally immature. The unlucky breaks inseparable from golf got on his nerves and he became convinced that the world was against him. To win his first tournament became such an obsession as to make it all the more difficult.

Nor perhaps did the sort of party to which he invited a number of fellow professionals to his suite in a St. Paul hotel, and eventually finished by opening the window and driving balls down Market Street, add greatly to his prospects on the following day.

Suddenly, according to Lema's own words, everything in his life fell into place. He still liked, as did Hagen, to travel through life first class, but the days of the wild parties were over. His golf rapidly improved: he learnt that "missing a short putt doesn't mean that I have to hit my next drive out-of-bounds"; he became, as all successful professionals must, a good "bad player"—in other words, on the inevitable off days he became able to squeeze his score down to 72 instead of 78; and above all, in 1962, he won his first big tournament, on the third extra hole of the playoff.

It was on this occasion that he earned his nickname of "Champagne Tony" by celebrating his victory in the press tent—an agreeable custom which he continued at St. Andrews last Friday evening, though I am afraid I was too occupied in other directions to go and draw my ration.

At St. Andrews he did everything well and really it was impossible to fault him. He drove exactly where "Tip" Anderson, the best caddie in the town, directed him; his iron shots flew like rifle bullets, and his putting was a joy to watch. He is a tremendous "birdie putter," as they call it. One after the other, when he had a chance of a 3—and sometimes when he had not—he knocked them in. As for the short putts, Nicklaus, though he holes them, makes them look difficult. Lema was putting them in without giving the spectator the slightest twinge of sympathetic anxiety.

Above all, though, must rank his temperament, which carried him through one of the most dramatic moments in championship history. Going into the third round, he was nine ahead of Nicklaus. He opened with 4-5-4-5-5-4—three over 4's, though admittedly with the Loop, where you hope to pick up shots, to come. The sixth green adjoins the 12th, indeed they are all in one, and on the 12th at this moment was Nicklaus, five under 4's. Eight shots gone!

It must have been a ghastly moment for Lema. Perhaps the greatest tribute that I can pay him is simply to record his figures for the remaining 12 holes: 3-3-3-3-3-4-4-4-3-4-4-3. If that is not worth a case or two of champagne, I do not know what is.

DONE IT AT LAST!

I suppose the small fries of today want to be spacemen when they grow up, but in my day we all wanted to be engine drivers. Recently, some 45 years late, it fell to my lot to realise this ambition and I found myself, attired in a boiler suit [overalls], mounting the footplate of the steam engine Robin Hood to accompany (I will not say assist) Driver Peters—who, like nearly all long-distance train drivers, looks like a retired admiral—in hauling the Norfolkman from Liverpool Street to Norwich, 120 miles in 120 minutes with a stop at Ipswich.

I recalled a remark of Lord Brabazon's that it was "like driving a very powerful sports car—with two big ends [crankshafts] gone, and a puncture." We started quietly enough, with Robin Hood puffing and panting in a most human sort of way up the long 1-in-128 "bank" (as we railwaymen call it) from Liverpool Street to Brentwood, but it was not long before I realised that his Lordship had understated the case. It is more like driving a very powerful sports car with all the big ends gone, and four punctures.

Thereafter, as Mr. Peters coaxed his iron steed up to 90 miles an hour to make up time, I retain a confused impression of a deafening din, steam, smoke, vibration, blasts of heat as the fireman opened the hatch to feed the inferno blazing within, and a scalding sensation round the ankles as he periodically hosed down the cabin with jets of boiling water.

Above all was the feeling of superiority. This was a surprise. As a passenger, you mount one step and then sit down. On the engine you climb up four steps and then stand up. Both literally and psychologically you look down on the rest of the world. At some little crossing in rural Suffolk a little man was waiting in his little motor car. "Yes," I thought, looking contemptuously down at him as we thundered by, "and you'd better."

As for one's own passengers, they scarcely exist. They are coming along behind there somewhere, one supposes, eating, drinking, sleeping, reading, or whatever it is they are doing, but one thought monopolises the mind—to urge this great monster to Norwich on time.

Losing unregainable minutes through work on the new station at Colchester, we nearly did so. As the passengers streamed by without a passing glance for Driver Peters, I felt like rattling a collection box in their faces. I washed my hair in the stationmaster's office, but after the fourth immersion the water still came out like draught stout, so I gave it up.

How different was our return in the diesel! Padded armchair; sliding window out of which to lean a nonchalant elbow; uninterrupted, smokeless view of the road and the countryside; everything clean as a new pin and 2,000 horsepower throbbing behind the soundproof door—the Rolls-Royce of the rails.

"Yes," said Driver Williams, "but there's no interest in 'em. The old steamer's almost human. You've got to get something out of her."

There was another surprise, namely the number of birds that apparently prefer the railway line to the surrounding meadows, heaths and woods. Crows, pigeons, partridges, pheasants and innumerable sparrows. There being no vegetation on the line, one can only suppose them to be in search of grit. The crows, I noticed, are the wariest. They get up at a range of 200 yards. Pigeons step off with an offended air at the last moment—often, indeed, too late.

With merely a couple of levers, one in each hand, and a "dead man's pedal" which begins to bring the train automatically to a halt if one takes one's foot off it for seven seconds, I formed the impression, doubtless erroneous, that on a clear day I could safely be entrusted with a diesel train myself.

In open country one felt little impression of speed, but when it came to roaring between the narrow platforms of the suburban stations and over the points at 85 m.p.h. the feeling of superiority and "Out of my way!" became more insufferable than ever, and the temptation to seize the knob and give the peculiar two-tone diesel tootle to passengers waiting for mere "stopping" trains proved quite irresistible.

I retired to my bath in the Great Eastern Hotel with a smug satisfaction at having "done it at last," and the more humble conviction that, whatever the drivers of steam engines are paid, they deserve double.

1965

HIGHLIGHTS OF THE RYDER CUP

The Ryder Cup match which I should most dearly like to have seen was not a Ryder Cup match at all. It was the unofficial match at Wentworth in 1926—won, incidentally, by the British with the almost unbelievable score of 13 matches to 1—which led to

Samuel Ryder presenting his cup. I was a boy at school at the time but already in exhibition matches I had seen the two great British giants perform and one of them had become, and in many ways remains, my golfing hero. This was Abe Mitchell, and I still declare that if blindfolded, I could hear a dozen of the great players of today and yesterday driving a golf ball, I could tell you which one was Mitchell. The other was George Duncan.

Their opponents throughout the day were two equally redoubtable golfers: Jim Barnes, the lanky, sardonic Cornishman long settled in America, a past open champion of that country and now at this moment British Open champion; and the one and only Walter Hagen, also winner of the Open on both sides of the water. Hagen may on the surface have taken life light-heartedly but neither of these characters underneath their differing exteriors cared to be beaten.

I should, of course, have run round with the four of them all day, sticking to the pair of them in the foursomes and alternating frantically between the two matches in the singles. I should have had to hurry, too, for in the foursomes Mitchell and Duncan beat the Americans by 9 and 8, and on the next day Mitchell beat Barnes by 8 and 7, while Duncan beat Hagen by 6 and 5.

I did not see the first match for the Ryder Cup, which was played at Worcester, Mass., though when the British scored 1 point in the foursomes and 1½ in the singles it seemed to set the pattern for future matches in America for a long time.

The first home match for the cup was played at Moortown, Leeds, in 1929, and part of this I did see. Three of us who were in the Cambridge University team at the time climbed out of college at about four in the morning and arrived at Leeds five or six hours later. All the giants were there—Hagen and Sarazen, Duncan and Mitchell again, Compston, Charles and Ernest Whitcombe, and an already publicised newcomer, T.H. Cotton. Duncan, craftily forecasting where Hagen would play himself in the singles and anxious to prove that his previous win was no fluke, flashed his way round Moortown—he was undoubtedly the quickest great player of all time—to beat his man by 10 and 8.

The three of us became separated early on, as golfing spectators always do, it being really a one-man job, but soon we found ourselves following the same match, with eyes for but a single man. He was tall and slim and very goodlooking, and wore plus-fours, black and white shoes, and one of those grey garments that later became known as a windcheater. His name was Horton Smith. His swing was smooth and slow and beautiful, and he putted with the touch of a violinist. He was two or three down to Fred Robson when we picked him up but he won in the end by 2 and 1. I last saw him as he left our hotel after the 1963 match in

Atlanta to return to Detroit. Next morning I read in the paper that he had died that night. He was one of the classical scholars, so to speak, of golf.

The first match that I saw as a writer on golf was in 1933 at Southport and Ainsdale and this, in a sense, is "where I came in." It is common experience to remember more vividly scenes that took place when the world was new than what happened yesterday. My recollections of this match, however, have been sharpened by the fact that some years ago I assembled, from newsreels of the day, a film entitled "Great Golfing Occasions," and this match is one of them. We see again the thousands of people who rushed about the course, herded, not always successfully, by volunteer stewards brandishing long bamboo poles with pennants at the end, which earned them the name of the "Southport Lancers."

Many had come to see the golf but many, perhaps more, had come to see the Prince of Wales, himself a keen golfer, who had come to give the cup away. We see him in the end presenting it to dear old J.H. Taylor, non-playing captain of the British team, almost beside himself with pride, and we see Hagen with that impudent smile that captured so many male and female hearts saying, "We had the cup on our table on the Aquitania coming over and we had reserved a place for it on the table going back." Above all, however, we see what was perhaps the most desperate finish to any international match played to this day.

The match as a whole was all square; there was one single to come in, and this, too, was all square—with one hole to play. The protagonists were Densmore Shute (who later went on to win the Open at St. Andrews) and Syd Easterbrook. In the end Shute was about 4½ feet from the hole in 3 and Easterbrook a matter of inches inside him. I do not have to look at the film to remember the scene. It has been imprinted on my mind ever since I watched it. Shute, in the deathly silence that comes from the presence of a vast multitude, none of whom is making a sound, missed his putt. So now Easterbrook was left with his four-footer, with a nasty left-hand borrow at that, and the complete golfer's nightmare: "This for the entire match." Even at the age of 24 I remember thinking, "Better him than me." Nowadays I doubt whether I could have borne to watch it. Easterbrook holed it like a man, and the cup was Britain's.

I did not see the following match in America, but four years later we were back again at Southport and Ainsdale, with the ground baked hard and a wind of almost gale force blowing. Cotton in practise had done a 64 (his finest hour was to come within a few days when, against the full strength of the Americans, he won the Open at Carnoustie) and the general note was one of restrained optimism, in which I see that I shared at the time, though for a reason which I reveal with mixed feelings. It was, as I see that I wrote, that the Americans "have too many wives. Not that they have brought more than one each, but they have brought six in all, together with Master Revolta, aged two. And it is my experience, or rather I have observed it to be other people's, that women on these trips are an encumbrance equivalent roughly to conceding two shots per round." This forecast, coming, as it did, from a bachelor still in his 20's proved to be as inaccurate as it was ungallant, and the United States won by 7 matches to 3.

Then came the war, and it was not until November 1947 that the series was resumed, through the good offices of that perpetual friend of professional golf, Mr. Robert A. Hudson, who sponsored the match at his home club at Portland, Ore. I did not go over for this but I gather that it rained and rained and rained, and Sam King at the tail end of the procession was the only man to win a point for Britain on either day.

My memories of the 1949 match, which was played at Ganton, near Scarborough, are more of the voyage home from the United States, where I had been watching the Walker Cup match, than of the match itself. The American team came over on the Queen Elizabeth, and so did I. Every one of this team had seen some sort of service during the war—a notable record. The smallest of them, Johnny Palmer, had survived 30 bombing missions over Tokyo. For Chick Harbert it was his second crossing in the Elizabeth. With 19,000 others he had come over in her during the war. He was still marvelling at the organisation. He and his wife were now occupying a stateroom in which 96 men had slept, 32 at a time in three eight-hour shifts.

In February 1949 Ben Hogan had had his famous motor accident—it is an interesting reflection that had he been wearing a seat belt at the time he would now have been dead some 16 years—and as a compliment to his almost incredible, though still only partial, recovery, he had been made captain of the American team. His legs were still tightly bandaged and he could walk only with difficulty. We used to spend time in the Turkish bath together and it was here that I began to admire, and perhaps to begin to understand, this truly remarkable man. I referred to him once as the non-playing captain, which of course he was, but I could see at once that I had said the wrong thing. His steely blue eyes narrowed and his lips tightened. "This life is driving me crazy," he said. "I want to compete again." At that moment the only person who thought he would ever play again, much less compete, was Hogan. What he did later is a matter of golfing history.

I am told that he had some difficulty in persuading his team that the match was not a pushover. If they did think this, they were not unjustified, in view of the 1947 result. Two things combined to cause them to change their minds. The first was that the lowly British led 3 - 1 in the foursomes on the first day. The second—and it must be remembered that I am giving only personal impressions—was the unduly partisan behaviour of some of the spectators. It is all right to cheer when your own man puts his ball on the green: it is quite inexcusable to let out a roar when the opposition drives into the woods. At any rate, on the second day the Americans came out of their corner fighting and a formidable succession of 3's began to go up against their names, hole by hole, on the scoreboard. The result was 7 - 5 in their favour, and a match which had frankly proved unsatisfactory from the British point of view from more than one angle was over.

━━━1940━━━
THE LOTUS EATER

On the last night of the voyage I joined a party in what may be termed the Queen Mary's nightclub, known as the Veranda Grill—an establishment endowed with all the attributes of the modern bottle party: tiny, over-crowded, unbelievably stuffy, and opaque with the smoke of cigars. The band stopped nominally at 2:00, but were willing to continue so long as any of the patrons had any spare dollars. At the time in question it was about four in the morning.

A man sitting at the table I had joined, and whose name I didn't know, was quietly intoxicated—so quietly, indeed, that nothing would induce him to speak. In the centre of the table was a vase of gladioli. Waking from his torpor, my neighbour stretched out a listless hand and drew forth a large bloom. He then broke off the spikey green piece at the end, popped the rest of the flowers into his mouth, and solemnly munched and swallowed them. Without uttering a syllable, he ate three whole gladioli.

We then adjourned to someone's cabin, where my eye at once fell upon a bowl of chrysanthemums—great big white ones, seven or eight inches in diameter. Our friend sat silently on the table and ate two of them. He was starting on his third when I left for bed.

I have never met anyone able to account for this strange phenomenon. Lotus-eaters, yes; gladiolus- and chrysanthemum-eaters, no. Next morning, as we edged our way slowly up Southampton Water, I saw the fellow walking silently round the deck. He seemed as fit as a fiddle.

Some years later, having read the above, he reintroduced himself when our paths happened to cross again. He said he still enjoyed an occasional bowl of flowers—and he still looked as fit as a fiddle.

1968
CASTLEROSSE

It is difficult, since he has no counterpart today, to do justice to the unique reputation enjoyed in the 1930's by the monumental figure of Valentine Viscount Castlerosse, later sixth Earl of Kenmare, not only among the more sophisticated society of London, but in the minds of millions who never met him. To call him a columnist would be almost *lèse majesté*, since the younger reader might fall into the error of comparing him with the more sensational type of contributed column today. Castlerosse, in fact, every week for the best part of 15 years, wrote under the title of "A Londoner's Log" the whole of page two of the London Sunday Express. He wrote it all out in longhand with a battery of specially sharpened pencils—a mixture of people, places, philosophy, wisdom, satire and wit, interspersed with barbed allusions to the fickleness of women. Eventually he married the most beautiful woman in London and the rows they had have hardly been surpassed in the love-hate history of matrimony.

Castlerosse not only was, but looked, "every inch a Lord." He talked, wrote, ate, drank and had his being on the grand scale. His weight varied between 18 and 20 stone [252 – 280 pounds] and it seemed only proper for him to be attired in white waistcoat and spats and, in winter, a vast astrakhan-collared fur-lined coat. Low, the cartoonist, once drew an enormous cigar all by itself in mid-air, and even the man in the street knew it meant Castlerosse. Wherever he appeared he stopped the show, and never more completely than when he attended a huge fancy dress ball made up as Holbein's portrait of Henry VIII, whom in any case he almost exactly resembled.

He was the only columnist, though I still hesitate to use the word, who wrote from above his subjects. He was not to be summoned by some public relations man to wait upon visiting actresses, notebook in hand, at inconvenient hours. With Castlerosse it was he who was the celebrity. As a result, the first question asked by visiting firemen of either sex tended to be: "Can anyone get me an introduction to Castlerosse?" It may seem incredible today, but there it was. "Everyone" read his Sunday page and anyone who figured in it was made for the day.

I suppose one's "hero" is almost bound to be older than oneself and this was so in my own case by 20 years. You may imagine my feelings, therefore, on receiving a few years before the war a long, handwritten summons from the great man. Having made a modest mark in writing about golf, I was now to proceed to his ancestral home at Killarney, where he had ideas about making not only a golf course but, on account of the temperate climate and the adjacent Gulf Stream, a golf course in colour. His dream, I like to think, came at least partly true.

After an all-day journey across Ireland I arrived at the little station in darkness, but it was clear that something was afoot. This turned out to be His Lordship in person, complete with purple smoking jacket and slippers with the crossed C's monogram. In the morning I looked out with a lively surmise and found framed in the window a scene I can exactly recall to this day: the tall avenue of beeches, the white horse in the paddock, the meadows leading down to a glimpse of the lake and, behind it all, the purple mountains of Kerry. An air of total peace prevailed and you could almost feel it. No noise, no aeroplanes, no radio, no newspapers till tea-time, by which time they were meaningless. Despite the differences in age and background my hero-to-be and I hit it off together from the start, mainly, I fancy, because I fell so manifestly in love with the place, and the life, for which he would willingly have exchanged the fleshpots from which, alas, he had to earn the money to keep them up. Later he was to lend me the house for my honeymoon, and we were shown up by old Dennis, the butler, into separate rooms. It could only happen in Kerry!

His life in Killarney was still semi-feudal. The lakes "and all the fish therein" belonged to the family, and the ruined Ross Castle and the woods and demesnes as far as the eye could see; and his predecessors, as was the custom of the day, had thrown a seven-mile wall round the lot. At the farthest end we spent much time on the golf course and I began to understand the general spirit of the place when the estate foreman said that in a certain part there had been a road there before but it hadn't been used for some time. "How long ago would that be?" I asked. "Oh," he said, "t'would be about 400 years."

In the intervals we fished in the lake, or shot duck, His Lordship weighing down the stern of his boat so that the boatman could scarce get his oars to the water. I think it pleased him to think of me tramping down before dawn to get a shot at the geese while he lay in bed. One day he announced that on the morrow we should go stalking. We drove as far as we could and then set off in single file up the mountain, Castlerosse leading the way, followed by myself, two retainers carrying rifles and telescopes, and in the rear another man carrying only a pail. I did not like to display my ignorance by asking the significance of the pail. Later it turned out to be the ice for His Lordship's whisky and soda.

He drank on a scale in keeping with his person. In the first war, when he served in the trenches as an officer in the Irish Guards, photographs show him to have been as slim as a flagpole. He was shot through the elbow at the battle of Loos. It stiffened his right arm, so that he could never again extend it or hold it above his head, but it fitted perfectly for lifting a glass. It was nothing for him to pour half a pint of whisky into a pint tumbler, fill it to the top with soda, and then down it in a single draught. One day, after we had played golf at Ballybunion, he downed seven bottles of Guinness and five half-lobsters, and spent the journey home erupting like a minor volcano and cursing his long-suffering chauffeur Godfrey, whenever the car hit a bump in the road.

He had once been a scratch golfer but now his arm limited his game. We played together at Walton Heath one day and he topped shot after shot. "Pick it up," he would say to his caddie in a lordly tone. At the last hole he tried a final stroke, with the same result. He tossed the club disdainfully to the ground and stalked toward the clubhouse, uttering the memorable instructions, "Pick that up. Have the clubs destroyed, and leave the course."

Castlerosse, like royalty, never carried money and could go for long periods under the impression that he wasn't spending any. Towards the end of his life he lived at Claridges Hotel, and sometimes I used to lunch with him. A waiter would bring the preliminary drinks, for which of course no money changed hands. We would then proceed to the St. James Club, where he instructed the porter to pay the taxi. Lunch consisted of almost anything which was out of season, or vastly expensive, or both. He signed the bill, returned to Claridges, instructed the top-hatted lackey at the door to see to the taxi ("Of course, me lord! Certainly, me lord!") and went to sleep—happy in the knowledge that he had not spent a penny.

One day, in the absence of his equally long-suffering valet Welsh, he had decided, quite erroneously, that he was short of shirts. He had summoned the shirtmaker and I happened to be there when the man arrived, fawning and rubbing his hands at the prospect of a substantial order. Valentine chose the most expensive pattern of pure silk, making sure, of course, that each shirt would have his monogram on the breast pocket. How many? Oh, make it three dozen. At pre-war prices perhaps £200. The shirt problem, now solved, no longer existed.

Perhaps his most lordly gesture was when he tossed the entire morning mail into the wastepaper basket unopened. "But you can't do that," I said, with reluctant admiration. "Oh," he said, "if there's anything, they'll write again." Perhaps the shirtmaker was among them.

He left all his silk shirts and pyjamas, believe it or not, to the Convent of the Presentation in Killarney, and in the late 1950's the nuns were still wearing apparel which they had made from them. The Mother Superior used to wear a pair of his monogrammed slippers. "What little feet he had!" she said.

Relations between Lords Castlerosse and Beaverbrook, bosom friends, yet each, perhaps, envying the other for something which he himself did not possess, were sometimes strained—Castlerosse sweeping majestically through life, spending prodigiously and acclaimed wherever he went; Beaverbrook, his millionaire employer, knowing well enough who was eventually going to pay. One day when they were in Cannes together, there was a water shortage. Later Beaverbrook was taken aback to find on the hotel bill an item for 12 dozen bottles of mineral water. "Quite in order," said Castlerosse. He had had them sent up for his bath.

Eventually the debts and the creditors and the worry would catch up on him to such extent as to be no longer concealable from Beaverbrook's suspecting eye. Rows and recrimination would be followed by the usual promise of reform, but the result was always the same. Beaverbrook had to put his hand in his pocket once more, generally to the tune of several thousands. There are those who suspect that secretly in his heart, like a parent bailing out a profligate but well-loved son, he was happy in doing it.

"I see my moneylender has gone off to the war," wrote Castlerosse in 1939. "I only hope he charges the enemy with the same enthusiasm that he charges me." By now, however, rich living, the best of everything ("I never cared for the second class"), and burning the candle at both ends, even though it gave a lively light—all this, and sadness at the thought of yet another ghastly war—were taking their toll, and Castlerosse fell into an illness as melodramatic as London had known for many a long year.

Telephone calls poured in from all over the world and Claridges had to install a special operator to handle them. Flowers, get-well presents, messenger boys and actresses packed the corridors. His doctor, Lord Moran, prescribed "absolute quiet, no food, no drink, no books, no thoughts about women and no eroticism in your dreams." Castlerosse, "lying like a pink whale across the silken ocean of his great bed," as his biographer, Leonard Mosley, put it, received his visitors with caviar and champagne, while Beaverbrook, to relieve the patient's mind, slipped the more urgent creditors £1,500.

In the end Castlerosse pulled through, but the world in which he had been so conspicuous a figure was gone forever. He retreated to his beloved Killarney and from here began in 1942 to bombard me with fictitious telegrams, such as "Your aunt who lives here is dying STOP Will leave you her fortune STOP Come at once." Army Council Instructions, however, were only too clear. Nothing but the illness of a parent or "urgent business reasons" qualified one for leave in Ireland. Eventually Castlerosse wrote airily that he was "proposing to spend another £40,000 on the golf course," of which I happened to possess one £1 share. "This, sir," I said to an understanding Irish general who knew Killarney, "is urgent business reason."

September in Killarney! Fishing and shooting duck on the lake; the new golf course; scenery out of this world ("See what the Almighty can do when he is in a good mood"); and Castlerosse in his own home, the best company in the world. What a prospect to exchange for Anti-Aircraft Headquarters, the blackout and the blitz! With a high heart I reached the bright lights of Dublin. I rang up a friend. Where was I going? he asked. Why, to Killarney, to spend my leave with Castlerosse.

There was a long pause. "Alas," said the voice, "he died this morning."

―1965―
BITTER PILLS

How strange are the lapses of human memory—and none more strange than those suffered by people who play, attempt to play or watch the game of golf.

Among the many dramatic incidents, for instance, upon which Bobby Jones may have looked back, none could have been stamped more indelibly on his mind than the occasion on which, during his first visit to this country as a very young man, he tempestuously tore up his card at the short 11th hole at St. Andrews. It is an episode which has been quoted and requoted ever since.

He told of it in detail at the unbelievably moving ceremony at which he was presented with the freedom of the Royal Borough of St. Andrews. He recalled how he had driven into the Hill bunker, taken two or three to get out, gone over the green into the little bunker at the back where the ground slopes sharply down to the Eden Estuary, taken two more in there—and torn up.

Now, the fact is that within the memory of the oldest inhabitant, and indeed almost for a certainty within the 400 years during which golf has been played on the links of St. Andrews, there has never been a bunker behind the 11th green. Jones himself freely accepts this. "Nevertheless," he said, "I never took two shots in a bunker and failed to remember it yet!"

In 1926 Jones played another historic bunker shot—some 170 yards to the 17th green at Lytham—which won him the Open from Al Watrous, with whom he was partnered and was at that time level. This bunker is one of a series of sand traps, and some years ago the members of Lytham erected a sort of "tombstone" therein to commemorate his feat. Hundreds of people witnessed the stroke, but there remain to this day many who declare with hand on heart that the tombstone is in the wrong bunker.

Two correspondents wrote to say that they were standing next to Jones when he played this historic shot and that he was not in sand at all but in rough grass between two bunkers.

Among them is Mr. Norman Doley of Cooden Beach, with whom I was talking in the train on the way home. As Jones's ball flew, incredibly, to the heart of the green, he happened, he said, to be standing beside Watrous. 'There," said Watrous, visibly shaken, "goes $100,000!" And so indeed it proved.

A few minutes later Walter Hagen came to the final hole, needing a 2 to tie, and sent his caddie forward to hold the flag. Referring to this some time ago, I recounted, though I was not, of course, there, how his ball had missed the flag by inches and finished in the geraniums under the clubhouse windows. I was at once corrected.

It wasn't geraniums, said members who had been there at the time. It was a bunker. Though the bunker is now gone, they said, there was never at any time a flower bed at the back of the 18th. Others who were also present rallied to my support. Nonsense, they said. They could see Hagen to this day, hitting it out of the geraniums.

This fallibility of golfing memory extends itself to one's own play. There is an old story of the man who, on being asked how he had got on, replied that he had been off his game, and then added, "Come to think of it, I am never on my game." Yet all of us have moments, however fleeting, when everything goes right at once and we are "on." One would think that one could remember, possibly for as long as 24 hours, the elementary details of stance, grip and backswing, and possibly some single "secret" that brought about this happy state.

How many people, I wonder, on the basis that the only way to remember a dream is to write it down at the time, have resorted to diagrams and memoranda? Certainly I have myself. If so, we are in good company, for I even seem to remember some years ago, if he will pardon the disclosure, Mr. Cyril Tolley consulting some hieroglyphics which he carried about with him under the elastic band in his cigarette case. I can see him doing it. But perhaps, after all, it was Mr. T.A. Torrance.

My own tribulations in this respect, though of little public interest, may yet strike a sympathetic chord. Caught in the situation, familiar to every dedicated golfer, of being, in the late Mrs. Zaharias's brilliant phrase, "fouled up in the mechanics of the game," I have been straightened out, de-straightened and re-straightened by sundry distinguished advisers, not excluding Henry Cotton.

As I had sliced for 30 years, he said that the only thing, especially as our figures were not dissimilar, was to stand like Bobby Locke, i.e., aiming to the right, twisting round on the backswing till you are aiming direct at point [a cricket fielder's position roughly equivalent to first base], and proceeding from there. Then, however much you heave round to the left as you come down, you are still hitting "from the inside."

This was tried, and towards the end of the second bucket of balls at the golf school, a compromise between the Locke and the orthodox brought the desired result. Drive after drive flew painlessly into the distance as though fired from a rifle. The magic stance—distance from the ball, position of the feet, angle of approach, and so on—was measured and committed earnestly to memory.

The next day brought two bitter pills to swallow. Not only, as you may imagine, had I forgotten the formula and reverted to type, but I, the proud owner of the Clayton windmills known as Jack and Jill, failed to notice that Jack and Jill, ridden by Clayton, was running at Ascot. It won, while my back was turned, at 20-1.

1951
SINGING FOR SUPPER

I hope I shall not be accused of dwelling too much in the past if I confess to a sense of affinity with the ancient part of the Royal and Ancient game of golf. The minute books of long-established clubs always fascinate me, and I sometimes stop to wonder whether we shall seem as ancient in times to come as our predecessors sometimes do today.

I like, too, the sense of continuity that comes from sitting in the same chair, and looking at the same pictures as the members who played on the same course before the turn of the century.

At any rate, for a reason which will become apparent, my attention has been drawn, as they say in the libel actions, to the Minutes of the Kemp Town Golf Club, founded in 1893 and now the East Brighton Club, not far from where I live. I have spent an agreeable morning browsing among them and battling, in the imagination, to manoeuvre a guttie ball through the wind blowing in across the Downs from the Channel, with those long-headed, thick-gripped clubs now reposing in the glass case, I dressed in a tight Norfolk jacket, stiff collar and boots.

The amateur record for the green is set in 1894 by Dr. Bruce Goff with an 82, while playing Mr. H. Abbey, one of the founders, in the fourth round of the Abbey Cup—from which two queries arise in the mind. With those implements and those clothes how much better than 82 would the amateur record be today? And why the devil should not a course record still be set in match play, provided the players use the medal tees and hole everything out? Golf, after all, in this country at any rate, is a match-play game.

A running battle with the ladies' section, known throughout as "The Associates," lasts well over the turn of the century. They want among other things to be allowed to use the men's tees, but the men, ever jealous of their mystique as the stronger sex, won't let them.

The Associates offer in return to give up one of their days, but, no, they are to continue to play the ladies' course as laid out on the plan in the clubhouse. They try again, but the honourable secretary is instructed to "give notice that the decision of the Committee is final, and the subject will not be reopened." One would like to see him try that one today!

If only we had a tape-recording of the spirited discussion round the bar (opened on Sundays for the first time in 1899) and among the Committee which lay behind the Minutes. "Letter from Mr. Bechtel complaining of the conduct of Messrs. Tulk Hart and the Rev. Spelman, who were stated to have driven into Mr. B's party at the fifth hole. The matter was duly discussed, and it was resolved that Messrs. Tulk Hart and Spelman were right in what they did." What exactly, one would love to know, did they do?

Then there was another running battle, this time with Harris, who must have been some sort of professional or club-minder.

"*June 1899:* Secretary to arrange new terms with Harris. *September 1899:* Harris applies for increase in wages. Discussed and dismissed. *March 1900:* Complaints made of Harris and his brother being absent from the shop at the same time. Secretary directed to dismiss him if his orders not obeyed. *October 1901:* Mr. Clarkson and others suggest increase for Harris. Committee consider Harris sufficiently paid for services he renders. *December 1901:* Proposed by Dr. Burrows, seconded by Mr. Abbey, that Harris be given a month's notice. Carried unanimously."

Costs in the old days are always fascinating, even making every allowance for the value of money, incomes, taxation and the rest of it. Somewhere I have an old Army and Navy Store catalogue of the period when the great-to-be carpenter from Elie, Fife, James Braid, was a clubmaker there. The finest wooden clubs were about five shillings.

At the turn of the century the Kemp Town Club decided on an impressive programme of modernisation and instructed the secretary to obtain an estimate for the following—and present or past members of the house committee of any golf club today may care to estimate the present figure:

Conversion of earth closets and installing complete drainage, light and heat throughout, with gas. Furnishing ladies' room (one up to the Associates!). Erecting 75 new lockers. Painting the whole of the buildings.

The answer was £200 [$390 today], at which the secretary at once reported that it was "problematical if the increase in revenue would provide such a sum." The committee, splendid fellows, replied: "Order the lot."

One of the most difficult arts in golf, strangely enough, is that of running a successful dinner, and many and excruciating are those over which the chairman loses his grip. Our predecessors at the Kemp Town Club, assembled at the Royal Pavilion in 1900, had none of today's qualms about the festivities "going on too long." They were out for the evening and the carriages could wait. They expected not only a dinner fit for gentlemen, but also that between the courses—oh, ghastly thought!—sundry persons would "oblige" with a recitation or a song.

I feel that you may come to recapture their evening in the Royal Pavilion, which is quite unchanged over the intervening years and still the scene of golf club dinners, so here is what they sat down to in 1900 together with the accompanying speeches and "extras."

"The Queen" by Mr. Chairman. Tomato soup: Spring soup. Rule Britannia. Turbot. Sause Hollandaise: Whitebait. Song by Dr. Bruce Goff. Sauté Chicken and Mushrooms. "The Captain and Officers." Saddle of Mutton: Sirloin of Beef. Songs with harp accompaniment by Miss Mary Aukett: "Summer's Here." "Ye Banks and Burns." Roast Pheasant and Chips. Response by the Captain. Petites Bouchees de Chocolat, Poires Chantilly Glaces. Violin solo by L. Horner and (wait for it!) Song by H. Longhurst. Bloater Roes and Mushrooms on toast. Response by the new

Captain. Cheese. Song by A.V. Treacher. Song with harp accompaniment. "My Ain Gudeman," by Miss Aukett. Ice Pudding. "The Visitors." Dessert. Song by W.H. Southcomb. Violin solo by L. Horner. Café Noir. Response by the Visitors. Recitation by R.A.O. Fearon and (just to round off the evening) song by H. Longhurst.

Tail suits, of course, and very high, very stiff collars. How they stuck it out, my own and younger generations will never know, but what a bargain it must have been—all that lot, including two renderings by H. Longhurst, for precisely one guinea!

1949
A PERSON OF HARMLESS DELIGHT

They may indeed be all God's creatures, and those peoples of the East who on this account will not kill even a disease-bearing insect may well be right. I can only say that, with one exception, I do not share this view. The exception is the praying mantis, who sounds so sinister, but is, in fact, a person of harmless delight. The first I ever saw came and sat beside my soup one night in Rangoon. He was a beautiful shiny green and about 3½ inches tall. His grasshopper wings were folded neatly down his back and he sat back on his haunches against the salt cellar, looking towards my plate in the most comical way, and rubbing his little hands together as though about to partake of the feast. Sometimes he would close them in the prayerful attitude that earned him his name and, if you prodded at him with a spoon, he went through the most laughable defensive antics. From that moment my heart belonged to the praying mantis, and if it were not so cold in England I would have them all over the house.

COMEDY, TRAGEDY AND SHARP PRACTISE

It is always refreshing to read of incidents that emphasise the faintly ludicrous side of a pastime which tends, with golfers now joining the ranks of the millionaires, to be taken more and more as though it really mattered. Partly because stories of cheating at golf always delight me, though I am sure they shouldn't, and partly because I have entered into partnership with caddies of every race, colour and creed all over the world, I derived special pleasure from the episode in last week's tournament at Stoke Poges, wherein a caddie surreptitiously nudged his man's ball clear of an unplayable lie under a tree. Unfortunately, he was seen and reported by a spectator, so that all he got for this exhibition of loyalty beyond the call of duty was the sack. What is more, so ridiculously savage are some of the penalties in the Rules of Golf, the player was charged a total of three strokes—two for putting the ball back in the unplayable lie and one to pick it out again.

With large money at stake it is only natural that caddies should wish to help their men, sometimes in innocence, sometimes knowing only too well the enormity of their crime. I knew of one club before the war where, if a caddie did not have a hole in his trousers pocket and a correctly numbered spare ball, he was liable not to be employed again. James Bond's caddie in the famous match with Goldfinger at Sandwich (not, I hasten to say, the club I had in mind!) was taken strictly from life.

Just after the war I managed to get to what was left of the Royal Hong Kong Club at Fanling, whose tie by a happy coincidence, I happen to be wearing as I write. The Japanese had cut down all the trees and you had to take a picnic lunch, but one was at once surrounded by a crowd of enchanting Chinese children in huge, round hats, all clamouring for employment at nine pence a round. In the end, nine of them accompanied me, ranging ahead in the rough like beaters, and, of course, I never had anything but a perfect lie. In African countries, too, you are liable to be surrounded by would-be caddies, and here the test is simple. You choose the one with the biggest big toe.

Equally entertaining this week has been the story of the council [municipal] house tenant whose living room windows are so persistently bombarded and broken by errant members of the South Leeds Club that he has been forced to board them up to protect his wife and children. He estimates that in the 2½ years he has lived there at least 1,000 balls have landed in or on his house. I only wish he had asked me first and we could have gone into partnership. Instead of boarding the place up like an air-raid shelter, he should have erected a large, loose net—rather on the principle of the ones they stick out of mail trains to catch the letters without stopping. Perhaps it is still not too late.

This would catch up the balls, dropping them down to a funnel leading through into the sitting room via a flap which rings a bell to announce each ball's arrival, reminiscent of homing pigeons, and depositing them in a basket, from which he would collect them, like the eggs, every morning. As he is only beside the fifth hole, we might even get a few brand new ones. Furthermore, we should be in good company, for Bing Crosby, who once lived on the "slice" side of the 14th fairway at Pebble Beach, was reported never to have had to buy a ball in his life.

Golf balls and mushrooms not only look alike but bring out the same acquisitive satisfaction of "something for nothing." I wonder if any readers share my recurrent dream of looking for a ball, finding one, and then finding dozens more. Sometimes I am back in the chalk pit beside the Downs Club at Eastbourne, where I once found one as a very small boy. In others, John Morrison and I are searching among the millions and millions of smooth pebbles among which I have put our second shot over the sixth green at Deal during the Halford-Hewitt, all of which suddenly turn out in my dream to be golf balls. (When this situation did in fact occur, Morrison's shot sent up a shower of sparks and he later apologised with, "Sorry. Very unlucky. Got a stone behind it.")

In the old days people were constantly being hit by golf balls, or such is my impression, though I may have gained this from a little book by W.T. Linskill, the "founder of Cambridge golf." Writing of St. Andrews, where you used the same fairway coming and going, much narrower than today, he maintained that it was ridiculous to regard golf as a dangerous game, he himself having been "hit only three times this season." I suspect, however, that it was less painful to be struck with a guttie than the present missile. Indeed, it was common practise, if people in front did not get a move on, to "touch them up" by driving just, or not quite, into them—a practice which would highly commend itself in all too many quarters today.

I was about to say that golf was certainly not among the more dangerous games today when it struck me to consult that fount of all knowledge, *The Golfers' Handbook*, whereupon I was amazed to find how lethal it really is and how tragi-comical are some of the incidents recorded. In the final of the 1935 Yorkshire Evening News Tournament at Sandmoor, Leeds, for instance, Henry Cotton was dormie three on Percy Alliss when he hit his second clean over the 16th, struck a man on the head, and rendered him unconscious. The ball bounced back onto the green and Cotton got a half to win the match. I trust that the victim is still with us and that we number him among our readers—as we certainly do the gentleman I rendered unconscious in an exhibition match at Cotton's club, Langley Park. We remain on cordial terms and I still take out the golfers' insurance which he sold me while in the hospital.

The number of deaths from sundry causes on the golf course is quite extraordinary, ranging from the father who was instructing his son and was killed by a practise swing, to the man who broke his shaft against a tree and cut his throat with the dismembered half. Those who have lost an eye include that great sportsman and connoisseur, the late Jimmy de Rothschild, M.P., and a member of Fleetwood whose ball hit and rebounded from the wooden marker on the ladies' tee. An old friend of mine, Maj. Gerald Moxon, playing in the Army Championship at Sandy Lodge as a young man, was rendered unconscious by a wayward ball on the fifth tee. Next year he was standing within a few yards of the same spot telling his friends all about it, when he was knocked unconscious again.

In Australia a man hit a telephone pole with his drive and, under the local rule, played another. It hit the same pole, rebounded and knocked him out. In the same country a lady, excited at a good shot, stepped back, fell over her bag, and broke both arms. Johnny Farrell, one-time U.S. Open champion, who played in the first Ryder Cup match in Moortown in 1929, had his wrist broken by a pupil's practise swing.

It is human nature to laugh at the misfortunes of others, such as the proud father who during the boys' championship at Prestwick tried to rescue his son's ball from the Pow Burn, which was flowing particularly full and fast at the time, and fell in. Or the member of the Lewes Club, who shall be nameless, who overbalanced after his second shot to the sixth and somersaulted into a sheep trough full of water.

One may conclude with the episode of the two doctors sitting in the clubhouse at a championship which I will not in any way identify, when help was summoned from far out on the course. The junior of the two was dispatched and much later returned with the unhappy news that the spectator had been dead when he got there. "No fee then," said the senior man. "No. No fee, I'm afraid." There was a long pause. Then—"Did you get his watch?"

────1956────
"WILL I GIVE YE THE DAYLIGHT?"

I have been passing a week in Dublin, a city of strange contrasts. The breathtaking beauty of some of the old Georgian streets glowing in the evening sun with a sort of Italian light that we rarely see in England . . . and the utilitarian drabness . . . the tourist lures of Grafton Street, with the visitors in search either of seven-and-sixpenny steaks, or a bottle of E.V.M. (English Visitors 'Mixture'—any Irish chemist knows the formula) after too many of them . . . and the pale woman singing for alms in the gutter, carrying, like the London communists, a baby in her arms, possibly her own.

To an Englishman, though, Dublin offers escape by means other than the traditional steaks. The devil-may-care attitude towards life and the worries thereof is a happy contrast with the regimented queuing and solemn government posters in England. A happy instance of this carefree attitude occurred during a broadcast in which I was engaged after the final of the Amateur Golf Championship.

From an upstairs room in the Portmarnock Club we were meant to chip in to a programme run each Saturday evening by Angus McKay, covering the day's sport. An hour previously I had recorded a two-minute talk with Sam McCready, the new champion. On the strength of this and, I suspect, the fact that a good deal of cricket had been washed out, we were to have six minutes.

Eventually the voice from London said, "Over to Portmarnock . . ." This was greeted by dead silence—which was not surprising seeing that the only man who could hear London was at that moment making a telephone call. Eventually "Another try at Portmarnock . . ." said the voice, and away we went. In due course on went the record, revolving silently on its plate. A few seconds later it faded away, leaving four figures gesticulating feverishly to each other over a live microphone and a dead, but still revolving, disc. Complete shambles!

Now whatever you may say of the BBC, their outside broadcasts never go wrong. Their organisation in this direction is unsurpassed. I imagined the scene in the London studio: the tearing of hair, the subsequent inquests, the search for the culprit.

"Ah, 'tis over now," said the Irish, packing up their traps, "I wouldn't be worrying myself about that all."

That's the spirit!

Irishmen have a great gift for expressing commonplace things in a graphic way. A well-known English friend of mine, for instance, after a thoroughly Irish evening, lay slumbering heavily next morning. The elderly hotel valet shook him by both shoulders and, sizing up the situation, asked, not would he like the curtains drawn, but: "Will I give ye the daylight?"

I am afraid I started something by writing, just after the war, that it seemed, to say the least of it, peculiar to play the British Amateur Golf Championship in a neighbouring Republic which had been neutral during the war and now declared itself categorically to have "no connection with the old firm." Furthermore, that it was an odd prospect to take out a passport and go through the customs liable to interrogation and possibly search before being permitted to land to play in one's own championship.

This gave considerable offence at Portmarnock, and my last memory of that hospitable club is of being penned in against the wall by a ring of outraged Eireans busy celebrating an Ulsterman's success in the championship. Fingers prodded me in the ribs; amber-filled glasses waved before my eyes; a man seized me by the lapel.

"Is this the fellow? . . . Listen to me now . . . Leave him alone, man . . . I thought 't would be an older man . . . 'Tis not the British Championship anyway . . . Give him a drink, man."

It is all very well to say "Keep off politics in Ireland." You can't! If it is not the republic, it is partition. And if it's not partition, it's the Pope.

"There is no hope for Ireland," said one of the most renowned citizens of Dublin, "till they give them bullfighting!"

Earlier in the week a T.D., which is the Eire equivalent of our M.P., kindly arranged for me to visit the Dail, pronounced Doyle like the Irish boxer. This seemed to hold prospects of entertainment as well as instruction, for the paper that morning contained details of a happy little episode when Mr. Dillon, Minister of Agriculture, had made allegations regarding a Fianna Fail deputy:

Mr. Dillon: "Stand up like a man. Don't be snivelling there behind your hand!"

Mr. O'Briain (F.F.): "Can you tell us what a man is at all?"

Mr. Allen (F.F.): "You twisted-nosed cur!"

It was with lively hopes, therefore, that your correspondent passed through the stately portals in Kildare Street, and was ushered into the Strangers' Gallery. Here the first thing that strikes the eye is the wire caging which prevents the irate visitor from registering displeasure with any missile bigger than, say, a tennis ball. The pattern of this grille, after he has gazed through it for an hour or two, lingers in the visitor's eye long after he re-emerges into the outside world. The 21 deputies in attendance on the day in question, however, did nothing to displease each other or the 56 spectators in the gallery.

Mr. Morrisey, Minister of Industry and Commerce, presented the estimates for his department, reading from a typescript in a way that would not have done for the Speaker of the House of Commons, while Mr. Lemass, his opposite number on the other side, deplored that the Ministry had promised so much and done so little.

As I listened to the Minister closing his speech and heard the sonorous, familiar phrases, "no reason for complacency . . . only by wholehearted cooperation of all groups . . . enjoy that standard of living to which we all aspire . . . no time, however, to waste . . . much still to be done. . . ." I realized that Ministers do not change much in this world.

1967

GOLF WITHOUT GRASS

Golf, it has now long since been forgotten, is essentially a simple pastime wherein you start at A and hole out at B, overcoming as best you may such hazards as you encounter on the way, and I am always glad that this is in fact the way I started. My parents had decided to take their holiday in the little Dartmoor town of Yelverton and the year must have been 1921, since I so distinctly remember the man at Glastonbury, where we stopped on the way, with his monotonous chant of "Old Moore's Almanack predicts the coming events for 1922." The hotel at Yelverton overlooked the Common where two other boys whose parents were staying there had carved out three holes with penknives. Soon I had acquired a sawn-off club and together we used to sneak out before breakfast and play two or three rounds. I became completely "bitten" by golf and, although I sometimes suspect that I ought to have put such talents as I possess to a better use, the game has been uncommonly good to me ever since.

Both playing it and writing about it began to take me to some of the best, and therefore best kept, courses in various parts of the world, and continuous visits to America ushered me into a world of vast country clubs with swimming pools, masseurs, barbers and £1,000 entrance fees. It is excusable, perhaps, if I came to forget about the original simple golf, the sort of golf that was good enough for that great writer, naturalist and fisherman, the first amateur champion, Horace Hutchinson, at Westward Ho! where, if you found the hole becoming worn at the sides, you took out your pocket-knife and cut another, marking it with a gull's feather for the benefit of those coming behind.

I was brought back to the paths of truth and reality, and have not strayed since, by a visit to the oilfields in the foothills of Persia in the later stages of the war. New faces are always welcome in such parts—some fellows had not had leave for six years—and it was not long before I was ushered up to the Masjid-i-Sulaiman Golf Club, named after the ancient temple nearby. The clubhouse was a fine granite affair, just like home, and the accents of Fife and Glasgow predominated amid the tinkle of ice on a Sunday morning. It was not the clubhouse, therefore, but the course which brought me, literally, down to earth.

Not a blade of grass was to be seen: only a miscellaneous assortment of stones, boulders and slippery mud which bakes rock hard in summer. The greens were of asphalt (the "pitch" mentioned in the construction of Noah's Ark) and covered by a layer of fine sand, each one of them being attended by a man with a long broom who smoothed out the surface before each player made his putt. As you could not stick a peg tee into the ground, the barefooted caddie boys, some of them quite enchanting little villains, turned up with a lump of clay, out of which they fashioned a tee and presented it to you stuck on the bottom of the driver. Sometimes, as they departed for home, the lump of clay would conceal one of your golf balls.

Some of the views were stupendous, and sights and sounds not normally associated with the royal and ancient game enlivened the scene: a man in baggy trousers cantering across the course on a white horse, for instance, or half-a-dozen women walking silently past the green with pots on their heads. "*C'est magnifique,*" I reflected, "*mais ce n'est pas le golf.*"

And yet it was. It took only a few holes to bring home to me that here, once more, was the original golf—from A to B, overcoming without complaint the hazards encountered on the way, the complete reverse of the modern conception of playing the same shot with every club in the bag, all 14 of them, and a good shot being assured of a standard result. Here, as in all desert golf, of which I now regard myself as something of an authority, you have to "manufacture" shots, as indeed you do on the Old Course at St. Andrews. To cause a ball to carry an expanse of loose sand and pitch on a firm patch with just the right trajectory to run up through the gully and come to rest on a small circle of fast-running asphalt is true golf. Harry Vardon would have done it supremely well; Jack Nicklaus, I think, would not.

Later I went up to Teheran and here again the small European community had made a golf course. Not a blade of grass was to be seen and the course itself was absolutely flat. The greens this time were of a thick variety of grit, or granite chippings, all very tiny, and a ball pitching on them left a dark, bare patch where it landed and stopped dead. Strings of grave, supercilious camels, roped together, would wander across behind the tee or between player and green, their bells clanging mournfully, the drivers huddled up asleep in rugs on the creatures' backs. As we finished our round, maybe a couple of hours later, they were still to be seen, specks on the distant plain, plodding on.

The emigrating Scots have carried golf to the farthest and most unlikely quarters of the globe. A doctor friend of mine, whose practise encompasses several thousand square miles of the Western Arctic, landed to visit some isolated Eskimos. Clambering over rocks and ice on some barren, inhospitable island, he looked down and, beheld, of all things, a golf ball. The answer, of course, was Scotsmen. The number of holes had coincided with the number of members: three holes, two Scottish engineers and a Jesuit priest.

Some years ago I visited Das Island, which juts almost imperceptibly out of the middle of the Persian Gulf, little more than a mile long and three-quarters wide—the base incidentally for an operation destined to raise a few hundred millions for the deposed Sheik of Abu Dhabi. Never mind the drilling barge, said the accents of Scotland. You must come and see our golf course. There, sure enough, after only three months were nine holes already laid out, the tees built, the greens marked out, and three Indian tailors hard at work embroidering nine flags with the Company's emblem. There was also, by a strange coincidence, Mr. Terry Thomas, the film comedian, in whose company I later helped to eat a sheep in Bahrain.

Most of my grassless golf has been played, naturally enough, in the Middle East and many are the comical and poignant memories that return as I look back on it. The course of the Royal Baghdad Club is, or was, in the middle of the racecourse, and last time I was there the overnight rain had turned the alluvial deposit of which it, and indeed most of Iraq, is mainly formed into a kind of reddish glue. There were other excitements, however, since it was a race day. The jockeys ride halfway out to the starting post and there dismount for a walk and a smoke while the public bets on the totalisator, which, shrewdly enough, they decline to do until they see that their selection is actually alive and on four legs. As we played the short seventh, we had an audience of half a dozen jockeys leaning against the rails. Their comments seemed to be of a derisory nature but we finished 1 up, we thought, when the first three of us got on the green and the fourth man hit the stick and nearly holed in one.

Hard by the Eternal Fires through which walked that imperishable trio, Shadrach, Meshach and Abednego in the days of Nebuchadnezzar, and I myself in more recent times—the fires are reduced to a few feet high now but still stink as abominably of rotten eggs—you will find the Kirkuk Golf Club, the course broken up by a few eucalyptus trees and the terrain ideal for golf. A few years ago some bright spirit brought back from Cairo small quantities of a grass which it was hoped might not only survive the climate but also "creep." They made a miniature "green" on each "brown" and, when I was there, the 18th had already "crept" 60 yards back towards the tee. Perhaps the whole course is covered by now.

It was in Cairo that I had a mortifying experience of grassless golf in reverse. In the Egyptian Open Championship I was partnered at Gezira with a dignified sheik from a desert course who played in a nightshirt, from below which a pair of enormous boots protruded like skis. He beat me easily. What really hurt, though, was his comment at the end. "That is the first time, sir, that I have ever played on grass."

Quite a wide experience of desert golf leaves me with a strong impression that the keenness of golfers varies in indirect ratio with the quality of the course they play on. In other words, the worse the course, the keener they become and the more seriously they take their game. I think of the arid waste of Aden, with the camel sweeping the greens in circles; of Kuwait, which is just one massive expanse of sand, but where you still cannot ground your club in a sand bunker; of Tripoli-super-Mare with the white city dazzling in the distance; and of Royal Benghazi, often inundated by the sea ("but it soaks through and improves the fairways"), where a man told me of the house to which he proposed to retire beside a course in Hampshire and added solemnly: "I have given my wife a power of attorney so that, if the time comes when I can no longer play golf, she is to send for the vet and have me put down."

Above all, however, I remember El Fasher, in the heart of the Sudan, where they have nine greens, no tees, and one flag, which is brought out each time anyone wishes to play. No good having regular flags, since, if they were made of wood, the ants would eat them and, if of metal, they would be instantly melted down by the locals for spears. A boy holds the flag in the first hole till one is near enough for an enormous Sudanese caddie to angle his bare feet behind the hole, whereupon the boy rushes off to hold the flag in the second. One short hole among some particularly repulsive camel thorn, sharp enough to use as gramophone needles, was described by the Governor as "set in a sylvan setting." As we neared the end, it was noticed that one of the caddies, wearing a blue, diamond-shaped badge on the back of his nightshirt, was getting restive. It turned out that he was on ticket of leave from the local gaol and was anxious about getting back by lock-up. He was thereupon sent back in the Governor's car! I wonder if they miss the British after all?

THE UNIVERSAL AMATEUR

The death of Lord Brabazon of Tara will leave an absolutely unfillable gap in the lives of all who had the good fortune to know him. He was completely unique. His 80 years of life, 10 better than the established par of three score and ten, covered more radical changes in human existence than any other two centuries put together and it seemed as though he was in at the birth of them all. He was the most "interesting" man—in the sense of stimulating one's own interest—I ever met and I doubt whether anyone could remember having spent a dull moment in his company.

The walls of his office told his early story. Here, for instance, was Aviator's Certificate No. 1 of the Fédération Aeronautique Internationale, date March 8, 1910—30 years after which the holder started the craze for "personal" car numbers by securing FLY 1.

Next to it a young man with gum boots, Norfolk jacket, and slightly prominent teeth is seen grasping the levers of a Heath Robinson flying machine—none other than the "biplane pusher with bamboo and ash framework," which was the first all-English aeroplane to fly. With it Brab won £1,000 from the Daily Mail for a circular flight of one mile, average height 40 feet.

Another picture, surely a unique galaxy of aeronautical pioneers, shows, under the heading "First English Aerodrome, Mussel Manor, Shellbeach, Sheppey, 4 May, 1909," a knickerbockered group including all three of the Short brothers, Wilbur and Orville Wright, young Moore-Brabazon, and the handsome, ill-fated Charlie Rolls, of Rolls-Royce, who Brab was later to see killed in an air display.

"The only gentleman's way of leaving the ground," he used to say, "is ballooning," and in another picture he is standing in the basket with Charlie Rolls, waiting to ascend from Battersea Gasworks (45,000 cu. ft. £4 10s. "including labour and bags of sand: holders-down extra.")

Other pictures reveal him, in chauffeur's cap, waiting to crank the first Rolls Royce, with the Duke of Connaught sitting bolt upright as passenger; and at the huge, high steering wheel of the Minerva with which he won the Circuit des Ardennes in 1907.

Beside one of the most remarkable pictures ever taken of the Cresta toboggan run are, curiously enough, two of a main-line railway station. Only very close inspection reveals them to be models, reminders of younger days when Brab had the best model railway in England. He would have! He ran it with his brother-in-law, Clarence Krabbe, and when they had an accident they stopped and held an "inquiry."

One day I chanced upon Brab at Turnberry, at breakfast, poring over what appeared to be a football pools coupon. It would have been in keeping with him if it had been, as he would have undoubtedly just worked out a completely novel system of permutations and combinations. As it happened he was engaged in a chess match by post with Lady Powerscourt in Dublin and was filling in his next move. This was in mid-summer. I asked him how he was getting on. "I lost a bishop in February," he said, "and have been in difficulties ever since." I did not see him again till about September. I again asked him how he was getting on. He looked round with an almost conspiratorial air, as though to make sure that no one was listening, and said, "I was mated last week." We agreed that he might now add to his many other distinctions that of being the only peer ever to have been mated by post.

Among the many other firsts in Brab's life was that, as a boy at Harrow, he was walking down Grove Hill when a few yards away from him a motorist put on the brakes too hard, ripped the spokes from his wheels, and became the first man to be killed in a motor accident. While others stood back, waiting for the infernal machine to blow up, Brab stepped forward and turned off the ignition burners. He was the only person who knew what they were. Afterwards he gave a lecture to the school scientific society on "The Motor Car." "A treasure now lost to the world," he called it.

Brab was the complete pioneer. He was one of the earliest riders on the Cresta, and certainly, in his 70's, the oldest. In the first war he became without question the Father of Modern Air Photography. He once turned up at Cowes with a kind of rotor arm attached to the mast of his yacht instead of a sail. It was he who, somewhat ridiculed at the time, pulled the first trolley up the first fairway at St. Andrews.

Later he was to be led out by the past captains at 8 o'clock on a September morning to drive himself in down the same fairway, as captain of the Royal and Ancient. He had previously been observed making surreptitious practise swings in his shirt sleeves behind the bandstand, but, when he executed one or two on the first tee, I remember remarking to my companion that, if the real thing were to turn out like these, no great good could come of it.

In fact, he hit it all along the ground towards mid-wicket and the ball had long been stationary before the first of the caddies could reach it. Afterwards he described his opening stroke as a "noble gesture of self-denial which has given pleasure to thousands."

With his booming, unmistakable voice he would hold an audience anywhere, whether in the Commons, the Lords, after dinner, or, particularly, in the United States. Proposing the toast of the Open champion at a dinner, he opened with: "It is only appropriate that a Member of Parliament whose constituency borders upon Liverpool and Merseyside should be asked to get up on his hind legs and propose the toast of Cotton."

It was he who in the Commons likened the Opposition to "a lot of inverted Micawbers waiting for something to turn down." Nor did his own side escape, for it was them, I seem to remember, that he meant when he referred to the "snores of the Front Bench reverberating throughout the land." It was certainly the then Archbishop of Canterbury whom he accused, when His Grace had made a speech on finance, of "talking through his mitre."

When Prince's, Sandwich, was used as a target range in the war, Brab declared that it was "like throwing darts at a Rembrandt." When Royal St. George's was waterlogged and too little, he thought, was being done about it, he put a suggestion in the book "That the water in the bunker at the 13th be changed."

People who worked with him were always astonished at the variety of subjects on which he could truly be described as expert. Yet in many ways he was an example of that rare, invaluable, and almost extinct species, the Universal Amateur.

Of the more serious side of Brab's long life—his work as Minister of Transport during the blitz and later of Aircraft Production, as President of the Royal Institution, and on the board of many eminent companies—I must leave it to others to write.

For those who pursue the humble game of golf, however, it is nice to think that a man of so many parts and of such immense distinction should have written in his autobiography:"When I look back on my life and try to decide out of what I have got most actual pleasure, I have no doubt at all that I have got more out of golf than anything else."

BEWARE THE MARTINIS!

A "completely obsessed" golfer of 23 informs me that he has had the good fortune to secure a job in Denver, Colo.—"incidentally, at a ridiculously high salary and I cannot understand why more people of my age are not hot-footing it out there"—and asks if I will reveal to him "just what this game of golf is in America." Since American golf and golfers are so constantly in the news, I thought I would try to answer our enviable reader's question here.

He will find golf in America, I suspect, an almost completely different game, some aspects of which he will like, others perhaps not. The first difference, from which stem many of the others, is that the Americans are, and always have been since the very beginnings of golf in their country, of the opinion that golf is basically a stroke-play, rather than a match-play, game. This is a wholly logical approach. They set out to play 18 holes of golf and 18 holes they are jolly well going to play.

Their primary object is to see how many they can go round in, or "shoot." They are not interested in picking up their ball, as we do, because their partner has won the hole for their side. Indeed, I have played in four-balls where no sides were picked at all; we simply played round, each of us, or at any rate three of the party, recording all the scores at each hole—including, to my great mortification, my own. Mostly, however, they will make up some sort of match, but it is still their own score that they are thinking of, and the scores of perhaps a dozen others with whom they have made all sorts of complicated wagers, to be worked out later over drinks in the locker room.

This, of course, leads to the second, much-publicised difference, against whose influence we are fighting a none too successful rearguard action over here, namely, slow play. "Golf is not a funeral," Bernard Darwin once wrote, "though both can be very sad affairs." Four-ball stroke play, with four indifferent club players holing out at every hole, is bound to be funereal, and the first thing our young friend will have to do is to learn to live with it.

When after about three hours the usual messages begin to come up regarding the anticipated pint of beer at the 19th, he will have to send back the disquieting intelligence that they are only sitting on the 11th tee and there remain at least another two hours to go. Also that it is no good his stomach talking about pints of beer; all it is going to get is a rather weak form of lager, so cold as to freeze its very lining.

As to the golf itself, it is possible to portray a typical course more truly than could be done in this country. The picture is of a park-like country club course, quite hilly, tree-lined, cut perhaps out of the vast acreage of scrub and forest which took possession of the land when the original settlers just abandoned it and moved west. The greens will be bigger than in Britain, with separate "pin positions," and a straight or level putt will be a rarity. Though spectacular advances have been made by the agronomists in adapting grasses to the varying climates in the United States, the newcomer will find that on the whole the grass is coarser-bladed than here and, through heavy watering, more lush. The run-up approach will soon be but a memory.

The odds are that he will find himself playing at a golf-and-country club combined, for which the subscription will be anything from treble to 10 times what we pay in England. A comparatively modest country club, however, will have a pool, and a magnificent locker room, according to our undemanding and insanitary standards, complete with attendants, possibly a masseur, showers, and (what even we might soon aspire to) something to put on your hair afterwards. There will be a beautiful drawing room scarcely used except for formal occasions, a card room, and that most insidious of institutions, the men's grill.

I say insidious because the men's grill is open all day and is therefore one of the main causes of slow play among club golfers. It does not matter when they finish. Bar service (beware the martinis, my young friend—always look on the bottle and when it says "100 proof" have a care!), steaks, huge ribs of roast beef, three-decker sandwiches, the lot—are all perpetually "on." So if they take five hours, well, they have come out for a day's golf anyway, and have had more of it than if they had gone round in four. All the same, we should not hear so much about slow play in America if they stopped serving lunch on the dot of half-past two!

The pro's shop will be reminiscent of one of our better sports-goods stores and the pro himself, as here, an excellent and respected citizen. There will be no secretary, but instead a highly paid club manager, for this is no small business. With everybody signing chits for everything, even the caddie's tip—and after the first two 100-proof martinis signing blithely and with no pain at all—the turnover is liable to be very considerable.

This, I hope my American friends would agree, is a fair picture of a typical country club, lavish perhaps by comparison with our own, but then it is the playground not only of the golfer but of the family. There are, of course, extremes above and below. Many a public-course golfer, in order to be sure of a Sunday game, queues up at midnight on Saturday, but, if he does secure a starting time, he is at least sure of a day's golf. His round may take him seven hours.

At the other end of the scale one could quote the late George S. May's Tam O'Shanter Club outside Chicago, which, in his day at any rate, had 13 bars, a telephone on every tee, and a special "quiet room" where people could retreat from the otherwise incessant piped-in music.

Or a California club where a weekend's compulsory hire not only of an electric buggy but also a caddie to hold the flag costs more than a year's golf at most clubs over here, and a local rule declares that "a player on foot has no standing on the course."

It takes all sorts to make the world of golf. My prophecy is that our young friend will thoroughly enjoy his golf in America and the warm-hearted welcome that will assuredly go with it. His salary, he says, is ridiculously high—and so, for that matter, is Denver. The city, we may assume, will remain at its present altitude. Whether the salary will appear so elevated after a few months of golf is another matter.

1975
A PLEA FOR SMALLER GREENS AND TEES

There are certain situations in life in which every man has at some time imagined himself to be the central figure. Driving an express train, looping the loop, being electrocuted and walking Niagara on a tightrope are among those which come readily to mind. Among golfers, not less than 98 percent, of whom I am one, imagine themselves as designers of great golf courses. No island paradise, no mid-ocean atoll big enough to support a runway, is immune from the attention of golf architects, good or bad, and it irks me to think that I came on the scene too late, or perhaps too soon, to have got into the act with one or two masterpieces of my own.

Since earliest times, successful professionals, as their playing talents or interest wane, have turned to laying out courses. Willie Park Jr., British Open champion in 1887, was among the first. As the game suddenly spread inland from the original coastal links of Scotland, he laid out near London what is probably the course best known to our many American visitors, namely Sunningdale.

Most notable among today's champions-turned-architect is

undoubtedly Jack Nicklaus, who with typical thoroughness apprenticed himself first to two masters of the craft, Pete Dye and Desmond Muirhead. I look with respectful admiration on his efforts, partly because he assisted Mr. Dye in creating the excellent Harbour Town Course on Hilton Head Island, and partly because of the course at his new Muirfield Village development near his original home town of Columbus, Ohio.

Nicklaus is quoted as being in favour of small greens, smaller at any rate than on the innumerable so-called championship courses of the last 10 or 15 years. In this I am sure he is right, though we may have reached the same conclusion for different reasons, his being practical, mine largely psychological. Take, for instance, a situation which must occur several million times a day, and heaven knows how many more on Sundays. It is a par-4 hole with the usual huge green and you have made the edge of it in two, 25 yards from the hole. The long putt does not quite make the grade and you just fall with the resulting six-footer. Three putts = 5.

Compare, however, the man who is precisely the same distance from the hole in two, but off the edge of a smaller green. He pitches up within the same six feet (a much more entertaining shot, incidentally) and just misses the putt. Ah, well, he just did not manage to "turn three shots into two." He, too, took 5, but what a contented fellow he is, as he walks to the next tee, by comparison with the man who has just taken three putts.

If I were laying out a "members' course" today, I should go back to the old principle that the size of a green should vary in direct ratio to the size of the club with which it will normally be approached. Two-iron for the second shot—big green. Five-iron—medium green. Wedge—tiny green. For those who know that greatest of inland courses, Pine Valley, I would quote no. 8 and no. 10: the first a drive and a wedge, the other a microscopic short hole. Each has a tiny, sugar-loaf sort of green, almost wholly surrounded by sand, and it is a good man who has never taken a 10 at either of them.

Nowadays they tend to build huge greens with four or five little separate "pin positions," giving you, according to your approach shot, an outside chance of one putt or, more likely, the virtual certainty of three, or even four. Sometimes these greens are so fast and so steep that a ball merely set in motion will roll with gathering speed far past the hole. At the risk of being banished forever from the Masters I would mention in this connection the 15th and 18th at Augusta—and many, too, at Winged Foot.

Economy of upkeep, i.e., being able to mow it all in one "go," is a reason advanced to justify another architectural monstrosity to which I object on psychological grounds, namely these 80-yard-long tees. The first I saw were at the beautiful Peachtree Course in

Atlanta a few years after the war. So sensible, I thought. Later, however, as time marched remorselessly on, I joined the ranks of the innumerable club golfers no longer in the first flush of youth, who hit the ball less far than we did, and much less far than we like to think we did.

With an uneasy laugh we agree to play off the "white markers." No one mentions the fact that the markers for the "real golfers," on the same teeing ground, are so far back as to be almost out of sight. We are in fact playing what is virtually a children's course. So never mind the greens superintendents and their mowing. Let them separate the different tees again, as they used to do, and give us back our self-esteem.

I have from time to time ventured to press these points on that best known of golf architects, Mr. Robert Trent Jones, but he tends to blind one with science about his big greens being "only so many square feet," and so on. However, seeing that he once stood me and his entire family lunch at Maxim's in Paris and paid the resulting, hair-raising bill without flickering an eyebrow, who am I to argue?

---------------------------1957---------------------------

A HARD CASE FROM TEXAS

How strange that the toughest character one has ever met should be connected not with wartime deeds of violence and daring, nor even with the fraternity of peace, but with the sedate, pedestrian, old man's game widely known as "'ockey at the 'alt," namely golf!

Ben Hogan is what is known as a "hard case," a very hard case indeed. He hails from Texas, which is the home of hard cases. He is a small man, normal weight no more than 10 stone [140 pounds], height about 5 feet 9 inches with smooth black hair, wide head, wide eyes, and a wide mouth which tends, when the pressure is on, to contract into a thin, straight pencil-line. You could see him sitting at a poker table saying, expressionless, "Your thousand—and another five." He might have four aces, or a pair of two's.

Those who watched professional golf in recent times have noted that most of the current American "aces" are big husky fellows. Given the same degree of skill, a strong big 'un will hit the ball farther than a strong little 'un. Hogan, a very little 'un indeed, set himself to find some method by which he could keep up with the big fellows. In the end he found it. This kept him up with his rivals. How could be beat them? How could he, as the Americans so graphically put it, "get the edge" on this hard-bitten crew?

Coldly and deliberately he decided he would do it by superior powers of concentration. The process took some years, but he did it. He got his mind into such a condition that nothing, neither idiotic spectators, nor unlucky breaks, nor the trembling thought of "this for $5,000," nothing, ever, would put him off, nothing prevented him playing at crucial moments the same sort of shots he could so easily unloose on the practise ground.

The first time I saw him play was in the Motor City Open at Meadowbrook, Detroit, in 1948. Big "Dutch" Harrison, one of the most charming men you could ever meet in sport, was one stroke ahead of Hogan after three rounds, and had gone out first for the last round. Hogan was out last, partnered with Bobby Locke. Long before he was due to start, Harrison posted a 67, leaving him 66 to tie.

It was at the end of this round that I met him, with three holes to go. He now needed three 4's to tie, and two of them were long holes. Locke introduced us and Hogan chatted affably as we walked up the 16th. I faded away as we approached his ball and observed a steely, grey look come over him. He stood pondering over the shot, cigarette midway between thin pursed lips.

Then he flipped the cigarette to the ground, coldly drew out a club rather as a dentist picks an instrument from his tray, and hit the ball a colossal clout to the middle of the green. He did the same at the next, in each case about 10 yards from the hole, the sort of distance from which ordinary mortals hear small voices whispering "Three putts?" It was clear, however, that any voice that might whisper to Hogan at such moments would talk more in terms of "One putt?" He took great pains in examining the line, picking up tiny obstructions and such-like, and then, again flipping away the cigarette, whose smoke curled silently up beside him in the still summer afternoon, he hit the ball firmly at the hole. Up and up it came, "right between the eyes" as it were, and at the last moment faded off amid the groans of the gallery to lie two inches away. He tied, of course, and won the playoff, and, looking back, I realised that from the moment I set eyes on him it never occurred to me that he wouldn't. Thus Hogan reached the top; qualifying for a place among those whose names have become legends in the annals of sport.

Then in February 1949, Hogan and his wife Valerie, a pretty, dark, understanding woman who supported him on the tournament trail, drove off one sunny morning from the border Texas town of El Paso for the next tournament. A little way out they ran into a patch of ground mist. Fifteen seconds later they were lying in a tangled mass of metal on the roadside, given up for dead.

A bus had come out of the mist, bearing down on them in overtaking another car. Hogan threw himself to his wife's side and the steering column passed through the seat in which he had been sitting. He was badly mangled about the hips and legs. As to the driver of the bus, without even returning to the car he telephoned the police that two people had been killed.

Such was the story Hogan told me on the Queen Elizabeth on his way to Britain later. For some weeks he had lain pretty well at death's door, and when at last a few intimate friends were admitted to his bedside they were hard put to keep from their expressions the shock they felt upon seeing the pale, gaunt, little figure now diminished to about eight stone [112 pounds].

Largely due to the mental powers he had developed on the golf course, Hogan won his battle for life and was eventually taken home. Seven months later, on his way to Britain as captain of the American Ryder Cup team (anyone who mentioned "non-playing captain" soon knew he had dropped a brick), he was still wearing full-length elastic stockings and could walk only for about half an hour at a time. One talked of his being "temporarily out of the game" and so on, but I think there was only one man in the world who at that time thought Hogan might seriously play golf again, and that was Hogan.

It was in December that one of those highly coloured, pinch-of-salt American news agency reports filtered through to the effect that Hogan had not only played a round of golf, but had holed the Colonial Club's course at his home town of Fort Worth, Tex., in 71 and 72.

Telephone calls poured in. Hogan's reply was, "Nonsense!" He had hardly hit any long shots and had used a cart to get about on. They were "only newspaper scores," he said. Then, just a year after his accident, the news went out that Ben Hogan was to try his hand once again—in the Los Angeles Open.

Nine thousand people, then easily a record for the opening day, turned up to give the little man a sympathetic and emotional cheer. The other 128 players, said an American writer, "roamed the acres unmolested." They included Sam Snead, who had jumped to the top as Hogan, literally, fell by the wayside.

Right at the start there was trouble. Sharp words with the photographers seemed to show that Hogan's steely control was no longer what it had been. For a while stewards carried a sign, "No cameras, please—player's request," but the irate photographers prevailed and the sign was withdrawn. Pursued by his vast gallery, and seating himself between shots on a shooting-stick, Hogan got round in 73, well down the field.

Next day he shot a 69 and his position improved. On the final day bigger crowds than ever swarmed over the course. Hole by hole, as he kept up the 4's and 3's, the tension increased. Another 69. One more like this and he might not only finish once more with the leaders. He might even win.

Golf, perhaps through its very slowness, can reach the most extraordinary heights of tenseness and drama. Of all the great rounds ever played I would as soon have watched this last one of Hogan's. After a dozen holes he was well in the hunt, still shock-proof as ever but now clearly close to physical exhaustion. Over-weight at 11 stone [150 pounds plus] and hitting the ball less far than before, he was under pressure from all sides. I can see him so well—the tightening of the lips, the discarded cigarette, and one more shot dispatched on its way. Amid scenes of excitement unusual on a golf course, Ben Hogan finished once more in 69 for a total of 280.

As the day wore on, only Snead, the man who had stepped into his shoes, had a remote chance to catch him. At the 17th hole he holed a very long putt. On the 18th he sank an even longer one, this time almost semicircular, to tie. Snead won the playoff, of course, but that was an anticlimax no one cared about. The glory was Hogan's, for what is perhaps one of the most stirring come-backs in sporting history.

Among his comments in an interview afterward with Joe Williams of the New York World Telegram was: "This much I can tell you for sure, Joe. There's nothing about death that will ever frighten me again. . . ."

In the meantime, they say, he had settled with the bus com-pany for $250,000 free of tax, payable over the next 10 years.

And if that doesn't prove he is a hard case, nothing does!

─────1949─────
PRISONERS AT PLAY

A familiar sight in Lagos is the working parties from the local gaol. A great many of the prisoners, I was often assured, are far from reluctant to undergo a spell "inside." For people whose philosophy is that you work in order to eat and, when you have enough to eat, you no longer work (and what an admirable philosophy, too!), the steady security of prison life, the regular meals, the beds, made a strong appeal, and there was the story of one man who got left outside one night and spent two hours persuading the guards that he was entitled to come in.

These working parties intrigued me greatly. Mostly their job is cutting the grass, and beside the road you see perhaps a couple of dozen of the biggest and blackest men you ever imagined, each wearing a little pair of cotton shorts with his number stamped on the backside and brandishing a murderous implement akin to a billhook. They are standing in a row—all except two. These two stand behind and provide the music. The music consists of a pair of triangles, upon which two enormous men tap out a little refrain which has been jingling in my brain ever since.

> Ting ting *ting*
> Ting-a-ting *ting*
> Ting ting *ting* ting
> Ting-a-ting *ting*.

On and on they go, half asleep as they play, while the row doing the work takes a pace forward in unison, slash their bill-hooks, and rise up to repeat the process . . . forward, slash, up . . . forward, slash, up . . . "Hi-ya, hi-ya . . . Hi-ya, hi-ya." They keep perfect time—but without the ting-a-ting-ting, I was told, they might easily cut each other's feet off. With their billhooks flashing in the sun these vast men looked a pretty bloodthirsty crew and one glanced instinctively for the guard. Ah, there he was! A little fellow propped up against a tree, nonchalantly swinging a small stick.

I mentioned this to a friend at home who had spent much of his life administering large tracks of West African territory and he confirmed the tale. He went further. In his day, he said, the guard sometimes carried a rifle. On one occasion he was to be seen marching his prisoners back for the night, when he suddenly remembered that he had left his rifle leaning against a tree.

So he sent one of the prisoners back to fetch it!

GAME WITHIN A GAME

The art of putting at golf resembles that of goalkeeping at soccer, in being "a game within a game." Furthermore, as I remember so often reflecting as I leant nonchalantly against the uprights—having played in goal since the age of 8—both are games which enable a fellow with a certain crafty cunning to neutralise the efforts of stronger, braver men, and this in any walk of life is a source of much inward satisfaction.

On the other hand, both putting and goalkeeping may lead to an embarrassing immortality not to be endured in other departments of the games. The poor wretch who lets it trickle slowly between his legs in a Cup Final is remembered long after missers of sitting goals have sunk into merciful oblivion. A yard putt missed on the last green may also live forever.

Thoughts of putting come to mind because I have recently mentioned the four secrets of putting, as outlined to me one day years ago by Bobby Locke, who was presumably the greatest holer-out in the world in the postwar years, and one or two people have asked to be let in upon them.

I hope that I am not poaching on Locke's professional preserves in revealing them. A good agent, I should have said, could have got him £1,000 for them.

One: You must hit the ball clean. This does not involve any nonsense about "topspin" or "trying to make it roll." If you flick a Ping-Pong ball off a table, you take aim with your fingernail and flick it cleanly. Touch the table and you "smudge" it. It is the same with brushing the putter along the grass.

"You can tell a good putt," says Locke, "by the noise it makes"—and very remarkable it is to hear him demonstrate, interspersing clean hits with an odd one just touching the grass. Ping, ping, PUNG, ping, ping, PUNG, they go—and so on. It occurs to me that Locke was probably the loudest putter in golf.

Two: Every putt you will ever have in your life, on any course, in any country, of any length, is dead straight. Elementary, when you come to think of it, but had you thought of it that way? Of course, on a sharp slope the ball may roll almost in a semicircle, but you did not make it do so.

All you can do, time and time again, is to hit it dead straight— not necessarily, of course, straight at the hole. A bullet fired in a high wind will travel in a slight curve. The man who gets a bull's-eye with it adjusted his sights and aimed straight. The mental relief on grasping this simple conception is unbelievable.

Three: Hold the putter very loosely. "Ha!" I remember saying, "and what about when you have a four-footer to tie for the Open?" Said Locke: "Hold it looser still!" Touching wood, in a good hour be it spoken and all the rest of it, I do verily believe this may be at least partially the cure for the "jitters."

Four: Any fool can putt through a hoop four feet wide from 10 yards or more. In other words, you take three putts through getting the distance wrong, not the direction. So when Locke wanders slowly between ball and hole, he is not, as one might suppose, pondering on the infinite. He is making up his mind how far it is. See also Rule One.

If you sometimes hit it clean and sometimes touch the grass, it may make a difference of four or five feet in distance—the difference between two putts or three.

Five: This is my own, based merely on observation. Locke evolved a drill—never mind the details—we can all evolve our own. In other words, for every putt he ever made, irrespective of distance or circumstances, once the machinery was set in action he went through the same motions. No extra waggle, no extra look at the hole. For better or for worse. Which is yet another reason, I fancy, why it was almost inevitably for better.

────── 1966 ──────
"YOU CAN'T LET THEM DO IT, BARBARA!"

My curious and occasionally envied way of life involves a considerable amount of travel, fortunately at the expense of others, and this takes three forms. This week's by air to Augusta for the Masters via Washington, Atlanta and all points south, is the fastest but by far the most uncomfortable. It is now many years since the tailor at London's Olympia, thrusting a tape measure against my chest for my Army discharge civilian suit, turned to a colleague and announced in a loud voice, "Forty-two, short, portly." I fear that I have not decreased in the meantime, and to sit for seven hours cramped in a little seat, seeing nothing and in the end hearing practically nothing is not my idea of heaven, even if I am being miraculously carried along at 500 m.p.h. in the process.

---

*Mrs. Barbara Castle, the then British Minister of Transport.

Aeroplanes at the moment go either too fast or not fast enough. Thus, on arrival at Augusta at what I am pleased to call 3:15 a.m. "stomach-time" tomorrow, one sets the watch back six hours and calls it 9:15 p.m. today. This is not so bad, as one can soon retire to bed. On the way back, however, after a long day in America and most of the night in the aeroplane, one is brought down to earth at 3 a.m. "stomach-time," only to be told that it is 9 a.m. and that a bright new day has just begun. Experience shows that one pill of a particular purple shade will carry me over till lunchtime, after which the favourite drops in his tracks and is comparatively useless for 2½ days.

The second form of transport, though not across the Atlantic, is the motor car, of which I possess a notable specimen. It gives me conscious pleasure every time I get into it, but to sit in it for four days in order to get to Scotland and back, harried by maniacs and compacts is, again, not my idea of heaven, though it might well lead to it. As a believer in the law of averages, I take the view that, if you expose yourself long enough, they're bound to get you in the end.

No, there is only one way to travel, and that is by train. I have long known this and have more than once written of the good sober driver, the private butler and chef and, when necessary, the bedside attendant, with whom I like to be accompanied when I make my way about the country. The only trouble is that too many of the Philistines are beginning to cotton on to what was previously known only to connoisseurs. However, one may still remain "1 up" with certain expertise.

They don't yet realise, fortunately, that you want to make a beeline for a corner seat in a middle compartment (where you get waggled about less than in the end ones), back to the engine (so that the scenery flows away from you instead of at you) and, of course, non-smoking (in case someone lights up one of those ghastly little imitation cigars).

They don't even know to bring with them for the sleeper the pink pill and the cotton wool for the ears—which the airlines provide and the railways still don't—and to put the plug in the basin, up through which comes so much of the noise.

I am not the first of those who follow the golfing scene to write nostalgically of the sleeper to Scotland—the anticipatory dinner at the club; the bustling scene at Euston or King's Cross stations, with the sorters already at work in the great mail train and the nets now folded back on the sides, later to reach out in the night and grab new cargo as they pass; and, finally, the moment of waking in a new world of hillsides, burns, a dashing river and air like champagne.

Sometimes as you look out over the last miles of uninhabited moorland before Gleneagles, you see skein after skein of geese in the sky. At Kilmarnock you may be forgiven the unworthy temptation, as the long row of sleepers trundles away, of thanking the Lord that you are not as other men are, since they are being taken on to Glasgow, while you are going to Ayr and thence over the coast road, past Culzean Castle and one of the noblest views in Britain, to Turnberry.

Supreme among journeys to Scotland, however, is that of the golfing pilgrim to Mecca, in other words St. Andrews. I still cherish the bound volume of *Railway Wonders of the World* collected as a boy, with the wonderful coloured picture of the express roaring over the Forth Bridge and, in order never to miss it, I have fallen into the way of catching the earlier train to Edinburgh and thence the breakfast train at 7:30 from platform 15, in which almost as a ritual, I have finnan-haddock while crossing the bridge. There used also to be the Navy, with battleships looking like toys in the bath down below, but now there is the magnificent road bridge whose single span exceeds, unbelievably, the length of the two longest holes at St. Andrews put together.

Soon we hear the familiar cry of "Leuchars! Change for St. Andra's" and we board the little two-carriage train waiting at the buffers between the two main lines. It used to be hauled by a veteran steam engine called the Kettledrummle, but now it is a diesel, which is better really because, by sitting up in front, you can see where you are going. For golfers from all the nations—and I like to think, for many of the students in the ancient and ever-growing university—this is the most memorable train journey in the world.

Round the corner to Guard Bridge, past that fellow's immaculate vegetable garden and the paper mill, across the bridge over the Eden—the driver having already twice leaned out to exchange those big rings with leather pouches attached in order to secure his right of way—and alongside the estuary with, at low tide, its innumerable birds on the mudflats. In the distance now the singular, unforgettable outline of the "Old Grey Town," with its spires and towers and the ruins of the cathedral.

We pass on our left the far end of the Eden Course and soon we are hard beside the Old Course itself. The 16th tee is right against the railway fence and so is the 17th, and on the farther side of the big double greens the early starters are already on their way out. From the train I once detected on the second a four-ball consisting of three peers and knight! Passing behind the black sheds over which you drive at the Road Hole, we see the little Road Bunker, in which every great golfer has at some time stood, with the same thoughts running through his head, and behind the green the dreaded road itself.

A quick glimpse of the Royal and Ancient clubhouse standing foursquare behind the first tee and we are rounding the bend with a cheerful toot to announce our arrival at the little station, where dedicated hands have traced out on the bank in white stones the legend: "St. Andrews. Home of Golf." The golfer is home indeed.

Soon more and more pilgrims will be coming to St. Andrews, for the railways are to replace the old black sheds and the coal yard, into which we slice out-of-bounds at the 17th.

In the meantime, quietly, almost furtively, and in very small print, they propose—believe it or not, and you scarcely will—to abandon the railway and close the station.

You can't let them do it, Barbara. You can't, really!

P.S. Sadly, and as ultimate proof that nothing is sacred in this world anymore, she did.

1966

CHIPERS, SMUDGERS AND JIGGERS

My own relations with the golfing insurance world remain cordial, but will not, I am afraid, have labelled me as a model client. In the days when I was actually invited to play in exhibition matches (interval for incredulous laughter) I struck a spectator on the head with a high slice—we remain friends to this day—as a result of which he not only went to hospital but also sold me a golfer's insurance policy. Within a week I had broken a steel-shafted 2-iron and recovered twice the amount of the premium.

Later I decided to add an expensive shooting-stick to the policy and an extra premium of half-a-crown was duly negotiated. A few days later, I left the stick in the electric train on returning to Liverpool from the Open Championship at Southport, and my claim for £12 10s crossed in the post with the insurer's receipt for the half-crown. They suggested that perhaps "in view of the circumstances, it would do if they only paid half," but I stood firm.

I recalled for them the case of the well-known London golfer playing a young fellow in a continental championship. Having driven into the rough, he first tried his brassie behind the ball but eventually worked his way down and played out with his niblick. His opponent having cleared his throat rather suggestively, our friend replied, "Look here, son. If I am going to cheat I start with the niblick and work up to the brassie."

I often think that what one might call modern golf—that is, the sort of game which may validly be compared with today's—started after World War I, though I should not be surprised if senior observers better qualified to express an opinion assured me that the Great Triumvirate of Vardon, Taylor and Braid, despite the methods illustrated and described in their books, played the game in its modern version.

One thing is certain, namely, that for all talk about "craftsmen," the clubs used not only by Vardon and his contemporaries but even by Jones and Hagen, right up to the very late 1920's, made the game more difficult and a more delicate work of art.

Two of these clubs come to mind. I have often, for instance, taken out of its case at the Royal and Ancient the driver with which Vardon won his last Open in 1914, incidentally, one of the eight clubs he carried on that occasion. It is, I suppose, a "modern" club, certainly beautifully made, but one feels somehow that, even in its original condition, a couple of bashes by Nicklaus must have broken it in half.

Again, the mashie-iron with which Bobby Jones played his immortal shot from the bunker at the 17th to win the 1926 Open at Lytham hung for many years in the clubhouse for anyone to take down and waggle. (Ethical standards in Lancashire being presumably not what they used to be, the club is now nailed to the wall!) At any rate, it seems impossible with its thin grip, its thin, delicate shaft and lightweight head to think of hitting a ball 170 yards from a bunker. If Jones could do that with that, what could he not have done with the supremely effective clubs they make today—and none better, if I may strike a commercially patriotic note, than some of those made in Britain.

I am sorry, of course, that, apart from driver and putter, the old names have disappeared and we no longer get those maids-of-all-work of doubtful parentage, which had names all of their own. The pride of my undergraduate life, and later, too, was a sort of deep-faced mashie known as the Benny, invented by and named after Ben Sayers of North Berwick.

My father's dubious 16 handicap was based largely on a sort of scuffling club known as the Chiper, which rightly or wrongly, he pronounced to rhyme with "viper." Presumably if they had meant it as a club for chipping with they would have called it a chipper, but he made it sound much more crafty as a chiper. My father also used another most descriptive expression that seems to have gone out of the game. Halfway through the downward swing, sensing that no good was going to come of it, he would exclaim, "Ach! Smudged him!" It strikes me that, whatever they may now call themselves, a great many smudgers are with us still. Roses by any other name . . . .

"MY, BUT YOU'RE A WONDER, SIR!"

Every instinct tells me that Bobby Jones ("Bobby" to us on the British side of the Atlantic, not "Bob") was the most popular and well-loved games player to visit our shores during my lifetime. We all, I suppose, while lifting our hats to the professionals for their skills, their prowess and their millions, to say nothing of their inevitable good manners, reserve the warmest spot in our hearts for the gifted amateur. Jones was the gifted amateur par excellence.

How good was he? How would he stand beside the heroes of today? Well, it does not seem to matter at this moment and, anyway, he himself settled this hoary old locker room argument when he said, "All that a man can do is to beat those who are around when he is around. He cannot beat those who went before or those who are yet to come." To my generation Jones will always be the greatest, and we can leave it at that.

It is a matter of history that he retired in 1930, with all worlds conquered, at the age of 28. Six years later, his game now rusty, he came over for the Olympic Games in Berlin and, having met some friends on the boat, accompanied them to Gleneagles for some golf. Being so near to St. Andrews, where he had won both the Open and the Amateur, he went over on a sentimental pilgrimage to play a round on his last morning. He arrived, unheralded, just before lunch. By the time he reached the first tee, the word had spread round the town—"Bobby's back!"—and no fewer than 2,000 people were assembled to greet him.

"I shall never forget that round," he wrote later. "It was not anything like a serious golf match, but it was a wonderful experience. There was a sort of holiday mood in the crowd. It seemed, or they made it appear at least, that they were just glad to see me back, and however I chose to play golf was all right with them, only they wanted to see it."

So he did the first nine holes in 32 and on the eighth tee was paid "the most sincere compliment I can ever remember"—one which he did not reveal till about 25 years later. As he put his club back in the bag, his young caddie looked up at him and said, "My, but you're a wonder, sir!"

In 1958 Bobby, now in the throes of that crippling spinal ailment which took so tragically long to put an end to his life, was back at St. Andrews, mainly to captain the United States in the first World Amateur Team Championship for the Eisenhower Trophy, and partly to receive the Freedom of the City, only the second American to do so, the first having been none other than Dr. Benjamin Franklin 199 years before. Already, though, the people had accorded to him the freedom of their hearts. "It is a wonderful experience," he wrote, "to go about a town where people wave at you from doorways and windows, where strangers smile and greet you by name, often your first name, and where a simple and direct courtesy is the outstanding characteristic."

The ceremony at which he received the Freedom of the City from the Provost, in his red and ermine robes of office, and became an Honourary Burgess of St. Andrews (thus becoming entitled, among other things, to "cart shells, take divots and hang out washing on the first and last fairways") was one of the most moving occasions in the memory of those of us who were lucky enough to be there. It was well summed up by Herbert Warren Wind: "Bobby spoke for about 10 minutes," he wrote, "beautifully and movingly . . . He said near the end of his speech 'I could take out of my life everything except my experiences at St. Andrews and I'd still have a rich, full life.' He left the stage and got into his electric golf cart. As he directed it down the aisle to leave, the whole hall spontaneously burst into the old Scottish song 'Will Ye No' Come Back Again?' So honestly heartfelt was this reunion for Bobby Jones and the people of St. Andrews (and for everyone) that it was 10 minutes before many who attended were able to speak again in a tranquil voice." I know I was certainly one of them.

Next morning, almost completely crippled now, he was driven out onto the Old Course in the same electric buggy—the first, I believe, ever to be seen at St. Andrews—and once again huge crowds assembled to wish him well. And who was privileged to drive him on that occasion? Well, it was me. A proud experience, indeed.

BATTLESHIPS, BLASTING POWDER AND GOLF BALLS

I note with interest and amusement the promotion of various devices to discover the true center of gravity of a golf ball, so as to be able to place it accordingly. I had thought, believing everything I read in the papers, that all balls these days are ballistically perfect. Apparently not.

The reason for the incessant picking up and cleaning of balls already spotlessly clean is, a British Open champion assured me some time ago, to enable tournament players to replace the ball with the seam in line to the hole, believing it will run more truly this way.

When I referred to this in print, a ballistics expert promptly shot me down. "Each ball," he said, "has a bias or weighted side and will run accurately when this bias side is on top or bottom of the ball. If the bias is on the side of the ball, it will curve.

"The professionals use the brand name as a marker—not, as you state, with the seam in line to the hole but across the seam of the ball. In fact, some balls have long names which form a distinct arrow on the ball when used for lining up the putt. This name is no accident but a carefully designed thing, enabling the player to take advantage of this alignment aid."

This theory in turn was knocked in the head by a super expert in the person of the technical manager of an internationally known firm of manufacturers. "If there was sufficient bias in a ball to affect a five-foot putt," he said, "what on earth do you think would happen to a 250-yard drive?" And yet . . . .

Many devices have been made to test putts of makeable distances on super-perfect surfaces and not one of them, so far as I know, has holed 100 percent, thus showing, one would have thought, that even now not every ball is identical.

The most entertaining experiments within my own experience were conducted, in deadly earnest, by a low-handicap ex-naval captain, whose knowledge of ballistics was such that he was assigned to one of the great naval armaments manufacturers, in the days when Britain had a navy, to supervise the production of those colossal 16-inch guns and shells used on battleships.

The guns had long been outdated when I asked him whether you could really hit anything with those monstrous missiles. This simple question produced an almost perfect throwaway line. "Oh Lord, yes," he said with perfect seriousness, "I guarantee they'd hit a tennis court six times out of eight at 12 miles."

The captain's "golf gun" that he used for the experiment was a mere pistol with a barrel 18 inches long and a bore of 1.622 (the British ball is 1.620). I first saw the apparatus in action in 1958 during the initial tournament for the Eisenhower Trophy, when the captain shot off a salvo of balls from the steps of the Royal and Ancient clubhouse at St. Andrews. Several shots easily carried the Swilken Burn 370 yards away, but one was inaccurate enough to land on the ladies' putting course some 60 yards adrift. (Our more mathematically minded readers may care to work out by how much this would have missed a tennis court at 12 miles. Something to do with equal triangles, I suspect, but my geometry is even rustier than my golf.)

When he first began experimenting, the shots were fired with a 12-gauge cartridge and the ball flew out so fast he never saw it. It was later recovered by chance 800 yards away. He therefore reduced the charge from 23 grains of nitro to 7½ of black powder, which is much less powerful than nitro, loaded in a shortened .410 cartridge. This 7½ grains is no more in bulk than you could balance on a dime and, when touched off with a match, goes up with a pleasing flash and a hardly audible "poof." Incredibly, this tiny amount will send a golf ball 240 yards.

He first thought that he was up against the same problem of swerve that baffled 18th-century gunners and was proved by the Germans in 1840 to be due to the center of gravity of a spherical missile not always being in its geometrical center. Though he discarded this theory, it now seems that he may well have been right.

The answer, as he thought at the time, turned out to be spin. By projecting a shallow rib over the end of the muzzle he was able to catch the ball on its way out and set it backspinning, as it does when hit with a golf club. The effect with and without the "spin-brake" proved to be most revealing. Without it, a ball aimed horizontally hit the ground 20 yards away; with it, 200 yards. Aimed with elevation, the figures were 150 and 250.

His first shot with a very old ball was probably the most perfect played in Britain that day—about 300 yards dead into the wind and not veering an inch either way. The next was with a new ball, which slipped down the barrel without touching the sides. It had just enough hook to take it into the bushes, where it was lost. Perhaps its center of gravity was amiss. We shall never know.

The captain's theory of spin, however, seemed abundantly proved. With the brake adjusted just to the left of centre the gun hooked; to the right it sliced. I then induced him to double the charge to 15 grains and see if he could drive the green, 421 yards into a freshening wind. The result was a tremendous, high, towering slice—a shot with which, on a much reduced scale, I am sure most of our readers are only too familiar. It soared into the bushes well over 400 yards from the tee.

In the end he reckoned that with two clubs—gun and putter—and a pocketful of selected charges, he was almost in a position now to take on the Open champion.

──1969──
CHEATING

As a rabid fan of my colleague, Ian Fleming, and James Bond, I am naturally delighted to find that in the latest episode the second of the latter's three skirmishes with the villainous Mr. Goldfinger takes place on the golf course. Furthermore, those who know Royal St. George's—professional, Albert Whiting, short sixth hole known as the Maiden—will have little difficulty in following the play at Mr. Fleming's Royal St. Marks, Sandwich, where the professional is Alfred Blacking and the short sixth is known as the Virgin.

Mr. Goldfinger, as might be suspected of a man with creases down the sides of his plus-fours, cheats. I will not reveal the subterfuge whereby Bond outcheats him at the 18th, but will say that the account of the match adds materially to the fictional literature of golf and sheds light on an aspect of the game which has always fascinated me and on which I have often thought one day to write one of Sherlock Holmes's "trifling monographs."

In fact, though both Goldfinger and Bond had cheated outrageously at the 17th, Goldfinger did not, according to the Rules of Golf, cheat at the 18th. Bond called him for doing so and took him for $10,000.

I always think that it was more to Bond's credit to make Goldfinger cough up for infringing the Rules when he wasn't, than it would have been if he had. The truth is that with 93 pages of the Rules, to say nothing of heaven knows how many decisions upon them, neither Bond, Goldfinger, nor Fleming—nor, if I may class myself with so distinguished a trio, myself—know them.

Cheating at golf, like cheating at solitaire, is mostly so pointless as to have something rather splendid about it. There are, of course, exceptions, when there is very considerable point in it. Probably the outstanding example in the game's history was the singular incident in what we should call a selling sweep at a highly respectable American club some years ago, when Mr. A, handicap

17, and Mr. B, handicap 18, made a net return of 58 and 57, a total of 115 for 36 holes.

This notable score won for the talented pair and the man who had bought them in the sweep some $16,000. Inquiry revealed, however, that Mr. A's handicap was not 17 but 3 and that Mr. B was not in fact Mr. B at all, but a young Mr. C, also handicap 3, whom Mr. A. had invited to come along and play under Mr. B's name and handicap. (On second thought, I am not at all sure that Mr. A was in fact Mr. A, either.)

Money is, of course, the root of nearly all major cheating at golf and nearly always the caddie is suborned into being an accomplice. I knew one club where too much money was habitually played for by people too keen to win it, and most of the caddies were reckoned—though I personally did not have occasion to prove it—to have holes in their trouser pockets and a spare ball.

Women golfers, I am often assured, cheat nearly all the time, but I suspect that this may be the sort of unfair generalisation that is usually levelled against women motorists. When you see a particularly abominable piece of driving by a man, you tend to say "Look at that fellow." If it is a woman, you say, "These women!" Perhaps it would be fair to say that women in ordinary day-to-day golf do not adhere quite so meticulously to the rules—which is, of course, quite a different thing.

Far and away my favourite story is of a former Cambridge player, now dead, who really did cheat flagrantly and was known to do so. He was playing with Dale Bourn in the foursomes against a very well-known London club—I never go there without thinking of it—and at the last hole Dale drove into the bunker on the right, while the club pair were over to the left. Dale arrived in time to find his partner busily teeing up the ball in the bunker.

"I say. Look here," he said, or words to that effect. His partner looked up. "What?" he said. 'They didn't see me, did they?"

1967
ARNOLD PALMER–
A VERY CONSIDERABLE MAN

I find myself in the course of duty writing from my balcony overlooking the blue Atlantic surf rolling in upon Puerto Rico, which, in case your geography is rusty, is an island 1,600 miles southeast of New York, level with and on the right of Jamaica. It was discovered by Christopher Columbus in 1493, colonised by the Spanish and protected by the great fortress of El Morro and San Cristobal which you can see, unchanged, today. Drake had a crack at it in 1695 and Sir Ralph Abercromby in 1797, but eventually the Americans captured it in 1898. Later they turned it into a commonwealth and now you'll find New York populated largely by immigrant Puerto Ricans.

The purpose of the present visit has been to attend the fourth and final round of a tournament between the "Big Three"— Palmer, Nicklaus and Player—which, if you will forgive the advertisement, is for the BBC television. The course here at Dorado Beach is a typical creation of America's best-known architect, Robert Trent Jones, and probably one of the best. When we were here in 1961 for what was then called the Canada Cup, but has now promoted itself to World Cup, Trent Jones took me round the second course he was building, which now seems as though it has been here for years, and I remember being impressed not only with the number of artificial water hazards, but also with the fact that they were all on the left. He regards this as the "professional" side. He said that the ordinary run-of-the-mill visitor, whom he is out to please, is more likely to be a slicer, and I suppose he is right! Like most American resort courses this one has virtually no rough, so there is little or no looking for balls, and the main hazards are the tall palms.

In framing a constitution for Puerto Rico, the Americans specifically included the right to strike, and four years ago the caddies at Dorado Beach took them at their word and, technically, are on strike still. The club in reply installed dozens of electric carts, which are hired out at about £3 a round. Even with these and allowing for a balmy temperature of 80-85 degrees, it still takes, believe it or not, between four and a half and five hours to get round.

They have 10 days of rain a year here, so they say, and had one of them just before we arrived, with the result that the course for our match was rather "holding" and presented what we, in a slightly superior tone of voice, are liable to call "target golf." Both

Palmer and Nicklaus told me that this is the sort of golf they prefer, and one can hardly blame them. When you are playing for tens of thousands of dollars, you do not take kindly to the 'umps and 'ollows of the seaside golf we like so much in Britain and the crazy bounces that sometimes arise therefrom. You want to know that where you pitch it there it will stick. All day the three of them were pitching shots right up to the flag and stopping the ball dead in its tracks—just like throwing darts at a damp dartboard.

Palmer really is a remarkable sporting phenomenon, quite apart from being one of the wealthiest athletes of all time. He is recognised by the man in the street in pretty well every country in the world, not least in Japan, where there is even a tea shop named after him. He is the man that everyone wants to win. His "army" follow him around in thousands, sometimes even carrying banners. While winning the Masters, he was once encouraged by an aeroplane droning round and round over the course, towing a banner with the legend "GO, ARNIE, GO."

Player can't wait to get back to his farm in South Africa; Nicklaus can't wait to go fishing; but Palmer's real love remains golf—even if he is at the moment just about the most over-golfed man in the history of the game. His main hobby is his $800,000 aeroplane, probably the most highly publicised flying machine in America. Naturally enough, he is agent, among innumerable other interests, for the firm that made it.

These interests are handled by manager Mark McCormack, author of a book, *Arnie, The Evolution Of A Legend,* which I cannot commend too highly if, as I do, you like books which enable you to enjoy another man's life without the trouble of living it, so to speak.

Among Palmer's many sidelines is a chain of laundry and dry cleaning centres. When he opened the first one, the other pros made such comments as: "The only pro golfer I would send my laundry to is Chen Ching-po," but the answer is that he now has 100 and at the present rate will in 10 years' time have 2,000. Almost anything he puts his name to turns to gold and the requests he has had for personal endorsements include houseboats, a yacht basin, children's toys, coin-operated games, walking sticks, creme de menthe, African safaris, poultry farms and a one-act play, to say nothing of an option to buy an apartment house in Pittsburgh for a modest $5,080,000. When McCormack was quoted in the Wall Street Journal as saying, "If a good orange grove came along, we'd buy it," more than 30 offers of orange groves came along within a fortnight.

One of Palmer's more endearing characteristics is that he is "amateur" enough at heart to need some form of challenge to bring the best out of him. In the 1966 U.S. Open, for instance, he was seven strokes ahead of Casper, with whom he was playing, with nine to play and momentarily "went to sleep." Then everything happened at once; he lost all seven strokes and Casper won in the playoff.

McCormack quotes a splendid example of this sort of thing from our own Open Championship at Troon in 1962, when after three rounds Palmer was leading by five strokes. His wife, knowing his fallibility in such circumstances, was heard asking: "What can he play for this afternoon? The tournament is as good as over," to which a British newspaper man—not yours truly—replied: "Perhaps you could tell him that only two or three people in history have won it two years running." "That's good," said Mrs. P., "I'll tell him that. It will give him something to shoot for." He thereupon won by six shots.

McCormack writes charmingly of Palmer's happy marriage, which began with an elopement when Arnold was a penniless amateur-turned-pro and neither party could have had an inkling of what was to come. The engagement ring was founded on a round at Pine Valley, where some friends wagered with Palmer on the basis of his paying $100 for every stroke over 80 and winning $100 for every stroke under 72. He went round in 68 and has never looked back.

Another, perhaps the principal, characteristic that draws people to Palmer is his maxim, "Hit 'em hard." He is one to let it fly, to have a go, and, when it goes into the woods, to hack it out, bash it onto the green and hole the putt. As McCormack says—and I do recommend this book most strongly, not only to golfers—his epitaph might well be: "Here lies Arnold Palmer. He always went for the green." Judged by any standards, a very considerable man.

—1966—
SIX OF THE BEST

Elementary calculation shows that there are rather more than 150,000 holes of golf in various parts of the world and the other day some of us fell to debating which were the greatest, and why. The late Tom Simpson, a golf architect of somewhat controversial distinction, always maintained that no hole could be truly great unless it began to operate in the player's mind for some time before he actually came to play it.

Incidentally, how he would have delighted in the great Sam

Snead's observation on the Olympia Fields course, near Chicago, before a championship some years ago: "These golf architects make me sick. They can't play golf, so they rig the courses so nobody else can play, either." At any rate, as I look at my own choice of the half-dozen best holes out of the 7,000-odd which I have played in a misspent—no, hang it, well-spent—life, I find that Simpson's adage applies certainly to five of them.

Most of the great holes, it seemed to be agreed, were not necessarily "natural" in the sense that nature created them, but "naturals" as boxing promoters use the term. In other words, given the chance, anyone with golfing intelligence, whether a professional architect or not, would have detected them and laid them out as they are. This again applies to five of mine, the other one being on the Old Course at St. Andrews where, so far as one can gather, the holes just "arose." It seems generally accepted as part of the true greatness of the Old Course that no architect in his right mind would have laid it out today!

The hole in question is the long 14th, which to my mind has surpassed the more celebrated 17th or Road Hole, now that the latter has become "meadowy," as the principal hurdle to be over-come by would-be champions at St. Andrews—as played, that is, from the championship tees hidden away far back in the whins. A former Lord Rosebery, I believe, made the memorable utterance, "No man can be wholly free of worry until he has lost the last of his teeth and all interest in the opposite sex." On a more mundane level, no man in the Open Championship can be wholly free of worry till he has got past the tee at the 14th.

He must hit it at least 240 yards to reach safety. On the right a low out-of-bounds wall awaits the ever-so-slight fade; on the left, invisible, the cavernous bunkers known as the Beardies, from which he may well have to play out sideways. All this and Hell bunker still to come. Both Locke and Thomson have taken 7 at this hole at crucial moments in the Open.

As a three-shot hole for "us" and a two-shotter—though not always—for "them," I take the Azalea Hole, or 13th at Augusta, Ga., the home of the Masters. This is a right-angled dogleg to the left, and on the left, running along from the tee and round the corner and then broadening out in front of the elevated green, is a stream. To have a chance of reaching the green in two, "they" must not only drive past the corner but also risk the stream. All along the left is a high bank surmounted by colossal pines and at the foot of them a vivid mass of multi-coloured azaleas. It really takes your breath away.

No Cambridge golfer could, I think, fail to place in his first six the short fifth at Mildenhall, so humble at first sight as to escape the stranger's notice. Just a narrow hump of a green backed by fir trees. No bunkers: just this tiny target with a sharp slope running away on either side, so that a man may go to and fro till driven to a frenzy. Here on the right is also a stream and among my more cherished memories is that of an undergraduate, up to his knees in excruciatingly cold water, fishing for the putter he had just hurled from the green.

My other three holes, now I come to think of it, also take your breath away, so perhaps that, too, is a quality of greatness. Walking along a wooded path to the fifth at Pine Valley, for instance, you come upon a deep ravine, with a lake full of turtles at the bottom. At eye level on the far side, a full drive distant, you perceive a long, narrow green, sloping to the right, with the flag in the far left-hand corner. Miss it on the left and you are in a sand pit. On the right your ball trickles down among the pine roots and you may be down there for a long, long time. I once did this hole in 2. For several days life had nothing more to offer.

At the eighth at Pebble Beach you drive in humdrum fashion up a slope, little suspecting that, as you mount the crest, you find the fairway suddenly ceasing to exist at the edge of a 100-foot drop. The cliff works its way inland and back again, leaving a shot of at least 180 yards across the bay to the green. I can see my brassie shot now, soaring over the chasm, white against the blue California sky and pitching with a thump on the green. Unfortunately, its two predecessors had pitched into the Pacific and I was by now playing 6.

Only a few miles up the road lies my final choice—rather obvious, if you like, but, after all, the seven wonders of the world are no less wonderful because so many people take pictures of them. Here we are, then, reaching for our cameras on the 16th at Cypress Point, with the green perched on a rocky promontory 220 yards away and nothing in between but the beach, the surf, and several hundred golf balls not worth retrieving because the crabs have been at them overnight. Hook, and you are in the ocean on the left; slice, and you are down among the rocks, where the noted American professional, Porky Oliver, when about to win a tournament, took 14.

Beyond the green a strange barking reveals the rocks to be covered with enormous, comical and, if the wind is wrong, malodorous sea lions. After them, next stop Hawaii. What a game it is, to be sure! Six holes out of 150,000, and many a competent connoisseur of golf, I dare say, would not agree with my choice of a single one of them.

1976
PRACTISE MAKES PERFECT? WHAT RUBBISH!

I take the revolutionary view that all this talk about the virtues of practise, for the average club golfer at any rate, is a snare and a delusion.

"Practise makes perfect," they say. Of course, it doesn't. For the vast majority of golfers it merely consolidates imperfection. And if you are already near-perfect, like Jack Nicklaus, there is no need to hit hundreds of balls to prove the fact—and at the same time risk knocking yourself off your game through boredom and fatigue.

Gary Player once remarked that he had hit a thousand practise shots in the last week, or some such. "Whatever do you want to do that for?" I asked. "You know how to play golf already." I think he was quite taken back by such heresy.

The other day I noted a piece about the American professional, Jim Colbert. Last season, it said, he practised so long and so hard that he damaged his back for a while and was knocked out of the game altogether. And Babe Hiskey, it went on, now in his 40's, reckoned on a daily quota of 200 practise balls, then a large steak breakfast, a 4½ hour round of golf, then another 150 balls.

Not all the great men of golf have been ardent practisers: not because they were lazy but because, as Hagen observed, he "did not see the point of leaving all those good shots on the practise ground." He recorded how, desperately anxious to prove that his 1914 U.S. Open victory was no fluke, he arrived in Boston in time for the 1919 event, but, what with one thing and another, did not get much practise on the Brae Burn Course. "Missing the practise did not bother me too much, for practise always took some of the zip out of me. I preferred to be keen, fresh and eager when the play actually started . . . ."

Having won the PGA Championship three times in a row, he decided not to compete in 1927. He was up at his camp in Michigan, he says, "enjoying the fishing and the lakeside breezes" (and, I dare say, one or two other diversions!). "Only two days before the matches I decided I owed it to my fellow pros to give them a chance to beat me—if they could. I rushed down to my golf factory, picked up a new set of clubs and hopped on a train to Dallas. I arrived at 4 o'clock on the afternoon prior to the start of the matches . . . ." And who won? Why, Hagen of course!

Bobby Jones, perhaps the greatest of them all, held the view that apart from hitting a few shots to get the muscles moving before going out to play, there was no point in practising unless to iron out a specific fault.

On the other hand Macdonald Smith (presumably the greatest golfer till Sam Snead never to win the U.S. Open) maintained, logically enough, as it seems to me, that you should practise only with those clubs you were playing well with—to work the good stuff into the system, instead of trying to work out the bad.

I suspect that the best form of practise for the rank and file golfer, if he gets the chance, is to settle down and watch some of the best professionals before a tournament and let them do the work. I think especially of the Masters at Augusta, where they provide grandstands for the spectators' comfort behind the players in the two practise areas.

One thing I have always thought important, and that is to choose as a model a player of something approaching your own stature. A short, stocky individual, for instance, would not have so much to pick up from George Archer as from, say, Gene Sarazen, who in his 70's still makes golf look so simple.

In the United States the practise ground is, in my opinion, rightly known as "Maniacs Hill." How much more pleasant to sit quietly in the grandstand watching the maniacs breaking their backs for our edification.

——— 1956 ———
TAKE A PINCH OF SAND

The simple, elementary amenities of course and clubhouse which satisfied the gentlemen golfers of early days have always fascinated me, perhaps because my own first introduction to the game was on three unmarked holes on Yelverton Common.

At Westward Ho!, the great Horace Hutchinson recorded, they used to cut the hole with a dinner knife—what Army quartermasters, I seem to remember, call a "nine-inch, cookhouse, large"—and when one hole became too dilapidated one of the players would get out his clasp knife and cut another. To tee your ball you took a pinch of sand from the bottom of the hole, which thus got deeper and deeper, until "it often happened that one had to lie down so as to stretch one's arm at full length in order to reach the ball at the bottom of the hole." To mark the hole they stuck in the feather of a rook or a gull.

Their first clubhouse was a room in a farmhouse, but they graduated to a bathing hut containing food and drink, which was dragged out to the first tee by coastguards. Then, till it was washed away, they had an iron hut on the Pebble Ridge and this was the setting for a scene surely without parallel in golfing history. They had, to quote Hutchinson again, "many old Indian officers, with livers a little touched, who, when the golf ball would not obey their wishes with the same docility as the obedient Oriental, addressed it with many strange British words which I delighted to hear and yet stranger words in Hindustani which I much regretted not to understand."

One day a gallant but dissatisfied colonel was to be seen stark naked, picking his way daintily with unshod feet over the great boulders of the Pebble Ridge. He waded as far as possible out to sea and one by one cast his offending clubs beyond the farthest line of breakers. "That the waves and tide were sure to bring them in again, to the delight of the salvaging caddies, made no matter to him. From him they were gone forever and his soul was at rest."

—1968—
HOW FRED RUINED GOLF AND WON AN AWARD

It used to be my custom to go up to a much-loved golf course on a Sunday morning and, instead of playing, knock about with a dozen balls. The course would be almost deserted and, apart from letting the occasional couple pass by, one had the place to oneself.

The other day I went back with an old golfing companion, only to find a continuous procession of players and, since there are several alternative starting points, every single hole occupied. Apart from hitting a few half-hearted wedge shots in the fringe of the rough, there was nothing we could do. "It's people like you," said my friend sourly, "and this damned television, that have ruined the game."

In a sense I suppose we have, though I like to think that in encouraging so many people to play that courses are full instead of empty, we may have contributed to the sum total of human happiness. A far more ruinous culprit than myself, or my fellow scribes, however, is another old friend of mine, Fred Corcoran, whom I see has just been given the annual Walter Hagen Award for "Distinguished contribution to the furtherance of Anglo-

American golfing relations."*

Corcoran, an Irish-American entrepreneur who has spent a lifetime in golf, managed the American Ryder Cup teams in 1937 and 1953—the former of these under the captaincy of Hagen himself, being the first to win on British soil—and he now runs both the World Cup, which used to be called the Canada Cup, and the Westchester Classic.

His main claim to fame, however, is that, as one-time tournament manager to the American PGA, he is virtually the founder of what has grown into the present "circuit"—I wish someone could think of a more congenial word—in which these golfing entertainers will play in this year alone for more then $5 million. It is these gladiators who, more than anything except perhaps the spread of the motor car, have caused the so-called golfing explosion all over the world.

Corcoran has been in it all, right from the start. Nowadays we have electronically operated scoreboards and placards carried round with every match—only too often at the "secure arms" position with the vital information facing the ground—and here again we have to thank Corcoran as the pious pioneer.

As scorer in the U.S. Amateur Championship in the 1920's, he produced, greatly daring, some coloured chalks, and became the first man to mark pars, birdies and bogeys in different colours. He declares that in our own championship at Prestwick, as late as 1934, the only scoreboard available to the public was a sheet of notepaper tacked to the starter's table.

When Sam Snead won his first tournament at the age of 25, which must be 35 years or so ago, the prize was $1,200. Nobody quite knows how many tournaments he has won since, or how many millions he has put away, but at any rate he told me in the aeroplane coming back from the PGA Championship at San Antonio that he had just won $24,000 in the Milwaukee Tournament, the one which clashed with our own Open, and that this was the biggest cheque he had ever picked up in his life—for finishing second!

Just before the war, when Snead won another tournament, the first prize was still only $5,000, and Corcoran presented it to him in the car park. The sponsor, an amiable golf enthusiast with considerable resources, refused to be photographed during the proceedings or to present the prizes in person. Later, when the gendarmerie came for him, it transpired that he was in the printing business—printing bogus whisky labels.

Corcoran was managing the PGA Tour when a man came up to him and said:"I have a friend who will put up more money for

---

*Corcoran died in 1977.

one tournament than you play for on the whole circuit," and thereupon entered on the scene another villian who, according to my earlier companion's way of thinking, helped to ruin the game by filling the golf course. This was the late George S. May, a spectacular and, to me, grotesque figure who laid out more than $1 million in prize money in the so-called world championship at his Tam O'Shanter Club outside Chicago.

May was an efficiency expert and, as such, eliminated caddies and compelled members to hire out his electric carts, thus getting as many as possible on the course at the same time. Furthermore, if they did not spend a minimum of $100 a month in the club, he billed them for it just the same. His club had "seeing-eye" doors, a telephone on every tee, 13 bars, incessant music and a small silence room with couches, where members who felt themselves going up the wall could recover and come back for more. Anything further removed from what we in Britain know as golf would have been impossible to conceive.

It was George May who first suggested numbering the players for the benefit of the spectators. The result was an immediate sit-down strike. Tommy Armour walked off the course, declaring that he had worn a number in the first war, and was damned if he would do so again on the golf course, while the rest of them simply declined to tee off. May compromised by pinning numbers to the caddies, and this, of course, has become universal practise, except that we have now advanced to having the players' names instead of numbers. Even so, it is extraordinary how long it took to get round to informing the paying customers who it was they were watching.

Corcoran has managed many of the great figures of golf, including Snead himself, who, if only he had won the 1937 U.S. Open instead of being nosed out at the last moment by the now forgotten Ralph Guldahl, might have won half a dozen more and made an even greater fortune, plus 10 percent for the manager. Two years later, needing only a 5 to win, he took 8.

Also in Corcoran's stable was that delightful fellow, Tony Lema, who won the 1964 Open at St. Andrews, only to lose his life later in an aeroplane crash. In the last round at St. Andrews, it was seen, when Lema was putting on the sixth, that Nicklaus, who was putting on the double green only a few yards away, playing the 12th, had picked up six shots on him. Corcoran, unable to bear it any longer, retired to Gleneagles. When he got there, the television informed him that his man had just done six 3's in a row, and he came rushing back in time to see him triumph.

Television is, however, a somewhat sore point with him. In the early 1950's he swopped his contract with the PGA for the televison rights in all their tournaments. He has often shown me the contract—50 percent of the first $25,000, one-third of the next $25,000, 25 percent between $50,000 up to $125,000, and 10 percent of everything thereafter. He hawked it round the various television companies, and not a soul would look at it, so in the end he let it lapse. How many millions it would have been worth to him today is anybody's guess.

I always think that we have largely to thank Fred Corcoran for our post-war successes in the Curtis Cup, for it was he who helped found the U.S. Ladies Professional Golfers Association, thus giving the best of our opponents an opportunity to retire from the amateur scene and turn pro. Formation of the body, he has recorded, "Touched off a national storm of indifference." In their first tournament they had six players, but one-sixth of the entry scratched at the last moment—because her dog was ill.

What really got women's professional golf off the ground was his promotion of one who was probably the most extraordinary all-round woman athlete in history, the late Babe Zaharias. She could out-drive most men, and when she turned pro, Corcoran, ever alert to give the sports writers something to write about, had it announced that she intended to play in the U.S. Open. There was nothing in the rules to stop her, but the USGA in almost unseemly haste created one, and within 24 hours the Royal and Ancient had followed suit.

In 1950, Corcoran brought her and five other "proettes"— delightful word— to England, and somehow there came to be fixed up a match against half a dozen highly distinguished London amateurs, many of them Walker Cup players. They played at Wentworth on level terms, and from the same tees, and the women won every single match. It was not an occasion, I fancy, when my old friend Fred Corcoran would have received many votes for "Distinguished contribution towards the furtherance of Anglo-American golfing relations."

DEATH IN THE FOREST

It was almost at the top of the highest mountain in the forest that the grand success was at last accomplished. We overtook our quarry, a big, solitary stag, standing majestic and unaware in a glen below us. I squirmed my way down to the point where a ledge of rock jutted out over the glen, and knew that the moment had come.

I drew a bead on the stag. Then, instead of pressing the trigger, I laid down the rifle and gazed at this magnificent creature I was about to kill. Death seemed a monstrous penalty to exact for his negligence. We had won the game, according to the rules, and had crept successfully upon him without revealing our presence. Who was I to say that the beast should die?

Here was no mere verminous rabbit or sparrow or pigeon, no enemy of man, but a noble specimen of God's handiwork—Monarch, indeed, of the Glen! My mind was a turmoil of opposing emotions. I could kill him, that was certain. He was nearly 200 yards away, but I knew that I should not miss. A squeeze of the trigger and the deed would be done.

Had I been alone I should have taken a photograph of the beast to prove my victory and let him go. But faced with the prospect of explaining away such fainthearted unorthodoxy to my host and, more especially, to old Dan, my courage deserted me. I raised the rifle again and a second later the stag was dead.

As it fell, there rose from the grass beside it a second stag. I shot that, too. And I knew how the Ancient Mariner felt when he shot the albatross.

Dan Donohue was beside himself. "Good, gentleman, good," he kept saying. We went down to examine the victims and found that the first was a royal; in other words, it had 12 points to its antlers, and this was indeed a memorable début, for to shoot a royal ranks high among deerstalkers—though, as I imprudently pointed out, you shoot first and count up the points afterwards.

My guilty conscience seemed to detect a puzzled, reproachful look in the glazed eyes of the two dead beasts. I reflected, with little satisfaction, that they had died not because I had been clever enough to shoot them, but because I had not the moral courage not to.

No such thought, however, entered the mind of Donohue and he launched himself with enthusiasm into the usual operation with the jack-knife. Moved perhaps by the same strange primitive instinct that inspires the Abyssinians, he attacked first the stags' genital organs, and with a wild frenzy flung them over his head.

The operation complete, we returned to the valley for congratulations.

I have shot my stag. I shall never shoot another.

1964
SLUGGERS' PARADISE

Throughout and after the U.S. Open Championship last year at The Country Club, Brookline, piteous cries of protest were heard to the effect that top-class golf was becoming a game strictly for "muscle men" and that the day of the true artist was done. Harrowing tales of a similar nature appear to be issuing from the Congressional Club at Washington, where this year's U.S. Open has just been played, and I think that, although they may not affect you and me, there is something in them.

Among the chief complainants is Jerry Barber, who captained the last American Ryder Cup team to play in Britain. He is, I suppose, one of the greatest short-game players in the world—but he is also 5 feet 5 inches in height and weighs a pound or two less than 10 stone [140 pounds].

"Golf course architects," he says, "drunk with sand, length and big undulating greens, are running the little man right out of the game. They are not changing the size of tennis courts . . . and football fields are still the same, but they feel they have to make changes in golf courses . . . Today an architect does not think he has made a good course unless at least three of the par 3's are wood shots."

Furthermore, Barber adds, two-thirds of the par 5's have water in front of the green, so that, while the Nicklauses of this world can pitch onto the green in two, the little man has to play well short and may be faced with a 100-yard approach instead of perhaps a 30-yarder, from which he might well have got a 4.

Many of the courses on the U.S. tour are municipal and therefore almost wholly devoid of rough. This makes them a pure sluggers' paradise and the devil take the hindmost. For the Open, however, and one or two other events, the rough is allowed to grow and courses are stretched to about 7,100 yards.

Barber cites Oakland Hills, Detroit. "In 1935 it was one of the finest courses I had ever played. In 1961 at the Open I hardly recognised the place. They had added more than 60 bunkers. They had made it fit the modern pattern. Everything has to be bigger and better, especially bigger."

Billy Maxwell, U.S. Amateur champion in 1951 and long a successful professional, though not a mighty hitter, blames it all on the real-estate men. Everyone wants to live beside the fairway, so on new courses you get extra-long fairways, with more building lots to sell. "Some of these new courses are ridiculous. They're not golf courses. They're just distance.

"The game itself is changing," he adds. "When I was growing up they would tell you not to worry about distance; just to concentrate on keeping the ball straight and in play . . . It does not matter any more if you swing pretty, like the old Scotsmen wanted to. What matters is how far the ball goes."

It is the custom on many American courses, understandably enough, to water a belt of the fairway at the distance from the tee at which most players' drives will finish, but there are times when the muscle men can carry this belt and pitch on the harder ground beyond, in which case they may be as much as 80 or 100 yards ahead.

It is no fluke that the "Big Three"—Palmer, Nicklaus and Player—are big hitters; the first two mostly by nature, but Player because he realised five or six years ago that he needed at least another 30 yards, or else. He worked continuously on his physique for two years and then made a whole million dollars from winning the Masters.

Deane Beman, who has won the Amateur Championship on both sides of the Atlantic, is in my humble opinion every bit as good a golfer as Nicklaus, and an even better putter. Furthermore, nobody could call him a short hitter, but, unless Nicklaus plays below his best, Beman can no longer live with him.

A good example of the complete change in the problems which a championship course presents to an Open champion is afforded by a comparison between the clubs used by Willie Auchterlonie to win on the Old Course at St. Andrews in 1893 and those used by Palmer at Troon in 1962. Over the Old Course, which then measured 6,487 yards, Auchterlonie had to take a wooden club for his second at no fewer than 12 holes. There were six which he could not reach in two and at two of these he had to take the equivalent of a 4-iron for his third.

At Troon, on the other hand, which we may take to have measured a minimum of 7,000 yards, Palmer reached five greens with a drive and the smallest club in the bag, the wedge, and six more with anything from a 6-iron down to a 9. Of the two very long holes, he reached one with a 3-wood and the other with a 1-iron and a very short chip.

So, while Auchterlonie took a wooden club for his second shot 12 times, Palmer needed nothing more than a 6-iron to a wedge 11 times. In between them came the great master, Harry Vardon. I did not know him well, though I did see him play, but it is my impression that this supreme golfing artist would today have been nowhere—unless, like Player, he could somehow have found an extra 30 yards.

Perhaps it does not matter what the few exceptional performers do, for what are three of them against millions of us? If it comes to that, though, we are not very good at cricket or tennis, either, but it would be a poor day for us humble fry if the artistry of the great slow bowler were lost to the game because he was not a Fiery Fred, and if the only man who could win at Wimbledon was the one who could serve so fast that no one could get it back.

1955
"WHAT CLUB DO I THROW?"

Golfers are not what they were. When I began the game, the public image of the golfer, in Britain at least, was that of a red-faced, white-moustached, plus-foured gentleman, presumably a colonel (Indian Army, rtd.) hacking away in a bunker and uttering appalling and unprintable oaths. Now all, or nearly all, is sweetness and light, so much so that in the best circles you do not even knock your opponent's ball away when you concede him a putt. Instead, you pick it up and with elaborate courtesy walk across the green and place it in his hand.

The thoughts occurred to me because I have just chanced upon details of rather a splendid competition which was staged at the Druid Hills Course, at Atlanta, before the war and recorded by Bobby Jones's "Boswell," the late O.B. Keeler. From time to time, people are kind enough to write to me and ask whether I can suggest any different form of competition with which to interest the members of their clubs. This might be the answer.

It appears that Harry Stephens, who was then professional at the Druid Hills Club, in the course of reading the riot act to a junior member whom he had observed throwing a club, said, "One of these days I'm going to put on a club-throwing contest to show you boys just how stupid you really look." The idea took root and the contest was duly staged. I would rather have witnessed it than many a solemn tournament of today.

After a couple of practise days, part of the first fairway was duly marked out with an out-of-bounds area on either side. Sixty contestants turned up, old and young, and there were prizes of three golf balls for different events calling for distance, altitude or accuracy, for left-handers and right-handers. The first question that arose, before any consideration of style or method, was: "What club do I throw?"

Instinct would have led me to put my faith in a good, solid driver. In fact, the most effective weapon proved to be that which I imagine is most often thrown in earnest, namely the putter.

Each player—for the benefit of anyone who may wish to promote such a contest, possibly on the morning after the club dinner—was allowed three shots, as in a long-driving competition, and some of the results were far from orthodox.

The professional himself, whirling round in the fashion of a man throwing the hammer, released his missile at the wrong moment and it pitched on the clubhouse veranda, fortunately without killing anyone. Several others, presumably right-handers, hooked out-of-bounds.

The result, judging by memories of my own club-throwing days and the efforts of some of my friends, were, I think, remarkable. How far would you back yourself to fling a golf club? I should have thought perhaps 45 yards would represent something like a handicap of scratch. This, however, would have turned out to be very much of an also-ran.

The right-handed winner achieved a magnificent throw of 61 yards. The accuracy award went to a man who flung a mashie-niblick within 7 feet 8 inches of a marker at 50 yards, while the altitude record was set by a player who hurled a pitching iron about 20 feet over the top of an 80-foot pine tree.

Golf is the most infuriating of all games, with the possible exception of certain card games—which I have recently resumed after all too long an interval—and I am not sure that we get the best out of it by bottling up our emotions for the sake of etiquette. I have always had a sneaking sympathy with Tommy Bolt, who was constantly being fined or suspended in America for throwing or breaking clubs or for other conduct calculated to cause a breach of golfing peace.

I am not, I hope, libelling that elder statesman of Australian professional golf, Norman von Nida, when I recall that in his more explosive days he threw his putter over the railway line at Southport and Ainsdale.

AS RENDERED BY NICKLAUS

I sometimes wonder whether the likes of me—I will not say us—can really be helped by the likes of Jack Nicklaus. He cannot have any conception, fortunately enough, of what it feels like to be me. Tuck a pillow in the front of his trousers, enfeeble his left eye, drain three-quarters of the strength from his hands and fingers, make him pant when walking up slopes and cause the blood to rush to his head if the ball falls off the tee and he has to bend down to pick it up again, and he might begin to get the idea.

On the other hand, it is nice for the likes of us to imagine what it must be like to feel like Nicklaus, who glories in his strength and cheerfully invites the young to do the same. My own generation was always taught to try to cultivate a good swing and let distance come later. Nicklaus thinks exactly the opposite:

"The first thing I learned was to swing hard, and never mind where the ball went. That is the way Arnold Palmer was taught, too, and I think it is the right way. A youngster first trying golf will enjoy the game more if allowed to whale away at the ball, and he will be developing the muscles he needs to become a strong hitter. Once he has achieved distance, he can learn control while still hitting a long ball."

The most important factor in long hitting, he thinks—and it would be interesting to know how many long hitters feel the same—is strength in one's legs, and this is developed by hitting hard when one is young. "If a golfer does this while young, he will get the leg strength needed to hit very long shots. I know that my distance is due more to the strength in my legs than to any power I might be getting from my arms, hands or fingers."

Meanwhile, spring draws us from our winter lairs and a few tentative swings may soon be made with the special weighted club, if we can find it. "Swing 250-270 yards to a fairway 35 yards wide; long irons over 200 yards to within 36 feet . . . ." I can see them all! As rendered by Nicklaus.

"SIC TRANSIT" GLORIA...

It was 10 o'clock on a lovely October morning and the scene was Westward Ho! The flat expanse between the clubhouse and the sea, which they call the Burrows, was shimmering in the sunshine, and red sails glided along above the level of the sandhills as the sailing barges and fishing boats made their way into the little harbour at Appledore. The world was at peace.

On the first tee down below the clubhouse a small group of people were waiting. Many were women, for the English women's championship was just beginning, but among them was a goodly sprinkling of men. Of the men, those that weren't caddies were golf journalists.

Golf journalists on the first tee at 10 in the morning? Yes, indeed. Every one of them. And what had lured them forth at this unaccustomed hour? Why, the rumour had gone round in the village that at 10 o'clock that day a lady intended to play golf in trousers.

One or two even went so far as to suggest that not only did she play in trousers but that she only used one club. This was ruled out as an unworthy attempt to paint the lily.

Trousers, yes; or one club, yes. But trousers *and* one club— come, come, sir!

No one you meet has ever seen a ghost; on the other hand, there's no one who doesn't know someone who has. So it was with the mysterious lady. No one had seen her, but every one had it first-hand from someone who had.

Ten o'clock came, and no apparition. The name was called once. No reply. It was called again. No reply. The know-alls wagged their heads with a chorus of "I told you so," and were retiring to the clubhouse for refreshment, when along the little lane that crosses the links a couple of hundred yards from the first tee, there appeared a big yellow motor car.

The car stopped, and out into the headlines stepped Miss Gloria Minoprio.

The deserters hastily retraced their steps from the bar, while among the ladies in waiting arose a clucking and fluttering as of an agitated flock of Leghorn pullets.

"My dear, do you see what I see? . . ." "What a figure! . . ." "What trousers!"

"Well, *really*!" cried the Ladies' Golf Union.

"Good God!" said the journalists.

Meanwhile, the object of their astonishment made her way composedly and with what dignity her costume would permit across to the waiting crowd. She was clad from head to foot in dark blue, and, yes, she wore trousers. Close-fitting, exquisitely tailored trousers, very tightly cut, especially . . . er . . . behind. She wore them, as did our grandfathers, with straps beneath the insteps of her blue suede shoes. A neat blue jacket and a little blue turban completed the streamline.

A slim, graceful girl, with delicate, sensitive features and figure divine. She had bumps, to quote Mr. Damon Runyon's rudely graphic description, where a doll is entitled to have bumps. Only one thing marred the picture. On her cheeks should have glowed the rosy bloom of youth and health. Instead, they were heavily, almost grotesquely, powdered in white. She might have been wearing a white mask.

With her was a young caddie carrying, rather sheepishly, a scarlet spare jacket, a ball bag, and . . . not one club, but two. But rumour had spoken truth, and she only used one of these clubs. The other was a spare in case of accident.

She said, "How do you do?" almost inaudibly to her opponent. At the end of the match she said, "Thank you." So far as I am aware that was all she did say.

Tapping the ground with her solitary cleek to show the caddie where she wished him to tee the ball, she prepared to play her opening stroke. It must have been something of an ordeal. If so, she certainly showed no sign of it.

She had, it turned out, a careful, precise style of play that might have been learnt studiously from the textbook. Nothing very dashing about it, no undignified vigour, but quite efficient. She did not hit the ball very far—no woman does with an iron club—but she hit it for the most part nice and straight.

That morning the champions played in solitude, their supporters lured away by magnetic Minoprio. I forget the name of her opponent, but there was no doubt as to which was the more nervous of the two. The prospect of losing to a lady in fancy dress using only one club is enough to shake the stoutest heart. Might take a lifetime to live down.

Recovering from their initial shock, those of the quickly gathering gallery who were interested in the technique of golf settled down to assess Miss Minoprio's capabilities with her solitary club. They proved to be considerable. Her long game was steady and, though the long shaft of her iron made her look rather clumsy, her putting was at least up to the average usually seen in a women's championship. Her approaches, low along the ground, were quite effective.

But the time came, inevitably, when she was faced with

strokes beyond the capacity of Bobby Jones, Cotton, or the devil himself, to execute with a straight-faced iron. She could not loft the ball, except in a full shot; she could impart no backspin; she could get no distance from anything but a smooth, clipped lie. To lob the ball over an intervening hazard was beyond her.

There was much speculation as to what would occur when she got into a bunker. The truth is that it is quite simple to remove the ball from a bunker with any kind of club if the sand is soft and loose. Hit hard, three or four inches behind it, and the deed is done. So in the fine seaside sand of Westward Ho! Miss Monoprio performed with no little distinction, and some who had come to mock remained to marvel. But on firm or rain-sodden sand or, indeed, on any hard surface, she was pathetically powerless.

That her average score would have been reduced by anything from half a dozen to 10 shots in a round by the use of a normal set of clubs, no reasonable critic could doubt. She went through the motions well enough, but the instrument she used was too ill-adapted for the purpose. She lost her match by, I think, 5 and 4, and I was able to telephone to the Evening Standard what I believe to be almost the only Latin tag to find its way into the sporting pages of that journal—"*Sic transit* Gloria Monday." (I repeated it shamelessly for five years with only one variation. One year she defeated a young girl who was so nervous that she could scarcely focus on the ball. So when she was beaten next day the tag became "*Sic transit* Gloria Tuesday.")

The yellow car had been driven across the Burrows and was waiting nearby. She stepped in and was whisked away, not to appear in public again until the next women's championship, and the company settled down to debate her reason for imposing upon herself the ludicrous handicap of playing with one club.

One school of thought held that she was doing it for publicity. Certainly, her unusual attire lent weight to that opinion. If so, she certainly succeeded, for her name and picture have featured in almost every newspaper every time she has appeared in a championship. But those who seek publicity like inevitably to bask in it when achieved. Miss Minoprio, so far as I know, has never entered a golf clubhouse during a championship; has never played in a tournament other than the two championships; has never made friends with other golfers.

And again, why the extraordinary outfit, admirable though it may be for golfing comfort? And why the mask-like countenance? Here a very strong school exists which holds that she plays golf while temporarily hypnotised, or entranced, either by auto-suggestion or by a friend. This is possible. And if she is not in a state of semi-hypnosis, that at least is as good a description as any of her appearance and demeanour.

She spent some months studying yoga in India (and, incidentally, she is a conjuror of the highest order, though the point is hardly relevant). After her debut at Westward Ho! she wrote to tell me she had bought 30 copies of the *Tatler*, in which I had written about her, to distribute to her friends. We exchanged three or four letters. Later, while walking round in a championship, I introduced myself as her correspondent. She blinked with surprise at being spoken to. She had the vacant, far-away look of Lady Macbeth walking in her sleep. She seemed scarcely to understand what I was trying to say. "Oh, yes . . . yes," she said, looking vaguely into the distance over my shoulder. I faded away.

The Ladies' Golf Union, aghast at her first appearance, issued a proclamation that they "deplored any departure from the traditional costume of the game," but the last laugh was against them. Nearly half the field in women's championships today turn out in trousers.

But none of them fit like Gloria Minoprio's.

The foregoing occurred in 1934—though I remember it as if it were yesterday. It is difficult at this distance of time to believe that an almost national sensation, far beyond the realms of golf, should have been caused by the appearance of a lady in trousers. Miss Minoprio later married, but, alas, died in Nassau in the late 1950's. It has always been my regret that I never really got to know this clearly remarkable person. When I won a continental championship in 1936, I was gratified to receive a telegram of congratulations from her and replied accordingly. It was only 15 years later that I learnt it had been sent by General Critchley.

1975
YANKS CHALLENGED TO RINGER MATCH

Since it is now manifestly impossible for Britain ever again to beat the Americans, professional or amateur, at normal golf, I venture to propose another form of contest in which I suspect that my lowly fellow countrymen might compete not only with success but to the general entertainment, and I hereby challenge readers to do their best. I refer to the Individual Eclectic Score competition. In case this sounds too much of a mouthful it simply means a "lifetime ringer," i.e., your best score ever for each hole on your own course. This produces extraordinary results and is not confined—indeed, far from it—to the Nicklauses of this world.

It first attracted my interest when some of us worked out that Jim Morris, in the course of 50 years as professional at one of my home clubs, had run up against a par of 70 an eclectic score of 44. Here, as a sort of celestial vision of golfing glory, are his figures:

$$313 \quad 231 \quad 233 - 21$$
$$331 \quad 332 \quad 332 - 23$$
$$44$$

As he recently, at age 78, easily defeated, level, a member who went round in 74 and, as they holed the course in 1 hour and 58 minutes, I am appointing him our British ringer team captain.

He is by no means, however, our best performer. Forty years of play over the Old Course at St. Andrews produced for that rude and rugged old Scotsman, Andra' Kirkaldy, a score of 21-22—43. Since so many visitors know this famous course, here are the old boy's figures:

$$232 \quad 332 \quad 312 - 21$$
$$212 \quad 342 \quad 332 - 22$$
$$43$$

Many of our American visitors who have toured that lovely stretch of seaside links east of Edinburgh, together with all non-exempt professionals who have had to pre-qualify for the British Open when it has been held at Muirfield, will remember the course at Gullane (pronounced "Gillan"), the one with the panoramic views once you have climbed the second hole. William Gilchrist, who owns a couple of hotels there, will figure high in my eclectic team. After what he estimates to be 10,000 rounds, he comes out with a total of 36—out in 29, home in 17: three aces, three 3's, and all the rest 2's. He has twice done the 17th (393 yards) in 2—"once a bit lucky, the other a good one."

Naturally the players of our two teams will tend to be veterans. Any bright young spark these days can do 69 or better but it takes a few years to accumulate an eclectic of 40! Thus I include on my team J.W. Nelson, of a well-known and full-sized club, North Hants, some 30 miles south of London. True, in 75 years he had done no better then 22-18—40 "and can hardly hope to improve on it now," but his figures for nine consecutive holes from the eighth to the 16th, including three par 3's and 3 holes of 454, 434 and 428 yards, make such reading that I cannot resist setting them down just for the pleasure of seeing them in print:

$$121 \quad 222 \quad 212 - 15.$$

Another of my team who will also take some beating is John Horden, of the par-72 Olton club in Warwickshire. It has always been the practise of American team captains to place a strong player, as a sort of "anchor man," at the bottom of the list. Indeed, I even remember the great Sam Snead in this humble-looking but important position. So Horden will bring up the rear on our side and, when you see his lifetime ringer, you will appreciate why I feel that he is a man who will not let us down in a close finish. Here it is:

$$222 \quad 222 \quad 222 - 18$$
$$222 \quad 222 \quad 222 - 18$$
$$36$$

Furthermore, every single one, or rather every single 2, was scored in a competition, and his various fellow competitors over the years presented him with a laminated scorecard to attest the fact.

Eighteen 2's and not a single hole-in-one! It seems incredible and only serves to emphasize the fantastic flukiness of holes-in-one. The record-holder, according to my handbook, is Art Wall, with 41. Art, an essentially modest man, would be the last to claim that he was, or is, 41 times as skillful as the legendary Harry Vardon. Yet, believe it or not, this giant had only one hole-in-one during his lifetime. And Walter Travis, three times amateur champion of the United States and once of Britain, never had one at all.

Golfers are taxed like anyone else—though I suspect that through crafty managers they suffer less acutely than some of us—and I have often wondered about the accounting when professionals win extra for holes-in-one. Recently, for instance, Maurice Bembridge, who once finished with a 64 in the Masters, won £1,000 and a £3,500 motor car for a hole-in-one in a tournament. The tax gatherer will doubtless claim this to be "earned income." If I were his lawyer, I should claim, with some confidence, that, since never in the long history of golf has anyone ever done a hole-in-one on purpose, it must be the purest fluke, and therefore counts as an "act of God."

---1975---

WHY NOT SUDDEN DEATH?

What do the Open championships of the United States and Britain have in common? Many things, indeed, but this year one in particular. Both ended in a tie, and all within the space of three weeks. Of all the accursed institutions invented by golfing authorities on either side of the Atlantic, the extra-day playoff is surely the most diabolical. All one can be grateful for is that, considering the number of players of approximately equal excellence, it does not happen more often.

Those who suffer most are those who complain the least—perhaps because they have not the means to do so—namely, the paying public. Streaming in by the thousands, walking half a mile or more from the car park and paying a hefty fee, they have come to see the final day of the championship. They have come to see the thrilling finish and to see the winner winning and to give him a friendly cheer as he is presented the trophy. Instead, when asked by non-golfing members of their family on their return, "Well, who won?" they have to reply, "Nobody."

I think it is not only ridiculous but of slightly dubious commercial morality to take the people's money to see the last day of the Open and then, at the end, tell them to come back tomorrow and find out who is the winner.

A playoff the next day is the complete anticlimax. On the evening of the fourth round, as the poet Rudyard Kipling put it, "The tumult and the shouting dies, the captains and the kings depart."

Nor is it only the captains and the kings who depart. The caterers, too, to quote this time the poet Longfellow, "fold their tents like the Arabs and as silently steal away." By the next morning not even the smell of a distant hotdog or hamburger stand is left to comfort the faithful spectator who has sacrificed an extra day in order to be in at the kill.

Blistering comments are to be heard in the press tent and it is even believed that critical observations, though pitched, of course, on a more gentlemanly note, are to be heard from those 300 or so connected with television. Hotel reservations have to be re-booked, if the rooms have not already been let to someone else. Airline offices are swamped with calls. For an hour or two all is shambles and bad language—just because a couple of golfers are not allowed to settle their differences right away, the same way they will be compelled to settle them the next evening should they tie again, namely sudden death.

In earlier times, if the replay ended in a tie, they played another 18 holes the second extra day and went on doing so until kingdom come, in other words, until one of them won. Indeed, for many years the playoff was at 36 holes, and if still tied they played 36 more the next day. I remember that in the British Open of 1963 the playoff was over 36 holes. Having duly won it against Phil Rodgers, Bob Charles in his acceptance speech suggested with the utmost courtesy that, after the long grind of 72 holes, it was asking a bit much to play half of it all over again in a single day, and would not 18 perhaps be enough? The point was duly taken and 18 holes it has been ever since.

The U.S. Open did away with scheduled 36-hole playoffs after the 1931 championship. That year at Inverness in Toledo, Billy Burke and George Von Elm tied at the end of 72 holes and each shot 149 in the 36-hole playoff. The next day they went 36 holes again, Burke finally claiming the title by the margin of a single stroke—148 to 149. Had Burke needed another stroke (or Von Elm one fewer), presumably they would have played another 36 holes the following day.

Even though the 36-hole playoff was voted out, the U.S. Open still couldn't get away from that route the next time there was a tie—in 1939 at Philadelphia Country Club. That year Byron Nelson and Craig Wood tied at 284 and each shot 68 in the 18-hole playoff. So they had to go another 18 the next day, Nelson winning, 70-73.

I suspect that the idea prevails among the authorities on both sides of the Atlantic that, while ordinary run-of-the-mill tournaments for a mere couple of hundred thousand dollars or so can be finished by sudden death on the final day, it somehow adds to the prestige of a championship if it finishes with an 18-hole replay next day.

This argument, with me at least, does not carry weight. I do not think that a championship would lose anything of its prestige, possibly even the opposite, by being finished off with a climax on the day set aside for the final round instead of an anticlimax the following day.

The real inescapable point, however, is that if the playoff ends in a tie, it is finished off by sudden death, and thus the principle of sudden death is accepted as part of the Open's constitution. If you accept it in principle on playoff day, why not accept it in fact a day earlier and send everyone home happy—except perhaps the loser.

Gary Player, who has had rather poor luck with sudden-death playoffs, is against playoffs of any kind. He says that, if at the end of the tournament nobody has beaten you, you are the winner and, if somebody else equals your score, then the two of you are joint winners. For ordinary tournaments there is much to be said for this, but somehow I do not think a national championship would be satisfactory to anyone without its producing an indisputable national champion.

Perhaps the last word on playoffs is to be found in the records of the British Open: "1876—Bob Martin, St. Andrews, 176 (David Strath tied but refused to play off)."

P.S. I confess that my chest swelled a little and I straightened my tie when none other than the late Clifford Roberts, the benevolent dictator of the Masters, confessed that it was largely this article when it appeared in *Golf Digest* that had convinced him of the merits for finishing the tournament on the Sunday and having done with it. He was particularly impressed, he said, by the argument that if, in the event of a Monday playoff ending in a tie, you were going to revert to sudden death and therefore, having done that, might just as well finish the tournament on the final day so that all the assembled masses could see the winner winning, instead of going home and having to reply, when asked who won, "No one."

Knowing the torment caused to the television authorities by these Monday playoffs, I reported to CBS, for whom I had the honour of working at Augusta for many years, with the expectation of a congratulatory pat on the back and thanks from all concerned. Instead, I got some very dark looks from Frank Chirkinian, CBS's talented golf director, who tends, like Frankie Ferocious, the hero of one of Damon Runyon's immortal stories, to look darkly at people anyway.

It appeared that Mr. Roberts was of the opinion that Bobby Jones would have wished the playoff to start at the first hole, and Mr. Chirkinian had had to arrange cables and camera positions for the entire course, just in case. So much for good intentions!

—1960—
CANNONBALL ACCURACY

Lawson Little was an appallingly difficult man to play against. He was only of medium height but his broad shoulders and barrel-like chest made him, in ordinary clothing, appear almost as formidable as a padded-up American footballer. His father was an Army medical colonel, so that Lawson had been brought up with a certain amount of reserve and was not at that time a natural mixer. He thought the game out step-by-step and took his time about it, including deciding between the five pitching wedges he carried among his 22 clubs. Unlike some of the other mighty hitters of the day, such as Jimmy Thomson, be managed to harness his great length. One cannonball drive followed another down the middle till at last even the most determined challengers buckled at the knees.

The experts tend to talk of a man being a good "birdie putter," or otherwise, and this is a point that all of us can appreciate, even in our own less-elevated sphere. In other words, do you reckon yourself more likely to hole a 10-foot putt offensively to earn a bonus in the shape of a birdie 3 or defensively to save a par 4? We are all one or the other, and it is a matter largely of temperament.

For myself, I admire the qualities of the former but have always, alas, belonged to the latter. By common consent Little was a great birdie putter. What with this and his huge straight driving and his iron play remodelled on the master himself, Tommy Armour, it was little wonder that they could not beat him.

1965

"✱✱✱✱✱✱✱✱✱✱✱!"

Being a traditionalist at heart and having been brought up in an age when the bad language of golfers was always good for a laugh in the humorous magazine *Punch*, I was secretly, and of course most improperly, delighted to read that the language of some of the golfers of the Rushmere Club at Ipswich had so much offended the susceptibilities of a number of passers-by as to cause them to make official complaint. Well done, gentlemen. Splendid stuff! This, as I once heard Mr. Churchill describe it, is a "mealy-mouthed, purry-purry, puss-puss age," and a few strong words do much to restore our self-esteem.

In my early days it was only the club golfer who permitted himself to give vent to his feelings; the professional never. In the intervening period we have had such characters as Tommy Bolt, a past U.S. Open champion, who was constantly being fined for failing to hold his feelings in check. But the conduct of the great millionaire professionals today, which sets the pattern for the rest, is almost solemn in its righteousness.

This "correctness" has now passed itself on to the golfing rank and file, but it still does not alter the fact that, to me at any rate, the most exquisitely satisfying act in the world of golf is that of throwing a club. The full backswing, the delayed wrist action, the flowing follow-through, followed by that unique whirring sound, reminiscent only of a passing flock of starlings, are without parallel in sport. Many is the time I have done it, and seen it done by better men than I—but now, alas, we should probably be drummed out of the club.

The classic club-throwing story is, of course, that of the fellow who, on returning from an unsatisfactory mission in Scotland, threw his clubs one by one from the carriage window into the

Firth of Forth while crossing the Forth Bridge. I never believed this to be true until I met a fellow who with the utmost seriousness assured me that he was the man. (Immediately on returning home, he confessed to me, he went out and bought another set.) There was also the hero who, on chipping three times into the Swilken Burn at the first hole at St. Andrews, when playing it as the 19th, beckoned silently to his caddie, lifted the clubs from his shoulder, and threw them into the burn. Then he threw his caddie in. Then he jumped in himself.

Many, many years ago, I was playing in a Bedfordshire Northants Alliance meeting in company with a partnership consisting of the then vicar of Northampton and a gentleman whose complexion indicated either good living or shortness of temper, or both. They were doing rather well and at the 17th were in with a definite chance. At this point the vicar's partner had only to loft a short pitch over the bunker onto the green, when, alas, up came his head, out came a lump of turf, and the ball dropped feebly into the bunker. The man lifted his niblick to heaven "*******!," he cried, and "*******!" and "*******!" Then, pulling himself up with a jerk, he began to make embarrassed apologies. The vicar's reply remains in my mind as though it were yesterday. "Brother," he said, slowly and gently, "the provocation was ample."

The best swearing "incident" in golf must surely be the conclusion of P.G. Wodehouse's story, "Chester Forgets Himself." (If any reader is so golfingly illiterate as not to possess, and be able to quote from, *The Heart of a Goof* from which book this story comes, and the original *The Clicking of Cuthbert* let him at once go out and get them.) Chester, it may be remembered, stifling his normal flow of strong language for the sake of the girl he hopes to marry, has to get down in a chip and a putt to break the course record. At the 18th he has at last managed to get through that immortal four-ball known as "The Wrecking Crew" and is about to play his chip, when one of them, I think it was the First Gravedigger, the one who "never spared himself in his efforts to do the ball a violent injury," took his usual swipe at the ball and for the first time in his life did everything right at once. His shot hit Chester on the seat of his plus-fours at the crucial moment, thus causing him to fluff his pitch, whereupon he let forth a blistering succession of asterisks and exclamation marks. The girl, wondering how all this time she could have "so misjudged this silver-tongued man," folds him in her arms and, a moment later, of course, he nonchalantly holes his final chip for the record.

The man who got really cross at golf—strange as it must seem to those who only knew him by the gentleness of his writing—was Bernard Darwin, who enjoyed, if that is the word, a kind of love-hate relationship with the game for the best part of 70 years.

A friend of mine was once playing in a foursome with him at Rye when, at a rather crucial moment on the 16th, Bernardo missed his second. He wandered off into the rough and started banging his club repeatedly on the ground. He thought he was out of earshot but my friend heard him muttering savagely to himself, "Why do I play this *****! game? I do hate it so."

It was Bernardo who told me what remains one of my favourite golfing stories, of a well-known Scottish amateur before the first war. Though a big man, he had made the discovery, as people do from time to time, that you can putt remarkably well, one-handed, with a little putter about the size of a carpenter's hammer. As always happens, it lasted splendidly for a while but proved fallible in the end. The climax came when he missed a tiddler with it on the ninth green at Muirfield. Raising himself to his full height, he flung it against the grey stone wall bordering the green. "You little ******!" he cried. "Never presume upon my good nature again!"

—1961—
LAW OF THE LINKS

"By special request," as the entertainers say when they have every intention of doing an encore anyway, I venture to produce an abbreviated set of golfing rules which I feel might cover the day-to-day activities of club golfers who require a common code and have no intention of cheating. No more is claimed for it than that, but it might, when its various inadequacies have been pointed out and corrected, serve as a basis of an official abbreviated version to replace the 93 pages of the present pocket edition.

It would be idle to deny that most people at the moment have only the sketchiest knowledge of the rules. Those that follow could be printed—albeit in pretty small type—on the outside portions of the scorecard and everyone could reasonably be expected to be acquainted with them. For professionals playing for thousands of pounds it might be desirable to produce a sterner and more detailed code. If so, I have no doubt that the Rules of Golf Committee would give them a hand in doing so.

Local rules such as picking out of specified streams, burns, etc., under penalty of one stroke, and improving the lie (but not the stance) between, say, November 1 and May 1, would remain the concern of individual clubs.

Perhaps I may note certain points in the suggested rules. There is, for instance, no limitation of clubs. Only in this way, it seems to me, can we hope to break down the absurd notion that a "set" of golf clubs numbers 14. A set is the number you choose to carry and would in most cases range from seven to nine. Again, I think that many minor contingencies, e.g., finding your ball on the wrong green or having a dog run off with it, would be covered, for club golfers at any rate, either by Rule 2 or by the words "in the traditional manner" in Rule 1. I envisage that the "background," i.e., form of clubs, amateur status, how to run a competition, etc., would remain available in a separate publication.

So here with due humility I set up to be shot at my plain man's Law of the Links:

1. The game shall be played in the traditional manner and with as little delay as possible. Penalty: match play, loss of hole; stroke play, two strokes.

2. If any point in dispute be not covered by the Rules, it shall be settled in accordance with equity.

3. Ball lost, out-of-bounds or unplayable. The player may drop a ball on the nearest edge of the fairway under penalty of stroke and distance, play another ball from the same place as the first, the second ball then becoming the ball in play irrespective of where the first be later found.

4. Impediments and obstructions. Without penalty (1) any loose impediment may be removed, (2) a ball (a) in any hole, mark or matter left by an animal, (b) within two clubs' length of any artificial obstruction, (c) interfered with by anything left by the greenkeeper, (d) lying on ground under repair or in sufficient casual water to interfere with stroke or stance, may be dropped or, if necessary, placed clear.

5. A ball embedded in its pitch anywhere except in a sand bunker may be lifted and dropped without penalty.

6. On the green. The ball may be cleaned, pitch marks flattened and impediments scraped aside. No penalty shall be incurred for hitting the flagstick, whether attended or not, or for accidentally hitting partner, opponent, caddies or equipment. If a player's ball hit another, there shall be in match play no penalty, in stroke play a penalty of one stroke. The ball struck shall in all cases be replaced.

7. The nearer ball, anywhere on the course, shall be lifted at the request of the player.

8. If a player plays one stroke with the wrong ball, he shall go back and play again without penalty; if more than one stroke, he shall in match play lose the hole; in stroke play lose two strokes and finish the hole with the wrong ball. If two players in match

play each play the wrong ball, they shall finish the hole thus and the scores shall stand.

9. The club may be grounded anywhere except in a sand bunker.

10. No penalty shall be incurred for, by mistake, (1) hitting a moving ball, (2) playing from in front of the teebox, (3) touching the sand in a bunker, (4) playing out of turn, (5) moving the ball. In the case of (5) the ball shall be replaced, the player ensuring, as always, that no advantage to himself accrues.

Following—I will not say as a result of—this article, Mr. Gerald Micklem, at the time of writing Chairman of the Rules of Golf Committee of the Royal and Ancient, produced for the Golf Foundation a short summary, of scorecard size, entitled "Some Guidance to the Rules of Golf."

—1962—
CHICAGO CIRCUS MASTER

George S. May was a singular character. Whether you liked it or not, you had to admit that he was largely responsible for turning professional golf into the "spectator" sport that it is in the United States and thus, by inference, influencing its character all over the world. It all began in 1940, by which time he had owned the "fabulous" Tam O'Shanter Club outside Chicago for three years. "What," he asked, "is the biggest prize in golf?" On hearing that it was the $10,000 offered in the Miami Open, he said: "I will give $11,000."

In a few years he had worked up an annual 10-day jamboree which drew the biggest crowds in the game's history and for which the total prize money reached $212,000.

The winner of his so-called "World Championship" collected $50,000 in prize money, plus a contract for a minimum of 50 exhibitions at $1,000 each, plus transportation and expenses, plus an option on 50 more on the same terms—plus $1,000 dollars to give to his caddie!

I have a remarkable film of the finish of one of these affairs. Chandler Harper holes a shortish putt for a birdie 3 on the last green, leaving only Lew Worsham with a chance. Worsham needs a 3 to tie and one sees him in the distance, playing his shot up to the banked and elevated green. Actually, I believe, he "skimmed" it a bit—as well he might—but it rolls up and runs straight into the hole for a 2, and rather more than $100,000. The gesticulating figure in the Harry Truman flowered shirt who dashes across the green to pick the ball out of the hole is George S. May.

What stuck in the throats of more conservative golfers was the circus atmosphere of May's promotions. He believed in keeping his public entertained and to this end even had his 27 "one-armed bandits" wheeled out into the open. These handed 30 percent back in winnings, but of the remainder May was relieved of 40 percent by a man called Julius, who called every Monday morning to collect it on behalf of Al Capone's successors. Julius, however, did not relieve him of any of the $50,000 a year that he made from the bingo and roulette.

George May started life as a Bible salesman and had the bright idea of following in the wake of the celebrated evangelist, Billy Sunday, who, by the time he arrived, had already softened up the potential customers. In later years he ran a business efficiency company, of which the American magazine *Fortune* reported: "Some May clients have been grateful for the company's help and have returned for more," but *Fortune* recalled some occasions when it had met with criticism. On reading this, May posted it on each of Tam O'Shanter's 12 notice boards. "Good publicity," he said.

Some years ago he escorted me round his club and it is an experience I shall not lightly forget. One entered by a series of "seeing eye" glass doors which were then to me a novelty, so that I was constrained to pretend that I had left something in the car in order to set them going again. We then turned immediately into a bar with a dark ceiling and artificial stars. This, he explained with pride, was one of 13 in the club and was handy if members were overcome by thirst while waiting to meet somebody in the hall or for their cars to be brought round.

Another bar was at the halfway house between the ninth green and 10th tee, and he made it a rule that you could not play through the people in front while they stopped and refreshed themselves. There was nothing for it, therefore, but to step and patronise the bar yourself. Subscription to the club was $560 a year and, if you did not spend enough money in it, George billed you for $364 a year just the same—a dollar a day for every day except Christmas, he explained.

Tam O'Shanter, he told me, was the only course in the world with a telephone on every tee. Members could be located on the course at any time or could stop and put in a call to ascertain the state of the stock market or to explain to their wives that they would be delayed. "Doctors, undertakers and other professional men," said a brochure, "find this service to be very valuable."

It was a certainty, of course, that in the clubhouse there should be that frightful piped-in music in every part of the building—dining rooms, locker rooms, card rooms, all 13 bars, everywhere—everywhere, that is, except two "Quiet Rooms," one for 12 men and the other for seven ladies, which he had just built at a cost of $14,000. "Many members," it did not surprise me to read in the brochure, "have said that these quiet rooms are the greatest improvement the club has ever made."

Discounting all the ballyhoo, there is no doubt that George May, with his annual jamboree and all the publicity it received, and by the winners' exhibition matches all over the country (preceded by a corps of his salesmen handing out free tickets to likely customers for the efficiency business), did introduce golf to vast numbers of new people and to that extent promote human happiness. As to the club of which he was so proud, I was delighted to have had him show me round. It is in no harsh spirit that I say it represented everything in golf that I cannot stand.

1966
THEM AND US

The thought of spending five hours plodding round a course of 7,000 or more yards casts melancholy on my soul. Nevertheless, it is equally wretched that the finest players of their generation should find no course in the world capable of demanding the full range of their talent and be reduced to walking 555 yards for the pleasure of hitting a drive and a 5-iron.

The solution, of course, is so blindingly simple that one would not expect anyone to give it a passing thought.

There should be a special and shorter "tournament ball" for "them" and another, the present one, for "us." They all could play happily together on the same course at the same time and might even do it as their fathers did, twice in one day.

"I CAN ALWAYS DIG DITCHES"

What one likes so much about Arnold Palmer, apart from inevitable courtesy and his ability to suffer fools and fans so gladly, is that he so genuinely loves the game of golf. "He has a deep affection for golf courses, a love of them, if you like." Wrote his manager, Mark McCormack, "He wants courses to fight back at him and considers them gallant opponents. This attitude of cherishing the game and the elements of it is, for a variety of reasons, an unusual one in a touring pro. Most of them come to hate golf courses, in part because it is the course that thwarts their ambition and in part because they feel such an attitude is helpful to their game."

I suppose that, though he certainly does not behave as such, Palmer is the wealthiest man in the history of sport, but McCormack finds it impossible really to convince him that he will never be poor again, that he is not only a millionaire today but will be for years to come even if he never hits another ball. He has main offices in five cities and corporations in countries all over the world—you can even walk down the street in Tokyo and see "Tearoom Arnie"—but money to Palmer in his agreeably direct and simple way still means money in the hand or the savings account. Mortgages to him are something that banks foreclose on and come and take away the furniture. Alone among his countrymen his maxim is: "If you can't pay on the nail, wait till you can."

Even now McCormack cannot convince Palmer that he is secure for life. Sometimes when he has one of his losing runs he will look at his huge hands with the stubby fingers and will say, "Mark, no matter what happens, I can always dig ditches." Instinct tells me they would surely be the finest ditches ever dug.

THE AVERAGE BRITISH GOLFER

A man was mocking at my work the other day and, among other things, chided me on the frequent use of the expression "the average golfer." This, he said, meant nothing at all: in fact, there was no such animal. He was nothing more than another mythical person like Colonel Bogey.

Now I think my friend was wrong, for I have a very clear conception of the man I mean when I talk about the average golfer. Here are some of his characteristics—and in case any reader should fancy that he recognises himself, let me assure him that no offence is meant.

My average golfer exists in his thousands in the suburbs of London, and he plays, for the most part, on the course that is nearest to his home. His club is definitely a club, in the sense that it is a meeting place for friends as opposed to a venue to which a number of persons, unknown to each other, come every Sunday for the purpose of playing golf. He prides himself that he and his friends are "a very cheery crowd of fellows."

He plays on Saturday afternoons, Sundays and sometimes on summer evenings, and, apart from the rare occasions when he enters for the monthly medal and the law will only allow him one partner, he plays four-balls. When cornered, he says that he believes the foursome [alternate shot team play] is the best form of golf, but for himself he prefers to hit his own ball.

He never practises and has never had a lesson or a game with the club professional, of whom he stands in some awe. His explanation for the continual humiliation of British golfers in the Walker Cup matches is that they never practise and they do not play enough with professionals.

His own handicap varies from 10 to 18, and, though he wishes he were better, he takes no steps to improve his game. He believes, when his ball goes farther in summer, that it is because he is hitting it better.

Golf is his only outdoor recreation (though he reads the soccer and cricket news), but he has never given a thought to the elementary principles of golf course architecture. Thus it does not occur to him that a hole which is a classic with one type of ball may be rendered futile by the introduction of another type that goes substantially farther. Any mention of a movement to restrict the flight of the ball rouses him to denounce it as an "attempt to deprive him of his liberty."

He is dressed in a plus-four suit of brown Harris tweed, accompanied by red garters, and sometimes, alas, by a stiff collar. He drives to the course in a 10-horsepower family saloon motor car, and he will be ashamed to admit that life has held a new meaning since the invention of the synchromesh gearbox.

So far as his game is concerned, there are times when he plays each of his eight clubs well, but these times have never yet coincided. Nothing, fortunately, will convince him that the moment will never come when they will.

His greatest pleasure is derived from the long drive, but most of his tee shots have a tendency to go out to the right—chiefly because he is generally aiming there. His putting is sound on the whole, rising to heights of inspiration and sinking next day to depths which he afterwards can scarcely believe to have been true.

At the moment he is somewhat perturbed by what he has read in the papers concerning a new type of whippy shaft, which he has a sneaking belief could hit the ball farther. A year hence he will still be meaning to try one.

Though he enjoys the fun of hitting the ball, he values the game largely for the exercise it gives him and the pleasant social intercourse afforded by the 19th hole, where his conversation turns on motor cars, his day's play, income tax, his day's play, the Minister of Transport, his day's play.

Finally, it is his proud boast that he is the backbone of the game—and, upon my soul, I am not sure that he is not right.

1955

HIS GOLF HANDICAP–NO LEGS

Having been asked to write about Douglas Bader and his golf, I do so with the natural pleasure of one who knew him when he was at the beginning of the golfing road and may even, perhaps, have helped him along it. Bader, whose name, incidentally, rhymes with "harder," not "Ada," lost both his legs in an air crash in 1931, but came back in 1939 to become one of the most outstanding fighter pilots of the war. At the moment, his life story, "Reach for the Sky," is being filmed in Britain, with Kenneth More in the leading part, and I only hope they do not "lay it on too thick," since his story itself is good enough for a wonderful film scenario without any artificial trimmings.

However, I am concerned here strictly with Bader as a golfer.

That he was able to play at all was due to the fact that, while he lost the whole of his right leg, he retained his left knee. I cannot help thinking that, without this, it would have been impossible—though, certainly, the things he does with what remains is remarkable enough. For many years he has played genuinely to a single-figure handicap, and, two or three years after the war, won a tournament at Camberley Heath, one of the hilliest courses in Surrey, with two rounds averaging in the middle 70's.

To be strictly unemotional, I suppose it is easier, if you are going to play legless golf, to learn the game after you have lost your legs rather than to try to recapture your form having played before. Everything in golf was new to Bader. He took it as he found it, not as he remembered it.

However, he took up the game in the early 1930's when he was not the supreme master in the art of legless walking that he is today, so that he was also in the process of overcoming many purely physical problems involved in walking round a golf course. To be able to do so for 36 holes, and occasionally an extra nine after tea, is a remarkable feat in itself and, in Bader's case, is attributable to the outstandingly fine physique of what is left of him.

To play golf on artificial legs requires, above anything else, two things: balance and simplicity. If you sway back on the outside edge of the right foot, as so many of us do, you cannot heave yourself back. You go down with a clatter.

You have slightly more latitude in the forward and backward sway (i.e., towards and away from the ball), but with no toes to assist in correcting such movement, you have to be a great deal steadier on your pins even than a good professional. It is conceivable that once you have mastered it, if you ever do, this may aid you to better striking.

Years ago, I played in the winter on the Royal Eastbourne Course, where the chalky turf can become incredibly slippery in wet weather. I found I had left my golf shoes behind, so I played in perfectly smooth soles. With the steep slopes and the greasy surface, my feet were liable to fly from under me at the slightest sway, and I have often thought that these conditions must have come very close to those under which Bader has always played. At any rate, I remember I played exceptionally well, merely through having to concentrate so much on remaining upright.

This concentration leads naturally to simplicity. You cannot afford frills, twiddles and turns if at any moment you are liable to fall down. You play and strike and "think" through your hands, which, in the end, I am sure, is the way to play golf anyway. This is certainly what Bader does, and the muscles in his hands and arms, like those of the blacksmith under the village chestnut tree, resemble iron bands.

Incidentally, he uses an extra-heavy driver. This has often been a matter for argument between us, but he must certainly know best. It keeps him steady, he says. At any rate, he hits the ball, without any charitable exaggeration, at least as far as the average single-figure amateur, and often a good deal farther—a fact which gives him a great psychological advantage over his opponents. Say what you like, there is something a little deflating about being out-driven by a man with no legs.

At one stage, Bader found that he hit the ball a great deal better through the fairway when he happened to be on a slightly uphill stance, that is to say, leaning a little to the left. As a result, he had half an inch taken off one of his legs so that, in effect, he would always be playing in this way. This again led to a friendly argument, which continues to this day. He had it taken off his right leg, whereas I have always maintained that it should have come off his left. However, the proof of the pudding is in the eating.

I should add that this refers to his golfing leg and that he does not walk about permanently with one leg shorter than the other. He has various spares, which he carries about in a container which might have been made specially for them—namely, a cricket bag.

Altogether, Bader's golf does seem to bear out a basic principle in which I have always believed but which, to my surprise, is not universally accepted, namely, that your hands are the guiding factor in golf. Harry Vardon called them "the chief point of concentration." Gene Sarazen said: "The great golfer plays with his hands." Bader shows that you can play single-figure golf with your hands and without your legs. We have yet to find a man who can play with his legs but without his hands.

———1945———

FISKE MEMORIAL

A little incident at a Birmingham gun site will always stick in my memory. Twice a week two kindly ladies used to appear in a Y.M.C.A. van and hoot encouragingly at the foot of our tower—whereupon the monkeys would down tools and rush down for their bag of nuts. They sold us chocolate and cakes and razor blades and tea, and lent out books, and were a cheerful and highly acceptable link with the outside world, and I hereby pay my humble tribute to the labours of them and their kind. One day, as I sipped my tea at the counter, I noticed the crossed Union Jack and

Stars and Stripes on the side of the van. Underneath were the words , "Fiske Memorial."

Billy Fiske! My mind raced back over the years to the time when we used to travel almost daily the 21 miles from Cambridge to Mildenhall in his mostrous supercharged green Bentley, and reckon it a poor journey if we did not touch 110 miles an hour on the long straight leading to Newmarket; and to the days when his father had helped to send a team of us to play golf in the United States. Fiske had a wonderful eye for speed, and for seven years he defied all comers on the Cresta toboggan run at St. Moritz. When he was 17, he captained the American bobbing team in the Olympic Games and won. Long before the United States came into the war, Billy Fiske gave his life for this country, the first American to do so, flying a Hurricane in the Battle of Britain. Now he lies buried in a little Sussex churchyard, and a plaque in St. Paul's Cathedral commemorates our gratitude.

I wondered what crisp comment this forthright little man would have come out with, if he could have seen me drinking a penn'orth of tea from the van that kept his memory alive.

──1968──
THE LITTLE MAN IN THE TREE

One of my favourite episodes in the long history of games-playing is that of the chess maestro who played 24 games simultaneously, blind-folded—and lost them all. I am reminded of it by an Edinburgh reader who sends me news of Mr. John Swanston, a 24-handicap golfer who has been playing at the nine-hole course at Eyemouth, near Berwick, for some 53 years and in his 70th year has just, I am happy to learn, won his first competition at Dunbar, where he is also a member. This has given much local satisfaction since he has never been allowed to forget another distinction gained 30 years ago and now at last cancelled out, namely that of being possibly the world's only player to be 9 up at the ninth in the final—and beaten at the 19th.

The philosophy of total collapse in golf has always had a morbid fascination for me. A cricket side can collapse but it takes a series of individuals to cause it. A soccer team can collectively collapse and so, indeed, can a golf team. Anyone, for instance, who attended the 1957 Ryder Cup match at Lindrick could sense the rot which conveyed itself, as mysteriously but as surely as foot and mouth, from one American player to another on the afternoon of the final day—though for reasons, let it be said, not wholly their own fault.

The full agony, however, falls on the individual and there can hardly be a golfer who has not in his humble way had the mortification of seeing a winning lead crumble away a stroke or two or a hole or two at first, then the gathering momentum, the avalanche, and the dread realisation that he is doomed. Always there is a turning point when the victim, ever hard he may struggle, can do nothing right again.

How much worse when you are destined to be not merely the talk of the club but to be written about as long as golf is played; when you wake up next morning into the certainty that, now you have missed that one, you will feature in the history books as the greatest golfer of his day who never won the Open. At home Abe Mitchell, Macdonald Smith and Archie Compston come to mind; in America even the great Sam Snead, once with 5 to win, 6 to tie—took 8.

Abe Mitchell, my boyhood hero, who gave the ball such a tremendous crack with his large blacksmith arms and wrists and hands, was in the end almost too gentle to win. Mitchell and George Duncan were the Nicklaus and Palmer of their day. They toured the world together and were the greatest friends, and with Ted Ray looked like becoming the Great Triumvirate of the postwar era. It was natural that they should be staying together at Deal for the Open of 1920. This, incidentally, was Walter Hagen's first visit to England, when he finished, with difficulty, 53rd out of 54.

Though Duncan would "go mad," and often did, it is quite possible that day in and day out Mitchell was at that time the best golfer in the world. At any rate, after two rounds only Jim Barnes and Sandy Herd were within six shots of him and Duncan, with "two ridiculous 80's," was 13 behind. As the pair of them walked up the promenade that evening they encountered the four-square, patriotic figure of J. H. Taylor, already alert to the American menace to come. "We shall want all your help tomorrow," he said sternly to Mitchell.

Back at the hotel Duncan told his friend, "J. H. is right. It's your championship. Two 75's and you'll win." Whereupon Mitchell, as Duncan later recorded, "said an amazing thing—it must have been some sort of intuition. He turned slowly towards me and rather sadly observed, 'I don't know, George. Suppose you do two 69's?'"

Duncan next day was due off at 8:45 a.m., Mitchell not till nearly noon. Knowing Mitchell, Duncan made him promise not to go down to the course too early to hang about and take the edge off himself with small talk and answering silly, if well meaning, questions.

"Imagine my horror when just as I was about to drive off, I saw Abe arriving in a taxi. I felt that everything I had planned for him would be ruined, little realising that I would help to do it." After hanging about for three hours Mitchell was at last on the tee, when a huge crowd swarmed down the 18th. "Duncan has a 4 for 69," a man shouted. Poor Abe! He got onto the first green in two and putted up to within 18 inches—and then came his moment of destiny. He not only missed the putt, he hit it only six inches. To the golfing psychologist one need not tell of the inevitable succession of 5's, the eventual 8, the total of 84. And all the time Duncan, if Abe only knew it, had finished with a 6!

I do not know at what moment Macdonald Smith at Prestwick in 1925, with 78 to win and 79 to tie, realised that he was "done" and that the loyally unruly Scottish crowd were going to be their own man's downfall and batter him into an 82, but with Compston at Hoylake in 1930 the moment of fate was as clear as Abe Mitchell's. In the third round, five strokes behind Bobby Jones, he started home 3-3-3-2 and, "playing like a frenzied giant and striding after the ball as though he could not wait to vent his fury on it," broke the record with 68 to lead by one stroke. "Watching him from the clubhouse as he swept past the 16th," Jones has recorded, "I had the feeling that spectators, tee boxes, benches even, might be swirled up in his wake . . . As he made his beaming way to the clubhouse through a myriad of well-wishers, he was about as happy a figure as I have ever seen."

Jones at this moment was due out in his final round. At the second he hit a high, towering slice which struck a steward on the head and careened 50 yards off-line into a bunker by the 14th. It lay clean in the sand, from which he hit a miraculous shot to the green and sank the putt for a 3. An hour later Compston appeared on the first tee—"photographed, congratulated and apparently full of confidence, he was good humoured and laughing." Anyone who knew him can picture the scene so well, but fate, or whatever you like to call it, lay in wait to take the smile from his rugged features. The Greeks had a word for it; P. G. Wodehouse sees it as the figure lurking behind the door with a lump of wet sand in the bottom of an old stocking; Francis Ouimet always called it "The Little Man in the Tree." A few minutes later, with a 30-inch putt on the first green, Compston was "standing staring at the ball, like a man dazed, when it stayed out." Five upon 5 followed," the series of terrible 5's which bled him white in the afternoon," says one account. He finished in 82 and was never the same man again.

Both Compston and Mitchell had started late. Would they have collapsed, I wonder, if all the leaders had been bunched together at the end, as they are today? Yet when Palmer lost seven strokes on the final nine to Casper in the 1966 U.S. Open—to tie and lose on the playoff—they were playing together. Still, that was different, for Palmer lost not by collapsing, but attacking. Casper started playing safe. "That's what really got me," wrote Palmer later. "Here was a guy trying to catch me and he was the one playing safe. I said to myself, 'There is no way that man can beat me. No way,' and I sure wasn't going to let it be said, 'There goes Palmer using a one-iron to be safe with a three-stroke lead.' Wouldn't that be a ridiculous sight? I would rather lose." So he took his driver, hooked twice into the trees, and did lose.

It occurs to me to compile a golf book with a difference, full not of deeds of daring and moments of triumph but of golfers great and small in times of calamity, ridicule and distress, a kind of Anthology of Disaster. Mr. Swanston of Dunbar and his 10 holes lost in a row shall, of course, have an honoured place, but I myself can make a modest contribution—8 and 7 over 18 holes in a championship; 10 and 8 in a University foursome: 6 up at lunch in a knockout final—and beaten at the 38th!

1970
EXTRAORDINARY RELUCTANCE

Hearing a man who has only recently discovered the game of golf holding forth on the beauty of what I should have thought to be a comparatively ordinary course, I fell to marvelling at the extraordinary variety of experience offered by this singular game, and the extraordinary reluctance of the average player to take advantage of it.

Every other game is played on the same kind of pitch the world over. One football field is like another; one cricket pitch like the next, except that in one case the background may be the village chestnuts and in another the gasometers.

Yet not only is every golfing pitch different from all others, but it consists of 18 little pitches within itself. Thus an almost inexhaustible supply of golfing problems presents itself.

How strange, therefore, that men of imagination in other walks of life so lack that quality as golfers that they will cheerfully play month by month, year by year, decade by decade, over the same 18 holes.

Ten to one, too, that they play with the same people every Sunday at the same hour, make the same remarks on the first tee, and, what is more, play a four-ball. Human ingenuity could scarcely devise golf in a duller form.

Their play, too, is highly conservative. Early in life they decide that the fourth hole is an iron shot. They are persistently short for 20 years. And still it does not dawn on them to take a driver.

—1964—
AGENCY OUTSIDE THE MATCH

The faintly embarrassing revelation in his speech at the prize-giving that on the previous evening he had "got down on his knees and prayed" showed the new British Open champion, Tony Lema, in a hitherto unsuspected light and raises a subject which must inspire in golfers a profound and, I trust, respectful interest. The possibilities it evokes are almost limitless.

The current U.S. Open champion, Ken Venturi, said after his victory a month ago that he owed much to a long letter from his local priest, telling him among other things, "If he asked the Lord for anything, to ask only for the faith and strength to play to the best of his ability."

Another American, Jack Fleck, who tied for the U.S. Open in 1955 with a rush of birdies at the end, when Hogan had already been acclaimed as the winner, and then beat the great man by three shots in a man-to-man playoff, also revealed later, in one of the magazines sponsored by that prolific evangelist, Dr. Norman Vincent Peale, that he had "conquered his inner self through prayer."

His wife, it appeared, had given him Mario Lanza's record "I'll Walk with God," and he "played it during the tournament whenever he needed strength"—though not, presumably, while actually on the course. We may infer that during the ensuing 12 months the record became somewhat worn, as in the next year's championship Fleck failed to qualify for the final day.

This unburdening of the heart by one of America's most respected professional golfers led to a similar reaction by an equally well-known amateur, Dick Chapman, who has won the Amateur championships on both sides of the Atlantic. His account of his experience appeared some years ago in the American weekly *Golf World*, and as a contribution to current discussion deserves a wider public.

Chapman's experience, which occurred in the final of the 1949 Canadian Amateur championship, may be briefly summarized. In the afternoon he found himself 5 down with 8 to play against the Canadian Phil Farley, who, having been in the final four times unsuccessfully before, was at least as anxious to win as his opponent.

"The oppressive heat and humidity," wrote Chapman, "were sucking my waning strength and concentration. Bad judgment and poor shots during the finishing holes were defeating me." He therefore resorted to a constant repetition of the Lord's Prayer. Whereupon—and to whom has this not at some time happened?—the small voice of conscience said, "If this means so much to you, you should make sacrifice in return."

Golf being the game it is, the elimination of bad language and profanity came at once to mind and the silent promise was accordingly made. "It has proved," he admitted, "very testing on many occasions since."

The promise having been recorded, so to speak, in the minutes, Chapman won three of the next six holes with birdies and was 2 down with two to play. His opponent duly obliged with three putts on the next, and on the final hole, 225 yards against the wind, Chapman hit a 1-iron to within a few feet of the green. Farley's 4-wood faded satisfactorily towards the out-of-bounds on the right, only to hit a spectator on the head and bounce back into a bunker, whence he put it 15 feet from the hole. Chapman pitched within three feet, Farley was one inch short with his putt—leaving Chapman, with what thoughts we may only surmise, an almost complete stymie.

"During the play of these last eight holes," he wrote, "I kept repeating the Lord's Prayer to myself. While looking at this apparently impossible situation, I observed the grain was left to right and that a cup putt might curve sharply round my opponent's ball into the cup, which is exactly what happened, to the astonishment of all."

At long last Chapman put another 1-iron three feet from the par-five 38th hole to win with an eagle 3. "Prayer had given me the strength, concentration and confidence necessary to perform a seemingly impossible task."

The story is not, however, over. A dedicated golfer if ever there was one, Chapman moved straight down from New Brunswick to the New England Championship where he was left to get down in two from just off the last green to win the qualifying medal. He took four more and failed even to tie. His reaction, it has to be confessed, was precisely that of the hero of

P. G. Wodehouse's classic, "Chester Forgets Himself."

"***!!!***!!!" he said, and more besides.

Suddenly the flow was interrupted by the reflection of a coin which someone had dropped on the ground. He bent to pick it up and there on the back of the coin was written—no, no, wait for it!—the Lord's Prayer. The inscription on the other side showed that it had belonged to a stunt driver. Chapman carried it with him thereafter, including during his Amateur victory here in 1951 at Porthcawl, as an "impressive reminder of his part of the bargain."

Well, there we are. Theologians will be able, I am sure, to instruct us on their aspect of the matter and I shall not seek to anticipate their findings. The man I am really sorry for is Farley. Five up with eight to play, he could have won peacefully by 7 and 6, had he only thought to invoke the aid of Rule 9(1)—the one about "accepting advice or suggestion from an agency outside the match." Penalty in match play—loss of hole.

1965

ADMIRAL BENSON
SAILS THE LINKS

If ever there were an argument for the theory that golf is a much simpler game than most people make it out to be, it exists in the person of Admiral Benson. Let us consider first the nature of his achievement in the May meeting of the Royal and Ancient Club at St. Andrews. The Old Course was playing extremely long—or so I thought, though this may of course be due to advancing years, lack of winter practise or what have you. At any rate, I do not remember seeing anyone get over the Burn at the first hole in 2, though I dare say some of them did. For me the strict par of the first five holes was 5-5-4-5-5—and then I am flattering myself that I could have reached the fifth in 3. The wind was strongly against for the first nine and got colder as the day wore on, and play was by threes, which meant that you were very lucky if you were on the course for less than 3¾ hours. In the best of the weather a distinguished international player, some 20 years younger than the Admiral, took 91.

Against this background Admiral Benson's gross 88 at the age of 81 becomes, in my opinion, a truly remarkable score, more especially when you think that he carried his own clubs. As he has recently been elected Captain of the Seniors, he is entitled to regard this as his "finest hour," or, perhaps one should say, his vintage year. I should add that last year, at the age of 80, he had his handicap reduced—from 17 to 16.

He carries six clubs, five of them in a patent contraption manufactured in 1893. This is made of wooden struts, with a canvas container at the bottom and a series of metal clips at the top, into which fit the shafts of the clubs. You set it down vertically on the fairway, raising the handle as you do so, whereupon a pair of wooden "legs" for it to stand on emerge from the front part. The sixth club, an enormous square wooden putter, is housed—since the bag was made at a time when it was not thought necessary for a gentleman to carry more than five clubs—in a special plastic container at the side. The other five consist of an orthodox driver, a wooden cleek, a short spoon, a kind of deep-faced mashie and an implement known as a "skibo," which is akin to a mashie-niblick or 8-iron. The wooden cleek is a beautiful club and has the shallow face which I have always maintained that wooden clubs should have in this country and did often have before manufacturers, not appreciating that conditions are so different in the two countries, began making wooden-club play more difficult by imitating American designs. All the Admiral's clubs, with the exception, I fancy, of the putter, have steel shafts. One feels really that, to complete the picture, they ought to be hickory.

At any rate, it was carrying this battery of half a dozen elementary clubs that he went round in 88, without a single 6 on the card coming home, and this brings me back to my original point of "simple golf." How does he do it? A friend gave the explanation, "Oh, I think he just 'sets a course' and continues to sail on it till he gets to the 18th," and perhaps this is as good an explanation as any. Whether he was a great "theoriser" in his earlier golfing days I do not know, but I have had the pleasure of playing with him at St. Andrews within the past year or two and it seems to me that he has few theories now. He has reduced the game to taking the club in two hands and making the same straightforward movement at the ball. In fact, though I am sure he makes no conscious effort in this direction, he has a "grooved" swing or, as they put it in America, a swing that "repeats."

I may of course be doing the Admiral an injustice, and perhaps he is in fact "thinking" all the time. At any rate, in answer to the question "How does he do it?" I should myself try gradually to gravitate to as simple a method as possible and to settle into a sort of drill, as Bobby Locke has always done, whereby one goes up to the ball, sets the machine in motion and carries out the same set of movements, time after time after time. I should read no more books, listen to no more tips and short cuts. By that time of life one ought to know that there aren't any.

Admitting that "fewer clubs" is a hobby horse of mine, I still think that the fact that the Admiral can go round in 88 from the medal tees on a really difficult day with only six does prove the point—if proof were needed. Would he have done better with seven? I wish I had remembered to ask him. Or with 14, or even with 16, which manufacturers in America are constantly urging as the maximum? I think I know without asking what his answer to that one would have been!

How absurd it has all become, when you come to think of it. Some of the bags wheeled round in a perambulator by, or carried on behalf of, competitors in the medal at St. Andrews were such a weight that one could hardly lift them and to hold them out at arm's length would have taken a professional weight lifter. Yet a whole "set" of 14 clubs does not weigh a stone [14 pounds]. The Admiral's entire set, together with bag, weighs, I should estimate, less than 10 pounds. Some of the bags I tried to lift, judging by memories of "full marching order" at 60 pounds, must have weighed 70.

The owners of some of this ironmongery and ancillary equipment took, many of them, 90 and 100 to get round. And the Admiral, carrying the whole damn lot in one hand at the "trail arms" position, got round in 88. If that does not make them think, nothing will. And I suppose the answer is just that. Nothing will.

—1977—
A GOLFER'S BEST FRIEND IS HIS DOG

The get-something-for-nothing experience in golf has intrigued me ever since I first saw it as a boy. This is the finding, or retrieving, of golf balls by dogs. Writing from the other side of the Atlantic, I wonder whether it is as common in the United States as it is in dog-ridden Britain and whether any American dogs have proved as profitable to their owners as some I have known over here.

Take, for instance, Dai Rees, 1957 Ryder Cup captain and three times runner-up in the British Open. Having been driver for General Montgomery when the latter accepted the German surrender at Luneburg Heath, Rees came back to his home club at Hindhead, England, to find the rough waist-high, a ball two yards off the fairway lost for a certainty, and balls as scarce as doubtless they were at that time in America.

An advertisement in the local paper brought him about 100 battered balls, which he and his wife duly scrubbed and repainted. These were soon lost, but Dai had an Alsatian called Rex. "In one night's hunting and sniffing," he later recalled, "Rex found 238 balls. The same balls returned over and over again to be scrubbed and repainted. One had a distinctive blue circle on it and could not be mistaken. Rex retrieved it 32 times."

How do they do it? By scent, one naturally supposes, and, knowing the tremendous keenness of so many American sportsmen on hunting with the aid of bird dogs, mostly pointers, which always point upwind, I suppose they would agree. And yet . . . I remember, years ago, walking around with the club professional and his ball-detecting spaniel. Suddenly the dog started digging feverishly in the accumulated leaf mould at the base of a boundary hedge and after excavating a hole nearly a foot deep, unearthed a ball—of a make that had not been manufactured for 20 years. Some of our older readers may even remember the name. It was the Chemico Bob, and what a splendid name for a golf ball.

This ball surely could not have lain for all that time exuding sufficient scent for a dog to detect it under a foot of leaf mould? All I could get out of the local veterinary surgeon some years later was that scent is a "curious thing." He thought it might lie in layers, since often, when fox hunting, he on his horse could scent a fox when hounds on the ground could not.

In a recent clubhouse argument on this topic a neighbour of mine credited his own Jack Russell terrier, which has been finding an average of 18 balls per round for several years, with one record day of 32. "This dog," he said, "normally appears to detect by scent, but there are some things that cannot be so explained. More than once I have seen him jump into a ditch containing a foot or so of dirty water and emerge immediately with a ball which, from the state of his nose, has clearly been dug out of the muddy bottom. Often he has been seen to drop a ball which he has been bringing me, dive several yards into thick bushes and come out with another ball. Normally, of course, he would not drop a ball he was bringing in, yet in every case the position of the second ball has been such that it would seem impossible for him to have detected it by smell or sight from where the first ball was dropped."

So much, it seems, for the scent theory. Can it therefore be some sort of detection by instinct, as with some people who can detect unerringly that there is a cat in the room, even if it is not in sight?

At a golf club a drive and a pitch, so to speak, from where I live, I remember watching the professional train an exuberant spaniel puppy in only about a fortnight and he found 4,000 balls the next two years. A friend of mine in the Channel Islands reckons that her poodle has found 12,000 to 15,000 balls in 10 years. Another neighbour swears that her spaniel not only detects balls in the bushes and trees high above its head but, when out in the car, gets wildly excited if they so much as pass a golf course. It is a sobering thought that we golfers should emit so powerful a scent as all that.

—1958—
THINKING OF SARAZEN

Gene Sarazen was the simplest golfer I ever saw. He stood with both feet rooted to the ground, grasped the club firmly in both hands with a couple of inches of shaft showing at the top, and gave the ball a tremendous, elementary thump. When I get fouled up in the mechanics of the game, which is more often than not these days, I can still produce a series of reasonable shots by forgetting the theories and imagining that I am Gene Sarazen.

—1967—
FLAT OUT FOR CHAMPIONS

Two of the world's greatest experts, each from his own side of the fence, having recently given their views on the subject, brings me to the question of the ideal championship course, and, if there is such a thing, could you and I play on it with any degree of pleasure, too?

The experts in question are Arnold Palmer, writing in the American magazine *Esquire*, and Robert Trent Jones, who has set out his ideas in the *Golf Journal* by the USGA. Mr. Jones, a native of Ince, near Liverpool, from which he was withdrawn at an early age to the New World, is probably the world's most prolific golf architect, simultaneously designing from his drawing board in New York courses as far apart as Spain and Hawaii.

Each seems to think it possible to extend the champions on courses which would still give pleasure to the club player, but, after seeing so many players make nonsense of the last two par-5 holes at Royal Birkdale, I begin to wonder. The operative word is "extend." Hitting the ball flat out is one of the joys of golf and the champions should not, in my opinion, be deprived of it.

If, however, they reach holes of 513 and 510 yards nonchalantly with a 5-iron, or even less, it is clear that nothing short of 800 yards will give them our own equivalent of a long hole—the kind of which the caddie observed, "It'll take three dam' good shots to get up in two today, sir." I wonder, for instance, how many times Jack Nicklaus in a whole year of tournament golf needs to take a brassie for his second? Half a dozen? I doubt it.

Palmer's ideal course is long, 7,080 yards in fact, because golfers today learn to hit hard and long before they learn any other aspect of the game. Like most people's ideal course it has four short holes, 10 par-4's and four par-5's—"long and lean," physically reachable in two but with so narrow a target as to make it not worthwhile going for the green.

I was brought up on the theory that the size of the green should vary in proportion with the length of shot with which you approach it. An example is the eighth hole at Pine Valley, where the second shot is no more than an 80-yard pitch. The green, as you play this little shot to it, seems to shrink to a tiny, microscopic hump surrounded entirely by sand and I remember being told how Roger Wethered—I hope I do him no injustice—plied his way to and fro for an 11.

Current American practise, as exemplified both in Palmer's perfect course and those which I have seen of Trent Jones's, is to make very big, undulating greens, each with anything up to five pin positions, some of them fantastically difficult, so that you are either hoping to get down in one putt or trying to avoid taking three. I was about to write how little this appealed to me by comparison with simply adjusting the size of the target, when I realised that it is the crafty pin positions which "make" the Old Course at St. Andrews.

"Rough," says Trent Jones, "will be very much a part of the penalty for misplaced shots in the Open Championship." This is certainly the policy of the USGA, who, two or three years beforehand, decide upon the precise height and extent of the long grass and often end up by leaving many of the competitors howling for mercy.

"There is no rough," says Palmer, on the other hand. "The grass off the fairways, instead of receiving the care of the green-keeper, will be allowed to grow, but not to a height which would interfere with play. I've long felt that high rough is unfair because it does not collect the same penalty from each man." He has, instead, trees, short and tall, dense and thin, and most of the rest of the trouble can be solved with "a good shot, or educated gambling."

Palmer's views on bunkers are novel and, as it seems to me, intelligent. His fairway bunkers—which do not worry the club golfer since he simply does not reach them—are shallow, with lips only about three feet high, so as to allow a long iron, perfectly hit, to carry out of the bunker and reach the green. Round the green, however, he uses "Scottish" traps (an expression new to me, this), from which the ball "must be struck so that it gets airborne quickly and only the sense of feel of the great trap shot will enable a player to get his ball close to the pin, since its point of landing almost surely will be out of his sight."

Though one can think of many historic water hazards in this country, they tend to be the exception, whereas, in American country club golf, ponds, lakes or creeks are almost the rule. Palmer's course has plenty of water and most of it, I notice, is on the right. Trent Jones is kinder-hearted, putting them chiefly on the left. He is a slicer, too!

As golf balls, according to the makers' advertisements, go farther and farther and Nicklaus reduces the great Augusta National to a drive and a pitch, I envisage eventually a "world-championship course" to end all championship courses, probably in the Californian so-called desert.

This course will be 15,000 yards long, so designed as to be capable of indefinite extension to accommodate later increases in the length of the ball, and the par-5 holes will measure 900-1,000 yards, thus giving Nicklaus the unparalleled experience of taking a long iron for his third.

The players will ride round in atomically propelled carts and alongside each hole I see a continuous moving pavement for the spectators, who will be able to step off from time to time for refreshment, or even, by missing the play at two or three holes, to take in a movie.

The press, it need hardly be said, will follow by helicopter, complete with bar.

━1961━
SERGEANT MAJOR SHERIDAN

The committee of the Sunningdale Golf Club in 1955 conferred upon a singular man a singular honour, unique so far as I know in the history of golf. They summoned their caddiemaster, Sheridan, and, handing him a club tie, declared him an honorary member. In thanking them he remarked quite irrelevantly but, as all who have known him will testify, with perfect truth, "Ah, well, I've been making my own rules and regulations around here for 45 years now."

Sheridan started at Sunningdale as a young fellow in his early 20's and grew rapidly into an institution. He came from the neighbourhood of North Berwick and his accent, despite nearly half a century amid the sophistication of Ascot, continues uncompromisingly to proclaim the fact.

The number of people who have waited in his little office, scanning surreptitiously the highly coloured and provocative picture postcards with which the walls are decorated, while Sheridan explains that there isn't a caddie and how anyone at that hour of the day could ever have expected that there would be defies his comprehension, must now run into thousands. They included for many years the Duke of Windsor, than whom no one, I am sure, will hail the honour done to Sheridan with greater acclaim.

As a "character" Sheridan has accumulated around him over the years a crop of stories, many unprintable, mostly apocryphal, which invited instinctive comparison with an equally outspoken Scot, the late Andra' Kirkaldy.

One of the oldest golfing stories is of the nouveaux riches who drive up to the club and inquire of the most influential member whether he is the caddiemaster. "No," is the reply," but I happen to know that he does not require any caddies today." It used to be told of "Pa" Jackson at Stoke Poges and "Aber" (J. F. Abercromby) at Addington and doubtless of many others. If it ever did really happen, I am sure it was Sheridan.

Nevertheless, his bark is worse than his bite. No club has more teenage caddies than Sunningdale and no one does more to help them start their golf than Sheridan. The Sergeant Major Brittain of the caddie world, he first frightens the life out of them, then presents them with an old set of clubs to start upon. He helps to set them up in permanent jobs and, when times are hard, he buttonholes the members on their behalf with, "Come on, I want a quid out of you!'' It is a bold man who does not reach at once for his wallet.

Mr. Brittain was a Regimental Sergeant Major in the Guards with a stupendous voice and a national reputation, who even played the part of himself in a film comedy. Officer cadets lived in great fear of him. "I call you Sir and you call me Sir," he used to tell them. "The only difference is that you mean it."

Sheridan's assurance that no caddie is available has, for the 27 years I have known the club, been instant and automatic. Once this preliminary gambit is over, it becomes a war of nerves. Weaker brethren go off muttering, carrying their clubs or fixing up a trolley. The stronger-minded leave their clubs leaning against the office and without further comment retire to the clubhouse, peering out from time to time to note that they are still there, unattended and ignored.

As the crisis nears, only those with years of experience have the nerve to make the correct move, which is to march out of the clubhouse and, turning the head neither to the right nor to the left, to proceed through the little iron gate, passing within two feet of the clubs, and thence, without a single backward glance, to the first tee. From here an occasional apprehensive glance may go undetected, but the master hand does not descend to it. He remains with his back to the office, facing nonchalantly up the first fairway. Meanwhile, the party in front have driven off and departed. One's partner and opponents have all got caddies and one of them has actually teed his ball. This is the acid test. Survive it—and you've won. All the same, as the Duke said, it was a damned close-run thing.

1966

THREE PENN'ORTH OF BARD

"Probably no one, not even the Bishop of St. Andrews, has ever yet surmised that Shakespeare was a golfer! Proof, however, is abundant that he was not only a distinguished player acquainted with all the hazards of the game, but that he knew every peculiarity of the St. Andrews links." Such is an extract from the preface to *Shakespeare on Golf*, 24 pages, published in 1887 by David Douglas, of 15a Castle Street, Edinburgh.

For myself, I am not so well acquainted as I ought to be with the writings of the Bard, whether on golf or other matters. I know, of course, of the Bishop (not, I think, of St. Andrews), having taken a gigantic divot, incanting, "O, pardon me, thou bleeding piece of earth," and I recall Richard III's "Put in their hands the bruising irons of wrath", and King John's more simple "Give me the iron, I say," but the thought that there may still exist 24 pages of Shakespeare on golf, and particularly on the Old Course at St. Andrews, is fascinating indeed.

Is it too much to hope that some reader of these notes may yet unearth a copy for me to pass on for our common enlightenment? I still await that copy, but other memorable golfing passages have in the meantime come to light. Our feelings towards the people behind, who press upon us and eventually have to be let through, could scarcely be better expressed than by, "Sweep on, you fat and greasy citizens!" from "As You Like It." Falstaff's "Three misbegotten knaves in Kendal green came at my back and let drive at me" (compare Chaucer's "Four rogues in buckram let fly at me") will also strike a chord. Again we are always told, and truthfully enough, that no man can succeed at golf until he has mastered the art of not permitting one bad hole, or indeed one bad shot, to affect the rest of his game. The following, from "Othello," put it better perhaps than it has ever been put before, and should be learnt by heart by all aspiring young golfers: "To mourn a mischief that is past and gone/Is the next way to draw new mischief on."

The details of the book in question came from an advertisement at the back of another little book published by David Douglas, called *Reminiscences of Golf on St. Andrews Links*, by James Balfour, who could at that time look back on 45 years' membership of the club.

Some of his experiences in the club gold medal were a little unfortunate. In 1863 he seemed a certain winner. Only Robert Clark (author of the first anthology, *Golf, a Royal and Ancient Game*, in 1875) had a chance, and he was in the neighbourhood of the road at the 18th with a single shot in hand to tie. He played a long shot with his cleek and not only holed out but won the playoff.

In another year Balfour tied with James Ogilvie Fairlie, only to have his opponent play, and win, the entire playoff without speaking.

It was also at St. Andrews, surely, that Bobby Jones relates having played with Harry Vardon in one of his more contemplative moods when, as he remembers, the great man uttered only once. "Did you ever see a worse shot than that?" cried the youthful Bobby. "No," said Vardon.

I am grateful not only to the correspondent who sent me the book but also to another who, by coincidence, lent me on almost the same day *Some Short Stories and Sketches* (1898), by Lord

Moncrieff of Tulliebole, two stories of which relate to golf.

If I delight in delving into the past, it is not, I like to think because my mind dwells permanently therein, but because it proves that, despite the 7,000-yard hand-manicured courses, the gin palaces and the electric carts deemed necessary today, the original simple thrill of propelling a ball from one hole to another and, especially, the foibles, failings and inner feelings of the golfers have remained unaltered through the years.

The scene is St. Andrews and one partner in a foursome has just lit a cigar and is walking along contentedly smoking it and admiring the scenery. In what year would you say that the following was written?

"This is a fatal sign. When a man smokes, he is either winning very easily or has given up all hope; when a man draws the attention of his companions to lights and shades, and the beauty of the scenery generally, it is tantamount to his saying 'as mere exercise this is a very pleasant and healthy occupation—plenty of fresh air, a charming day, and St. Andrews looks very well from here; but as to its being golf, to play with a fellow who puts you into a whin or a bunker every other stroke . . . .' " The answer is 1867.

Our manners on the course seem on the whole to have improved, if only for the more painful consequences of being struck by the modern ball. It is still true that golfers will "growl and murmur if they are kept an instant waiting by the party in front and remonstrate indignantly, nay even furiously, if a ball from the party behind comes anywhere near them," but at St. Andrews they cheerfully drove into the people in front, directly they had played their seconds, to "touch them up."

"Oh, let them out a bit, poor devils," one character is recorded as saying, "as though they were cheeping partridges and would not be fit for the table if taken too close." However, the author adds, "The most refined and effective form of cruelty is not to hit the party in front, but to keep dropping balls just behind them from a long distance. The effort on the nerves of a ball landing behind you with a thud after a flight of 150 yards, just as you are addressing your ball, will be readily understood by anyone who has endured this persecution." It will indeed!

One thing is certain. We are more democratic in our golf. "To St. Andrews," Lord Moncrieff declares, "where we breathe an atmosphere of pure golf, there comes occasionally some darkened man, to whom the game is unknown. If he is a distinguished stranger, pains are usually taken to enlighten him . . . If he is an undistinguished stranger, he is, of course, tabooed at once and handed over to croquet and the ladies, if they will have him."

We are kinder, too, to the ladies—though hardly an inch has

been yielded without a struggle. At St. Andrews they used to have a little course of their own, with drives limited to 70 or 80 yards—not because their ability to hit farther was doubted but because they could hardly do so without the unseemly gesture of raising the club above the shoulder. As to the real course, "If they choose to play at times when the male golfers are feeding or resting, no one can object."

As spectators they were regarded as the most frightful nuisance. "If they could abstain from talking while you are playing, and if the shadow of their dresses would not flicker on the putting green while you are holing out, other objections might perhaps be waived."

One man actually brought his wife to score for him three days running. His outraged opponent had the last word. "Yes, my good fellow," he said, "but suppose we both did it."

—1953—
TEMPTING THE FATES

Max Faulkner won the Open at Portrush and, as an inveterate toucher of wood and non-tempter of fate, I can still hardly believe that the gods of golf allowed him to do so. At the end of the second day he was two or three shots ahead of the field and I can see him now, surrounded by a bevy of schoolboys and young ladies in search of his autograph.

"Open Champion, 1951," he wrote—with two rounds to go. Someone asked him about his "pencil-gripped" putter, which had received a good deal of notice. "Oh," he said, stretching his hands four feet apart like a fisherman describing the one that got away, "I shall never miss another of those."

I moved silently away lest fate mistake me for an accomplice and in some way give me the hammer, too. Nevertheless, he went on cheerfully to win by two strokes.

1962
A BUNCH OF LOUSY GOLFERS

I was sorry, indeed, on returning from America in September, to find that Archie Compston had died. I remember my first meeting with him as though it were yesterday. Cambridge University, of which I had at that time the honour to be captain, had gone to play a Sunday match against Coombe Hill and had been duly defeated. A tall, dominating and extremely handsome figure, he was sitting in the fender in front of the fire. "You're just a bunch of lousy golfers," he said (he pronounced it "goffers"). "I could beat any three of you."

Feeling that this could hardly be allowed to pass, N.A. Keith, W.H. Bermingham and I took him on. I thought we were on to a good thing and wagered accordingly, but the result came under the heading of "Learning the Lessons of Life the Hard Way." Archie saw to it that we went off the farthest back tees and there were six holes which, in winter, we could not reach in two and which he could and did. He holed the course in 68 and beat us on the last green, and I had to sell my motor car.

Gambling was high at Coombe Hill in those days and Archie, who could survey the course on any given day and be certain within a stroke or so of how many he would take to get round, reckoned to make anything up to a couple of thousand pounds a year—equal to at least five today—from betting on his own matches.

The income tax people tried to tax him on it but he retorted that it was his own money and they wouldn't think of paying him if he lost. He took them to court and, to the general delight, won the match.

Later I rashly remarked in his hearing at Coombe Hill that I would give a fiver to anyone who could show me how to hook instead of slice. He hauled me straight out in rain and semi-darkness to his teaching hut and within minutes had me hooking them round my neck into the gorse. His terms were cash on the nail, he said—and I hope he paid tax on it.

Archie was then at the height of his powers. Two years previously in a 72-hole match against Walter Hagen he had pulverised that great player into a humiliating defeat by 18 and 17. Hagen, I fancy, did not care what happened on the second day, but he certainly did not mean to be 14 down at the end of the first.

Within months of my first meeting him, however, Archie Compston was to suffer an experience which, I always think, prevented him from achieving the heights of which he was so obviously capable. In the third round of the 1930 Open at Hoylake a brilliant 68 had gained him six shots on Bobby Jones and he now led him, and the field, by a stroke. In the afternoon, disaster followed disaster and he took 82. It left its mark on him and he never looked like winning the Open again.

Archie was blunt, direct and forthright in both his ideas and his speech, and on occasion tactless and even rude. When some inoffensive club golfer came to him for a lesson, he was liable to gaze down from his great height at the man's club and yell to his clubmaker in the next room, "George, show this gentleman a proper set of golf clubs!"

If you survived the initial exchanges, however, and told him not to talk nonsense but to get on with the job, he would throw his head back and roar with laughter, and you soon realised that under the rugged exterior he was just a great big, gentle, genial giant. He was the most inspiring teacher-cum-taskmaster I ever knew and I am sure that Pam Barton, who won the British and U.S. championships in the same year but was killed, alas, during service in the war, would have said the same.

I would give much to have been present when he was giving a lesson at the Mid-Ocean Club in Bermuda to Virginia, the then Marchioness of Northampton. So exasperated did she become with him that eventually she "did" him on the shin with the sharp edge of an 8-iron. "What did he do?" I asked. "He bellowed and said to me 'Now you hit a golf ball,'" she said.

I was, however, present on the occasion, later preserved for posterity in a drawing by Mel in *The Tatler*, when a rather officious little man with eye glass, long plus-fours and a squared-off sort of close haircut was holding forth to the company. Archie, about twice his height, rubbed the palm of his hand up and down on his head and in his booming voice said, "Gee, what a lie for a brassie."

On another occasion, having missed a short putt in a tournament before the war at North Manchester, he overheard a boy sitting at the edge of the green saying "Cor, do better myself!" Whereupon he strode over, yanked the wretched boy to his feet, paraded him onto the green, set down the ball, handed him the club and told him to get on with it. To his eternal credit the boy holed out—and no one laughed more loudly than Archie.

He was among the first of the "showman golfers." Women loved or loathed him—the former in the vast majority—and followed him round in flocks, but he never married. A lonely and, when you knew him, lovable man—ever searching for something he never quite found.

BABE ZAHARIAS

"All my life I have always had the urge to do things better than anybody else." So says that remarkable person, Mrs. Mildred (Babe) Zaharias. As a result of this urge she became what must surely be the outstanding woman athlete in recorded history. At the height of her powers she was stricken, in 1953, with cancer, underwent a major operation, finished third in the All-American women's golf tournament 3½ months later, to the astonishment of the medical profession, and in the meantime recorded on a tape machine the most uninhibited and completely self-revealing autobiography I have read for many a year.

Her parents were Norwegian and their name was Didrikson. The father, leaving home at the age of 9, spent his early life in sailing ships, among other adventures being wrecked off Cape Horn and clinging for some hours to the rigging with one hand while supporting another man with the other. The mother, when young, was the finest skater and skier in the district and, with a pair of skis made out of barrel staves, would "go like the wind from where she lived down into the city."

They emigrated to Texas at the turn of the century, but in the early days, with seven children, it was hard to make the money go round. "Never mind," said Didrikson, setting up a home-made gymnasium in the backyard, "we'll build good bodies for them." The baby of the family, in addition to keeping up with her brothers in the gymnasium, hurdled to and fro over the seven hedges between home and the grocery store.

She tells of her athletic triumphs naturally and without a trace of false modesty, and really they are fantastic. In the National Club Championship meeting at Chicago in 1932, several events of which were Olympic trials, some of the women's clubs had more than 20 representatives for the 10 events. Babe Didrikson represented her club alone:

"For two and a half hours I was flying all over the place. I'd run a heat in the 80-metre hurdles, and then I'd take one of my high jumps; then I'd go over to the broad jump and take a turn at that; then they'd be calling for me to throw the javelin or put the eight-pound shot." The net result of this feverish afternoon was that of the seven events for which she entered she won five, tied for a sixth, and was placed in the seventh. She won the club championship single-handedly with 30 points, the next best club gaining 22 points—with 22 runners.

Later, in the Los Angeles Olympics, entering for the maximum of three events, she set two world records—143 feet 4 inches for the javelin, 11.7 seconds for the 80-metre hurdles—and tied for a third, 5 feet 5 inches for the high jump.

When she took to golf she mastered it more quickly and more completely than a woman had done before or is likely to do again. It is not, I am sure, unkind to say that her outlook of the game and our own were some distance apart. She was not a connoisseur of golf, she was a competitor. She practised till "there was tape all over my hand and blood all over the tape."

To us in Britain there is a special interest in her trip to Gullane just after the war, when she made the Women's Championship her 15th tournament victory in a row. We know what impact she made on us.

It is intriguing now to find how curious was the impact we made on her—the almost complete silence of the galleries, which she later realised to be due not to hostility but to politeness; the venerable nature of her caddie who "looked about 80"; the capriciousness of the weather, which changed from summer to winter in a single day; the people on bicycles with the "clips on their pants' legs"; the tank traps in the rough and the sheep on the greens; the two little old Scotsmen who followed her for every hole "with their heads close together, gabbing and gabbing, and those kilts bobbing up and down"; and finally, it is nice to be able to record the manifold kindnesses and welcome which she received from the people of Gullane.

She called her book *This Life I've Led* and, although she took the knocks and disappointments inseparable from life in the limelight, in the whole of her story there is no trace of malice or resentment towards anyone. As she lay once again in the John Sealy Hospital in Galveston, Tex., it may have been some solace to her to reflect that her life story, and in particular the concluding chapters, earned her admiration all over the world.

1975
IT'S GETTING TOO COSTLY TO REMAIN AN AMATEUR

We look forward in Britain to welcoming yet another U.S. Walker Cup team to where many of us think this event should always be held, namely St. Andrews. Many who are seeing the Old Course for the first time may be forgiven for suspecting that those of us who deem it the greatest in the world are better qualified for the lunatic asylum. Our visitors may or may not have time to get the message. When that great and gentle man, Francis Ouimet, captained an American team at St. Andrews, all the players some years his junior, he briefed each to say, when asked an opinion of the course, "I'm mad about it."

The Walker Cup, though it cuts comparatively little ice with the golfing public in America, has long been a sort of Holy Grail in British golf. It is remarkable not so much that we have only won it twice but, considering the apparently inexhaustible supply of brilliant, young "unknown" amateurs in America, that we should ever have won it at all.

Nevertheless, the interest is not quite what it was, not through anyone's fault but through irresistible changes in the cost of playing golf as a top amateur and the potentially super-colossal rewards of playing it as a top pro. It may be said of the professional ranks, of course, that many are called but precious few are chosen. True, but a young man may be forgiven for likening professional golf to a lottery. You probably won't win the jackpot, but the only certain way of not doing so is not to enter. So they take their chance, and many fall by the wayside.

Thus the Walker Cup amateurs of today tend to be mostly what some bright American writer, to whom I would lift my hat if I knew who he was, described as "pre-pros," so that you may be sure that half the team you are seeing this year will have taken the plunge by the time the match comes round again.

Is it worthwhile, then, continuing the Walker Cup? Yes, certainly, say I. And even more so the Ryder Cup for the professionals, but with one difference. I should like to see the captains, instead of juggling the order, play their teams in order of merit. So that when the child asks, "What was the greatest thing you ever did in golf, Grandpapa?" the reply will not be, "In 1980 I won 8,796,360 dollars and 40 cents," but "My boy, I once played No.1 for my country."

To reach the top as an amateur—a legitimate enough ambition, surely, for any young man—you have to play a vast amount of golf and therefore spend a vast amount of money, which practically no one of that age has. The most worthy attempts have been made by the governing bodies to keep amateur golf "simon pure," but this has now become, like the conjuror's final trick, not only extremely difficult but actually impossible. Young fellows simply haven't the money.

Fortunately, the solution is simple and, though many may claim to have thought of it for themselves, it was in fact the poet Shakespeare who thought of it first, some 300-odd years ago. "All the world's a stage," he wrote, "and all the men and women merely players." Except, he might have added, those who actually belong to the PGA.

So I think that in the end something like a middle category of "player" is bound to come, something between amateur and pro, and, one would hope, limited to a certain age, like 25. I should include in this category all the college players who have golf scholarships. In fact, just the other day, no fewer than 94 of the leading women amateurs of Britain and Europe came out in favour of such a concept.

Their plan provides a good example of what might eventually become common ground for younger members of both sexes on both sides of the Atlantic. Mrs. Angela Bonallack, who has played in six Curtis Cup matches, is leading a drive for women's open golf. She recently returned for a spell of competitive play. "I was shocked by the expense of everything," she said. "Doing a tournament on a shoestring now costs as much as it did five years ago to play in style with a caddie and the best hotels everywhere."

After struggling to reach Curtis Cup rank, the girls can just no longer stay in the game; all they can do after reaching the top is get married and have babies (Mrs. B has four). So the women want open golf with prize money instead of cut glass or silverware or suitcases. They advocate sponsorship of players and low-cost tournaments with the equivalent of $500 or $600 for the winner.

Not all promising young golfers aspire to be pros, but if they are to continue to exercise their talents they must have either a legalised sugar daddy or modest-money tournaments or both.

It is grotesque to expect a young golfer living in, say, Seattle to be well enough off in his own right not only to reach the top but then to attend amateur championships in New York. His present alternative is either to abandon his legitimate ambition or become surreptitiously subsidised.

The "player" category, not totally amateur nor totally professional, with age limit of, say, 25, would make an honest man of him and certainly do no harm to the game. The time must surely come when golfers, as in other games today, can declare themselves merely players. A shock to us traditionalists maybe, but perhaps the sooner the better.

—1960—
SEVEN CLUBS ARE ENOUGH

Chick Evans, naturally enough, is one of the old school. He thinks that the number of clubs that people carry today is quite ridiculous—and so, of course, it is, but club manufacturers, like golf correspondents, have got to live. When Chick beat Bobby Jones at the 36th hole in the Western Amateur in 1920, Jones carried 22 clubs against Chick's seven!

This reminds me of a story told me by the professional at Buffalo, N.Y., when the Curtis Cup match was being played there some years ago. It appeared that they had some championship in which Chick Evans had been playing some time previously. When I remarked on some vast cabin-trunk bags belonging to ordinary members who could not even play to single figures, he told me how Chick had turned up with his seven clubs in a modest little bag and the young caddie to whom he, the professional, had handed them flatly refused to carry them. He could not bear the loss of face that would be involved among the other boys!

—1967—
THE GENIAL GIANT KILLER

I like to think of the small boy sneaking furtively across the fairways of The Country Club, in Brookline, Mass., sometime around the turn of the century, on his way to and from the little Putterham schoolhouse, built in 1768. Occasionally his pace is accelerated by the greenkeeper, but the risk is worth it not only for the time it saves but also for the fact that he so often comes across a lost guttie ball in the rough. By 1900, when he was 7, he had enough to last him for years. The only trouble was that he had no club—and, while people readily abandoned lost balls, to find a lost club was another matter.

Eventually his elder brother, who was old enough to caddie at The Country Club, discovered that a Boston store would exchange a new club for three dozen old balls. Thus he acquired his first mashie and the pair of them played incessantly round a three-hole course in the cow pasture behind their humble home. A few surreptitious holes at The Country Club at five in the morning, again until driven off by the greenkeeper, and then at the age of 13 he played his first real game—a mile-and-a-half walk to the tramline, three changes of tram, and nearly a mile to the public course, then 54 holes of golf.

His name, as you may have guessed, was Francis Ouimet, and his death in September will have caused innumerable people, in Britain as well as the United States, to say, as I do, that he was just about the nicest, gentlest and most agreeable man they ever met.

Scarcely seven years after his first game he changed the course of golfing history. In 1913 his heart was set on winning the National Amateur in the following year, but the Open was to be played at The Country Club, so he entered. On the eve of the tournament he played a couple of practise rounds at the Wellesley Club and in both took 88—or 22 strokes more than the record he himself had set. Yet a few days later his name was known all over the world, and the golfing flame he lit has been sweeping the United States like an unquenchable prairie fire ever since.

After three rounds he had the impertinence to be level with the British giants, Vardon and Ray, which is equivalent to a 19-year-old youth of merely local reputation tying with Nicklaus and Palmer today.

They did not in those days send the leaders out last and it so happened, to add to the pressure, that Ray finished, in 79, just as Francis started and that he heard while he was playing the fifth that Vardon had tied with Ray.

He heard Jim Barnes "had it in his pocket"—then that Barnes had blown up; then that a player called Tellier had it in his pocket—and then he had blown up. Now he himself took 5 at the short 10th and overheard a spectator saying, "Too bad. He's blown up."

It riled him, just as a similar remark riled Gary Player when he was 7 down to Tony Lema in a remarkable match at Wentworth. Ouimet rallied, and with six holes to play needed two under par to tie. He thought he might possibly get the shots back with a 3 at the 13th and a 2 at the 16th. At the 13th he missed the green altogether—and holed his chip. At the 16th, far from getting a 2, he had to hole a nine-footer for a 3.

Behind the 17th huge crowds had collected, blocking the road, and, as Francis got down to his curly 15-foot putt, an impatient motorist kept up a constant tooting of his horn. The putt went bang in the middle, and, when asked afterwards, he confessed that, such was his concentration, he had not heard a sound—perhaps the first, and true, version of the oft-told story of Harry Vardon and/or Joyce Wethered in similar circumstances saying, "What train?"

At last he was left with the golfer's nightmare, a four-foot putt to tie for the Open—which, he has recorded, "I popped in"—and so there they were, the three of them, next morning in the pouring rain, drawing straws for the honour and Francis drawing the longest. As he saw the great crowd, he trembled and wondered what he would do, but his 10-year-old caddie, Eddie Lowery (to become a prosperous West Coast motor dealer and until a few years ago a member of the USGA Executive Committee), carrying his eight clubs said, "Be sure and keep your eye on the ball"—and all was well. At the first hole he once again had a four-foot putt and "as I tapped it in almost instantly any feeling of awe and excitement left me and I seemed to go into a coma."

We may leave him in a coma and pause only for a glimpse of the great Ted Ray. At the long 14th he was the only one who could get up in two and we may imagine him with felt hat pulled down against the rain and pipe jutting from his mouth.

"He put every bit of power into the shot but his timing was poor and he hit the ball far into a grove of chestnut trees," and at the 17th, desperate now, he "tried to cut the trees on the left and hit a prodigious wallop that cleared everything, but finished in the long grass."

So, as they came to the end, the youth in the coma was three ahead of Vardon, seven ahead of Ray, and for the student of golfing psychology some rich moments follow. "It did not enter my head that I was about to become Open champion till I stroked my first putt within eight inches of the hole. Suddenly I became very nervous . . . A veil of something that seemed to have covered me dropped from round my head and shoulders . . . I was terribly excited."

His card was marked by our own Bernard Darwin and hangs in The Country Club today, where many a time I gazed upon it with awe. For the ensuing years Francis Ouimet was our constant visitor as player, captain or campfollower in Walker Cup matches, and in 1951 he was accorded perhaps the highest honour we have to offer, namely to become the first American captain of the Royal and Ancient Golf Club.

PARALYSIS BY ANALYSIS

Sixteen years ago when Ben Hogan, after being given up for dead by the roadside, recovered from the most frightful injuries to win both the U.S. and British Open Championships, the Metropolitan Golf Writers of America hit on the idea of presenting a trophy to the golfer whom they thought had done most to overcome physical handicap and remain active in golf. Naturally the first recipient was Hogan himself, and thereafter it became an annual award. They have now presented it to a 77-year-old expatriate Englishman, Ernest Jones.

Jones was born in Manchester and at the age of 18 became assistant at Chislehurst, largely on account of his skill, even at that age, as a clubmaker. He won the professional tournament known as the Kent Cup and then in 1915 went off to the war, where 16 pieces of shrapnel cost him his right leg below the knee. Then, having won the Kent Cup on two feet before the war, he proceeded to win it again in 1920 on one.

Four years later the late Marion Hollins, a past U.S. women's champion, invited him to go as professional to the new women-only club at Glen View on Long Island. People flocked to him for lessons, among them that greatest of all women golfers, Mrs. Babe Zaharias, who had become in her own phrase "fouled up in the mechanics of the game." Later, when the club was taken over by men, he established himself on the seventh floor of a building on Fifth Avenue and became undoubtedly the most popular indoor teacher in the history of golf.

Jones's phenomenal success with his pupils, at least one of whom came to regard his teaching almost as a religion, was due, I think, to its simplicity. "Swing the clubhead," was his maxim. Or, again, "You cannot move the club faster than you can swing it." As evidence of this, he would tie a jack-knife to his handkerchief and swing this and the club together. A good smooth swing brought the two "clubheads" to the ball at the same moment. Any form of jerk left the jack-knife behind.

There is no doubt that the ball can be hit both well and far with a solid head on the end of a flexible shaft. That supreme trick-shot artist, the late Paul Hahn, used to demonstrate with a block of wood on the end of a piece of garden hose. I tried it myself and can confirm that all you have to do, as Jones insists, is to "swing the clubhead."

Nevertheless, on the basis that a cat may look at a king, and admitting that my knowledge of physics is nil, I believe that it is his simplicity, rather than his mechanics, that has made Jones such a successful teacher. "Those who think in terms of golf being a science," he says, "have unfortunately tried to part from each other the arms, head, shoulders, body, hips and legs. They turn the golfer into a worm cut into bits, with each part wriggling in every-which-way direction." He calls it "paralysis by analysis."

Here I feel he is undoubtedly right. If we had an analysis, plus anatomical diagrams, of the muscles and movements involved in getting a fork into one's mouth—where one can't even see the "ball," let alone keep one's eye on it—most of us would either stab ourselves or starve.

On the other hand would the physicists agree with the following? "The greatest force you can develop with a given amount of power is centrifugal in nature. It is achieved by swinging. It is not necessary to quote from the science of physics for proof. Even ancient man understood that a swinging action developed maximum force. Remember David and Goliath and think: how did David get the force into the stone?"

It may be assumed that David, using rather a flat swing, slung the stone. He did, as the headhunting Dyak in Borneo observed to the missionary who showed him a picture of the incident in an illustrated edition of the *Old Testament*, "secure a particularly fine head"—and presumably by centrifugal force. One cannot help asking, however, whether he would not have done even better with the aid of some powerful catapult elastic.

Jones also cites the case of the pendulum, which, however long or short its backswing may be, applies its maximum force at the bottom of the swing, simply by swinging. This again is presumably true—but what if Arnold Palmer caught hold of it halfway down its swing and gave it the old one-two?

A photograph would show the shaft of the pendulum, if it did not snap in half, bent backwards like a bow. Surely if Jones is right, the makers of golf shafts have been wasting their time since the game began. Surely with a steel shaft, as against a handkerchief or a piece of hosepipe, Palmer can move the club faster than he can swing it.

Again, Jones says categorically, "There is only one swing: the correct one." Well, now, once more I take leave to wonder. I repeat the words of the 1964 Open champion, Tony Lema—leaving blanks since you may derive some innocent amusement in trying to detect the players before looking at the answers:

If you examine the swings that many of the successful players use, you might well decide that not one of them is any good.

1. _____ lunges at the ball and punches it.

2. _____ has the unorthodox habit of letting his right elbow

ride far out from his body as he takes the club back.

3. _____ has such a loop at the top of his backswing that it makes him look as though he were waving a flag. I myself loop noticeably at the top.

4. _____ is all hands and wrists like a man dusting the furniture.

5. _____ has his wrists almost completely cocked before he has even started his swing.

6. _____ braces himself with a wide stance that looks like a sailor leaning into a northeast gale and takes the club back barely far enough to get it off the ground.

If you lined all these players up on the practise tee, without knowing who in the world they were, and asked them to hit a few shots your advice would be simple: "Go back and sell insurance. You haven't got it."

None of which alters the fact that Ernest Jones is a very great teacher and thoroughly deserves his award.

(The answers are: 1. Arnold Palmer; 2. Jack Nicklaus; 3. Jacky Cupit; 4. Julius Boros; 5. Jerry Barber; 6. Doug Sanders.)

1971
GOLF GIVES ME UP

After the war I continued to play golf myself and quite well at that. I suppose I must have been scratch for about 20 years and I have no doubt whatever that in my line of country it helped if one got one's name in the paper occasionally as a player. It was also extremely good fun to combine business and pleasure in this way. What I enjoyed most of all, and still do, were the spring and autumn meetings of the Royal and Ancient at St. Andrews, and I would as soon have won the King William IV Medal as the English Championship, not that I was ever good enough to win either.

The more sensitive golfers, not necessarily of any great ability, get the most frightful attacks of nerves before setting forth in the Medal and the situation is not improved by the array of faces staring out through the windows of the Big Room just behind the tee, and the certainty, as you try to get your second or third shot over the Swilken Burn, that you are being observed through the binoculars. I myself have taken 90—off a then handicap of 5— which would have been unthinkable on any other occasion.

The sense of continuity is a great characteristic of the Medal

and one reason why I should so much like to have added my name
to the 130-odd people who have won it since His Majesty
presented it to the club. I like to think of them all, for instance, on
Medal day, 1861, gazing out of the windows of what was then the
Union Parlour and cursing the rain and gale in which they were
soon to set out. In those days the lifeboat was kept at the mouth of
the Swilken Burn. A rocket announced that a ship was in distress
and Maitland Dougall, member of a great naval family and later
himself to become an admiral, went down, found them a man
short, took the stroke oar, rowed for five hours in the bay, came
back, inserted some buckshot in his ball to keep it down against the
wind, and won the Medal with a score of 112. How proud one
would have been to follow a man like that!

As my travels, writings and broadcasting increased, to say
nothing of my age, my golf fell away and it became less and less
fun to do progressively more badly something that one had once
done reasonably well. I had had every reason to believe that I
should turn out in middle age, and even later, to be an accurate
and crafty player, always liable to beat an undergraduate, but it
was not to be. My swing disintegrated and I became quite
pathetically bad. I kept meaning to take myself in hand and go in
for a fortnight's serious practise, which I knew was all that was
needed, but somehow, with all the travelling about, I never got
down to it. If I played on Sunday mornings, I did not enjoy it, and,
if I didn't, I had it on my conscience that somehow I ought to have.
What settled the problem for me was what we call the twitch and
the Americans the yips.

I am afraid that by constantly writing about it I may have
served to spread the disease, in which context I am reminded of
my friend and neighbour Tubby Ionides, who incidentally won
the Grand National Irish Sweep on Sundew. Some people have
only to read about that other ridiculous golf shot, the socket, in
which the ball shoots off, knee high, almost at right angles, to start
doing it themselves, yet quite unable to do it on purpose. Con-
fessing to be one such, my friend added, "I am worse. I am a
carrier." So perhaps am I with the twitch.

In the end I think they will find the disease akin to vertigo, or
the case of the rabbit and the stoat. The rabbit can do 25 miles an
hour and the stoat, I suppose, about four, but the rabbit stands
paralysed like a man with a four-foot putt. Similarly you could
guarantee, drunk or sober, to walk down a road without touching
either side, but put the same road, unfenced, over Niagara and you
would be on your hands and knees within a few paces.

Thus I came one day to the last green in the Medal needing a 4
for a net 69 and a faint chance of defeating at last one of the most
tight-fisted bodies in the world, the handicapping committee of

the R&A. My second got on the green, only to roll back into the Valley of Sin, in which one stands at about eye level with the flag. I pitched up and the ball ran so straight that I had time to think, "By God, it's in! 68!" It stopped just short, a few inches perhaps—but when I got up onto the green the eye had been deceived from down below and it was a yard short.

I was standing idly thinking of nothing while my partner holed out when suddenly it came over me. "I can't do it." I looked at this hideous thing—just like the one you may have seen poor Doug Sanders missing to win, or rather not to win, the 1970 Open on the same green. I stood over it and remember with the utmost clarity thinking that I would willingly lay down a £5 note on the green not to have to make this putt. Suddenly I found that the putter had shot to and fro and the ball was as far away to the other side. I scuttled round and a moment later it had shot by again and we were back where we started. I doubled back, jerked at it again and this time, by sheer good fortune, it hit the back of the hole, jumped in the air and went in—but even as it disappeared I knew that my golfing days were numbered.

I forget where it happened but in the middle of a round, which I was regarding with the usual distaste, a small voice within me said, "You don't *have* to do this," and I thought, "No, by God, I don't." A great wave of relief came over me and on D-Day, 1968, I put the clubs up in the loft with the water tanks, closed the hatch, removed the steps and walked away.

Nor have I for one second regretted it. I had travelled a long and happy road since we had cut the holes with our penknives of the Common at Yelverton, but now it was rather like having sucked a very good orange dry and realising that you were eating the peel. Why not chuck it away and try an apple instead? Which is what I did.

1973
GOOD WISHES FROM HENRY LONGHURST

For several months after the 1973 British Open, Henry was on leave of absence from his writing assignments because of serious illness. On returning to work he wrote:

Well, well, now, where were we when so abruptly interrupted? Ah, yes—at Troon, watching the tall soldierly figure of Tom Weiskopf, smiling all over his handsome countenance as he strode up the last fairway to win the Open Championship and be duly embraced by his ex-beauty-queen wife.

If I offer a personal account of why I have been AWL, i.e., "absent with leave," for so long, it is only because I have been specifically requested to do so.

Life on the whole had been kind to me and enviable. I had achieved a certain notoriety both in writing and broadcasting about golf, and most people who remembered the frightful things I had done and said in the course of the past 40 years were no longer with us to recall them to a later generation.

During the course of the Open I was presented with the Walter Hagen Award, "for furtherance of golfing ties between Britain and the United States," which, if the truth be told, gave me infinite satisfaction, for I had been going to and from America since captaining a Cambridge University team there in 1930 and had in recent years been found acceptable on American television.

I had also during the Open taken part in a BBC chat show and had conducted various interviews, including one with one of the very great men of golf, Gene Sarazen. As U.S. Open champion, he had failed by one stroke to qualify on this same course 40 years ago and now had done the short Postage Stamp Hole in one in the first round and in two in the second. I had met innumerable friends and drinking companions, about a hundred of whom must have told me how well I looked.

I had even had the temerity to provoke providence by entitling an autobiography *My Life and Soft Times.*

Fate, however, had decreed that they had been soft for long enough. I tried to keep a bold face on it but the fact was that only two or three days before the Open I had visited the doctor with a complaint which, though a trifle coarse, proved to be so ludicrous that I venture to set it down. I had found emerging from my person what I could only take to be the end of a tapeworm, or some such unwelcome lodger, and, on pulling it, about eight inches came to the light of day.

"No," said the doctor, "tapeworms only shed half an inch at a time." I thought at once of Sherlock Holmes and the worm "hitherto unknown to science," but the doctor identified it as a piece of cellophane wrapping from a cigarette packet. "I have not smoked for 12 years," I said, with what dignity I could command in the circumstance, "and, furthermore, am not in the habit of eating and swallowing eight inches of cellophane wrapping without being aware of the fact"—but so it proved to be.

I then revealed that I had been conscious not of any pain but of a sort of "awareness" in the lower abdomen, as a result of which a day or two later a neighbouring surgeon, who turned out to be plus 4 at this sort of thing, and whom it still infuriates me to be unable to name, inserted his telescope and, at one of those moments when life stands momentarily still and you know it will never be the same again, said quietly: "Ha! A tumour."

This would mean a "colostomy," i.e., removal of part of the colon, and furthermore, if you will forgive me, an artificial orifice in the side of the body.

It was the thought of the latter which really decided me—though, to give comfort to others who face this, let me say that the modern apparatus for coping with it really is wonderful.

Lying soberly in bed during the Open, I decided that I had done all I had set out to do and that all good things come to an end. Like the late Errol Flynn, I felt "I've seen everything twice and am ready to go."

I enquired of three doctors (not, of course, including my own) as to whether I had obtained sufficient pills to exercise man's inalienable right, as Hamlet put it, to "shuffle off this mortal coil," and all said yes—one recommending, rather splendidly, "half a bottle of whisky and make sure they don't find you for 12 hours."

My life was prolonged, though he will be astonished and, I hope gratified to learn so, by last year's captain of the Turnberry Golf Club who, in an example that cannot be too widely followed by golf club captains, had presented me during the John Player Classic with a bottle of Highland malt whisky called Glenmorangie, which proved to be of such superlative excellence that I have never been without it since.

The fatal night, with my mind still made up, called clearly for a bottle of this powerful nectar with which to slide peacefully away and I attacked it with maudlin vigour, but alas, or rather hooray, I must have exceeded the stated dose and Glenmorangie got the better of me before I got round to taking the pills.

Thus the condition in which I was presented next morning to the Howard Ward of the Royal Sussex County Hospital and its devoted staff makes it all the more miraculous that I should still be here, restored physically to the "normal channels" and with, I am assured, a three in four chance of further survival, to offer our readers my good wishes for a Christmas, which in July I never expected, nor indeed intended, to see.

AFTERWORD

Well, in conclusion I can only hope that these miscellaneous writings of mine over the years will have brought the reader a certain amount of innocent pleasure. They cover the game, I like to think, in perhaps a wider aspect than today, when the emphasis has tended to shift almost wholly to the professionals and, in particular, to the amount of money they win, whereas of course the people who really matter are the millions, now perhaps even tens of millions, of ever-optimistic club golfers out of whose pockets the money originally flows—"the bravest, stupidest race in the world," that great writer Bernard Darwin once called them—"the unconvincible, inextinguishable race of golfers."

Few aspects of golf have changed so much in my time as the cost—but so, of course, have incomes. James Braid, five times British Open champion, started as a carpenter near St. Andrews and when he came to London as a clubmaker would make you a driver for the equivalent of two dollars and a half, and it would be one of a set of perhaps seven or eight clubs cherished for several years. Nowadays it would be one of 14, at a cost which I hesitate to set down. Nevertheless, much rubbish has been handed down about the days when clubs were made by "craftsmen." The first thing one did on visiting a strange club in my young days was to call in at the pro shop, where in most cases he himself had made the wooden clubs on show, and, believe me, many of them were positively awful. Most of today's factory-made clubs are master-pieces of craftsmanship and design.

Golf in my time has, literally, changed the face of the world. Remote beauty spots have sprouted tower block hotels and the air thunders with the roar of giant jets and package tours. The "Mysterious Orient" is mysterious no more, and even the Virgin Islands are not safe from my old friend, Robert Trent Jones, the golf architect, and the real estate developers. Yet who shall say this is a bad thing? Who shall deny the untold pleasure that all this has brought to thousands of people?

To me golf has brought a congenial life, as I hope these pages may have shown; a life spent among pleasant people, who have mostly been at their own pleasantest in the circumstances in which I have met them, often in some of the greatest beauty spots in the world.

Now it is time to lay down my pen and, alas, the microphone, too, and to reflect, in whatever time may be left, how uncommonly lucky I have been. And if I have managed to give a little pleasure on the way, well, what a happy thought that is, too.

Several weeks after writing these final words Henry died, on July 21, 1978.